Time-Lining

Patterns For Adventuring In "Time"

NLP And General Semantics On "Time"

By

Bob G. Bodenhamer, D Min
&
L. Michael Hall, Ph D

Published by The Anglo-American Book Company,
Bancyfelin, Carmarthen, Wales.

First published in the UK by

The Anglo-American Book Company Ltd
Crown Buildings
Bancyfelin
Carmarthen
Wales

British Library of Cataloguing-in-Publication Data
A catalogue entry for this book is available
from the British Library.

ISBN 1899836128

Printed and bound by Antony Rowe Ltd,
Bumper's Farm, Chippenham, Wiltshire

Table Of Contents

Acknowledgments

As we begin this exploration into the labyrinth of "time," we acknowledge our debt to the two geniuses who began NLP, Richard Bandler and John Grinder. Through the methodologies of NLP, they taught us first how to adventure forth as "time" detectives.

Then with the publishing of Tad James and Wyatt Woodsmall's classic book, Time-Line Therapy and the Basis of Personality (1988) we learned even more about exploring this Kantian category in human "personalities."

The text represents a composition of materials that each of us have brought from different sources. Bob Bodenhamer (BB) wrote the basic text of Chapters 2-6 as part of his ongoing NLP training in Gastonia NC. Much of it comes from his Advance Communication Course. Michael Hall (MH) wrote most of the materials in Chapters 1, 7-12 in the 1996 issues of Metamorphosis entitled, Adventures in "Time."

I (BB) also wish to acknowledge the following people without whom this work would have been impossible:

Richard Spencer whose vision introduced me to NLP, Gene Rooney, my first NLP trainer and inspiration,

Tad James who turned me on to Time-Lining and Language and the power they offer for personal change,

Wyatt Woodsmall who along with Tad walked me through Trainer's Training.

And most importantly, to my wife Linda, whose love and continued support has encouraged me throughout thirty-one years of marriage and ministry.

And I (MH) wish to acknowledge Dr. Carl Lloyd who has been "closer than a brother" to me throughout the years, Cheryl Buffa, my sweetheart of these many years who has proof-read more pages than I can count, and my daughter Jessica Hall, my other sweetheart.

E.T. Publications
1904 N. 7th. Street
Grand Junction, Colorado 81501-7418
(970) 245-3235

Foreword
by Dr Tad James

"We are at the beginning of a new era of understanding."

When I first wrote those words ten years ago, I was introducing my own work in Time-Line Therapy™. I was correct in saying that we were at the beginning of such an era. However, after using, refining and adding to the original concepts, I now realize that at that time I could neither fathom nor appreciate the sheer power of this revolutionary technology.

Throughout history, humankind has been aware of the passage of time. Aristotle was the first to mention the "stream of time" in his book *Physics IV*. William James spoke of linear memory storage as early as 1890. In the decades to follow, the concept all but faded into obscurity. It was finally revived in the late 1970's by the developers of Neuro-Linguistic Programming (NLP). In my own research and experience, I applied a therapeutic process to this concept of an internal storage system. The result was a collection of techniques called Time-Line Therapy™ which produced long-lasting transformations very quickly. These techniques have since become the method of choice to make fast, effective, long-term changes in behavior.

Readers of this book will most likely be familiar with the concepts and tenets of NLP. For those of you who are not, I recommend that you consult one of the excellent texts cited in the references at the end of this book. As for Time-Line Therapy™, allow me to offer a general explanation. Your personal "time-line" is how you unconsciously store your memories and how you unconsciously know the difference between a memory from the past and a projection of the future. It has been established that behavioral change takes place at an unconscious level and releases the effects of past negative experiences and changes "inappropriate" programming in minutes. This is deep, lasting change, documented by a decade of research and experience.

Now, we owe a debt of gratitude to Dr. Bobby Bodenhamer and Dr. Michael Hall for *Time-Lining : Patterns for Adventuring in "Time"*, their provocative, compelling new work about time-lines, NLP and general semantics. They have based their new work on my original theories, introducing us to their own cutting-edge analysis of "time"--a logical level model of time that integrates their concepts and mine with that of some of the finest semanticists, scientists and psychologists of this century. I am honored that in *Time Lining*, my work has found a place among the likes of William James, Alfred Korzybski, Edward T. Hall and Paul Ricoeur.

Both Bobby and Michael are highly skilled, infinitely capable trainers of NLP and Time-Line Therapy™. Each is an author in his own right. I admire both of these men for their integrity, their dedication, and the painstaking, conscientious research which has resulted in this excellent book. I am proud to be the one to introduce you their fine accomplishment, and, to paraphrase my own words of so long ago, we are still at the beginning of a new era of understanding. We are only now starting to understand the vastness of what we have yet to learn. I invite you to read this book, and join us on our exciting journey.

Everett W. "Tad" James, M.S., Ph.D.
July, 1997

Preface
by Wyatt Woodsmall

Time-Lining: Patterns for Adventures in "Time" fills a serious void in the literature on Neuro-Linguistic Programming. It is the first book on time-lines in nearly a decade. Much good work has been done since *Time-Line Therapy and the Basis of Personality* first appeared in 1988. I am excited that Bobby Bodenhamer and Michael Hall have taken up the challenge to move time-lines forward another decade.

The subject of time is one that has intrigued man since he first began to reflect on his own experience. This reflection has varied from considerations of memory and temporality to the age old questions of time, life and eternity. NLP's contribution to the study of time has to do with the question of how we subjectively experience and code time. Time-Lining allows us to bring under conscious control the way an individual internally represents his experience of temporality including his memories of the past, experiences of the present, and expectations of the future. This involves first eliciting the critical submodalities of how a person represents his temporal experiences. Once these critical submodalities are elicited, time codes re-adjust these internal representations in order to bring about change. This change may be remedial or generative.

There has been some discussion in NLP surrounding the origins of the idea of a time-line. The spatialization of time and the concept of time as a line are probably as old as mankind himself. They are deeply rooted in man's subjective experience of time (for reasons that will be made clear shortly). The idea of time-lines in psychology was discussed in detail by the psychologist William James in the 1890's; and in philosophy, the idea goes back to the Greeks and was discussed in detail by Edmund Husserl and Martin Heidegger in the 1920's and 1930's.

I have always been interested in the subject of "time." At Union Theological Seminary in the late 60's I had the opportunity to study "time" as understood by Paul Tillich, Martin Heidegger, Jean-Paul Sarte, Paul Ricoeur, and Alfred North Whitehead. After

Union, I studied Philosophy at Columbia University for eight years. This gave me an opportunity to continue my study of time from a scientific, philosophical and semantic perspective.

The discussion of different experiences of time in NLP can probably be traced to Leslie Cameron-Bandler. She taught a workshop on Meta Programs and Belief Systems in Illinois in September, 1982. At this workshop she discussed the distinction between "in time" and "through time." Anne Linden and Frank Stass attended this workshop. In struggling to integrate Leslie's material into their own understanding, Anne and Frank began to explore their own experiences of time. Anne experienced time on a line and wondered how other people experienced it. Anne and Frank began to experiment in class to find out how other people experienced time. I learned about time-lines from them in the fall of 1982. I also had the good fortune to attend a presentation on Time-Lines by Steve and Connirae Andreas at the second NANLP Conference the following year. I was excited about the possibilities of time-lines and took every opportunity that I could to explore them and to tell others about them.

In the fall of 1985 I began teaching an NLP Practitioner and Master Practitioner Training in Honolulu, Hawaii. This class included Tad and Ardie James, Marvin Oka and Richard Diehl. I soon had everyone as excited as I was about time-lines. Tad and Marvin began to experiment with time-lines in therapy and in personal growth. This led to the collaboration between the James's and myself to develop the material on time-lines that was published in *Time-Line Therapy and the Basis of Personality*. I have continued to develop and teach new ways of coding time up to the present.

It is very gratifying to me to see Michael Hall and Bobby Bodenhamer - who are two people who I have helped to train - become as excited as I am about time and time-line patterns. It is even more gratifying to me that they have accepted my admonitions that "NLP does not end with John Grinder and Richard Bandler" or "time-lines with Wyatt Woodsmall and Tad James" and that "It is up to all of us to further advance the field." They have done just that with this excellent book. The authors have both emersed themselves in NLP and time and also in general semantics and the latest developments in cognitive psychology and therapy. It is refreshing to find that the authors are not just cacooned in the field of NLP, and that they have extensively studied the origins of time and NLP in general semantics as well as other disciplines that bear on NLP and its applications in the real world.

It is also gratifying to see that the authors don't just quote Korzybski but actually use general semantics. This book is written in E-Prime and uses other extensional devices that Korzybski used to promote and maintain sanity. NLP has drawn much from general semantics and there is still much gold to mine there. Bodenhamer and Hall have been hard at work on this task and it has paid rich dividends in clarity and precision.

I have had the privilege of knowing both authors for several years and one thing that has impressed me about both of them is their integrity, their compassion, and their dedication to applying and expanding NLP into areas of the world where it has not traveled previously. This has not come easy. Both have made major sacrifices to pursue their interests in NLP.

Some people in the NLP community have informed me that they "were the first to develop and teach time-lines." Any number of people in the NLP community could have simultaneously made the application of submodalities to time-lines. It is unfortunate that in the NLP community people are so isolated from the rest of the intellectual world and from what everyone else is doing, that they continually feel the need to reinvent the wheel and then claim that they created it in the first place. It is particularly gratifying to me that Bodenhamer and Hall do not fall into this trap. They are immersed in the intellectual world as well as in NLP. Further, instead of arguing about who invented the wheel in the first place they are focused on moving it on down the road into new and previously unexplored territory.

In any case, it does not seem particularly relevant who first explicated time-lines. A lot of people dabbled in this area, felt that it was unimportant and went on to other things. Tad James and myself were the first to elaborate and expand on these notions and develop them into a systematic therapeutic system. It is gratifying that Bodenhamer and Hall are now advancing this system even further and exploring and testing the limits of its application.

The nature of time has been debated by philosophers, psychologists, and mystics from the dawn of civilization. The common-sense understanding of time interprets it as something moving towards the future or as something in which events point in that direction. Contemporary philosophy views time as the general medium in which all events take place (or appear to take place) in succession. Thus, all specific and finite periods of time (whether past, present or future) merely constitute parts of the entire and single time.

The English word "time" is derived from the Latin tempus which comes from the Greek temno meaning "to cut off." The Greek terms for "time" are *chronos* and *aion*. William James viewed the past and the future as existing in the "specious present" which he said was not a knife-edge but a "saddleback" with a certain breadth of its own; i.e. a duration. Bergson defined time as qualitative change, involving an irreversible becoming. He held that reason "spatializes" time, and that intuition is therefore a more adequate means of apprehending time. Whitehead also thought of time under the category of becoming. He viewed it as the movement into novelty or the movement from potentiality to actuality of events which thereafter retain an "objective immortality."

Heidegger distinguishes between two ways of experiencing time depending on whether one is living authentically or inauthentically. Einstein in relation to Minkowski made time the fourth dimension of the space-time continuum with the whole stretched out into world-lines with further occurrences as fixed as those in the past. This view holds that both space and time are two systems of relations, which are distinct from a perceptual standpoint, but insuperably bound together in reality.

Most people who have not been semantically trained hold a conception of time which philosophers call "the myth of passage." This view thinks of time as a stream that flows or as a sea over which we advance. But if time flows past us or if we advance through time, then this would be a motion with respect to a hyper-time, for motion in space is motion with respect to time; and motion of time or in time could hardly be a motion in time with respect to time. If motion in space is measured in feet per second, at what speed is the flow of time? Seconds per what? Moreover, if passage is of the essence of time, it would also be part of the essence of hypertime which would lead to infinite regress.

The idea of time as passing is connected to the idea of events as changing from future to past. Most people who have not been semantically trained think of events as approaching them from the future, being momentarily caught in the spotlight of the present, and then receding into the past. But in normal contexts, it does not make sense to talk of events changing or remaining the same. Roughly speaking, events are happening to continuants (to things that change or stay the same). Thus, it is possible to talk of objects as changing or remaining the same. But is it intelligible to talk of change itself as changing?

According to the article on "Consciousness of Time" in *The Encyclopedia of Philosophy* the spatialization of time is a mistake. The article concludes: "The besetting sin of philosophers, scientists, and indeed, all who reflect about time is describing it as if it were a dimension of space. It is difficult to resist the temptation to do this because our temporal language is riddled with spatial metaphors. This is because temporal relations are formally analogous to spatial relations...If we picture the passing of time in terms of movement along a line, we are led to ask "What moves?" and we are disposed to answer, like Husserl, "Events keep moving into the past" and to forget that "move" is now being used metaphorically, that events cannot literally move or change...Things change, events happen...Those who spatialize time, conceiving of it as an order in which events occupy different places, are hypostatizing events. The temptation to hypostatize events is presumably the result, at least in part, of the linguistic fact that the terms, which can be said to stand in temporal relations, like simultaneous with and earlier than, are event expressions. Those who ponder about time are forever using event expressions as their main nouns, and they frequently seem to forget what events are — changes in three-dimensional things. What we perceive and sense are things changing. Time is a nonspatial order in which things change...Our consciousness of time's "flow" is our consciousness of things changing." The fact that the spatial notion of time is so persistent (in spite of it being a conceptual error to the philosophers) must mean that it is deeply rooted in man's experience of temporality.

How do people normally represent their experience of the passage of time (temporality)? How does one denominalize the experience of time? How does a person tell what events in his past happened before other events? If a person can arrange the major and minor events of his life chronologically in time, then he has to have some way to do this. How is it possible to remember events chronologically? These are the questions at the heart of *Time-Lining*.

As was emphasized, the notion of time as being on a line has persisted throughout the history of mankind. The persistence of this idea is not just due to the fact that our temporal language is "riddled with spatial metaphors." This is to put the cart before the horse. It is "riddled with spatial metaphors", because the spatialization of time is part of the universal experience of mankind. It is one of the tasks of *Time-Lining* to un-code this experience.

Time-Lining is unique in several ways. First, it discusses time in the larger context of philosophy and general semantics. Second, it provides an in-depth discussion of time-lines and their applications. And third, it expands on the field of time-lines and makes a significant new contribution to the field. It is written by two people who have years of practice in applying these patterns to themselves and to others to produce successful results. Let us touch on each of these points briefly.

Time-Lining begins with an excellent discussion on the nature of time itself. The authors place time in the much greater context in which it has been explored in science, philosophy, semantics and religion. This provides an invaluable frame to understand its role in NLP. They then trace the origin and history of the development of time-lines in NLP. NLP is a process of "de-nominalization," and the authors begin their study by de-nominalizing time itself.

Time-Lining presents an excellent training in both basic and advanced time-line patterns. This book is not just theoretical. It is practical. These patterns work and can be used to bring about dramatic changes in oneself and in other people. They are presented with clarity and understanding. As with any powerful pattern, ecology is critically important and the authors stress it appropriately. They also avoid the trap that some people fall into of thinking that time-lines alone are sufficient to do therapy. They are a very powerful set of tools, and they are but one set in the pallet of any successful change artist.

Perhaps the most exciting part of *Time-Lining* is the major contribution that it makes to the development and expansion of time-lines. The authors challenge us to both understand and apply. Also they are continually giving us new avenues for further exploration and study. This is what makes this book so valuable. It is truly generative and will lead to the further development, explication and utilization of even more patterns as we strive to understand and apply its insights. This is perhaps its greatest contribution.

The subtitle of *Time-Lining* is *Patterns for Adventuring in "Time."* Bodenhamer and Hall provide us an opportunity to do just that. They make us familiar with the basic concepts and patterns and then launch us on our own journey in time. I urge you to take the voyage yourself. It may well be the most important trip that you ever take.

Wyatt L. Woodsmall, Ph.D.
July, 1997

Part I

Getting Started

Introduction

This work represents advanced models and patterns in "time" and time-lines using Neuro-Linguistic Programming and general semantics. As we begin this work, we assume that our readers already know the Neuro-Linguistic Programming (NLP) model. Rather than repeat the basics of NLP, we here refer the reader to our work, *Patterns for Renewing the Mind*, Bodenhamer and Hall (1997a), as well as the following. Each serve as excellent introductions.

> *Introducing NLP* by Seymour and O'Connor (1991)
> *Using Your Brain for A Change* by Bandler (1982).

For the more hardy, we recommend:

> *NLP : Volume 1, The Study of the Structure of Subjectivity* (1980) by Bandler, Grinder, Dilts, and DeLozier;
> *Timelines and the Basis of Personality* (1988) by James and Woodsmall,
> *Change Your Mind and Keep the Change* (1987) and
> *Heart of the Mind* (1989) by Steve and Connaire Andreas.
> *The Spirit of NLP* (1996) by L. Michael Hall
> *NLP : Going Meta Into Logical Levels* (1997), by L. Michael Hall

Most of all we express our deepest thanks and appreciation to Dr Tad James for his pioneering work in NLP around this very theme of how we code and represent "time" and time-lines. The work that he did with Dr. Wyatt Woodsmall, in that now classic NLP work, *Timelines and the Basis of Personality*, stands as the basis and foundation of this work.

NLP Overview

As a brief overview of this model about "the structure of subjectivity," we mention the following about how we use our nervous system (neurology and brain) to create our "model of the world" that creates our subjective sense of reality.

Our nervous system/brain inputs information from the world via our senses. Then we use those sense modalities of awareness for processing ("thinking") and storing ("memory"). NLP designates these as Representational Systems (RS) since by them we represent to ourselves information about what we have seen, heard, felt, etc. As notation, we designate the RS as:

V for Visual: sights, pictures, images, etc.
A for Auditory: sounds, noise, volume, tones, etc.
At — Auditory tonal (sounds)
K for Kinesthetic: sensations, feelings, etc.
O for Olfactory: smells
G for Gustatory: tastes
M for Motor: kinesthetic movements

These RS can refer to external or internal sources of data, hence sometimes we notate this by adding an e or i as in Vi (visual internal). These RS can also refer to remembered information stored inside neurologically (r) or constructed in the imagination (c).

r — Remembered information (VAK)
c — Constructed information (VAK)
i — Internal source of information (TDS, transderivational search)
e — External source of information (uptime, sensory awareness)

Then to denote that we have a meta-representational system, words and language, we use the notation:

Ad — Auditory Digital (the language system, words, self-talk)

In addition to these primary sensory systems that provide us **modes** (modalities) **for awareness**, we have the representation system above, or beyond, a logical level higher, that refers to the sensory systems—*language*. This symbolic system of words, sentences, phrases, enables us to talk about our sights, sounds, and sensations and to abstract at a higher logical level.

The domain below, or within, the RS and the meta-RS of linguistics refer to those *qualities, characteristics, and components* of the modalities—hence, submodalities (SBMD). Each system has its own list of submodalities.

Visual Submodalities:

Location: close- far
Size: small- large
Focus: clear - fuzzy
Structure: 3-D or 2-D (flat)
Tone: black-and-white - Color
In-Out: Associated- Dissociated
Motion: Slide-Movie
shape: contour- form
Brightness: low - high
Contrasts: many - few
Form: panoramic - bordered

Kinesthetic Submodalities:

Location: inside - outside
Nature: tactile - proprioceptive
Intensity: low - high
Weight: low - high
Duration: short - long
Size of area: small - large
Frequency: often, infrequent
Shape: configuration
Movement: none, some, much
Texture: smooth, rough
Rhythm: pattern to movement

Auditory Submodalities:

Location: source, direction
Volume: low - high
Tone: quality, style
Pitch: low - high
Distance: close - far
Rhythm: fast-slow,smooth-uneven
Tempo: slow- fast
Duration: short - long

This domain of submodalities provides the sub-structure of our subjectivity—the place of "the building blocks" of human experience and the place where we find "the difference that makes a difference" (Bateson). These coding cues inform the brain and nervous system about *how to respond* to information. Change or alter the submodality coding of an image, sound, sensation, word, etc. and you can change the whole gestalt of the experience. This feels "true with a vengeance" when you find *the driving submodality*. These submodalities critically determine and effect the experience.

In addition to the sensory and language modalities of ideas, understandings, beliefs, values and decisions, and their qualities (SBMD), NLP also identifies and distinguishes their *syntax*. This refers to the order and sequence of these qualities—the formula by which we put them together to create an experience. We call this order or structure of the component pieces of modalities a *strategy* in NLP (Dilts, et al., 1980).

Hence a guy who "runs the depression strategy," may make pictures in his head of the worst failure in his life—blow it up so that he sees it as large, close, in color, 3-D and "in his face." As he sees that, he immediately feels down, depressed, upset, frustrated, etc. his muscle tone in arms, legs and chest relax, he breaths high in his chest, he tightens his neck muscles. etc. Then he says negative things to himself in a critical tone of voice, close and using his dad's tonality, "I'll never amount to anything. Everything I attempt fails, what's the use?"

How different from those times when he "runs his excitement strategy." Then he makes a large and close picture, full of color and 3-D, but not "in his face," nor as large or close, of the content of this picture—how things will work out to fulfill his goal. So he feels energized, excited and says, "Great! Finally!"

Structurally, we find the same pattern in each: VKAd,t. But the limiting representations or resourceful ones differ. So do the kinds of beliefs and values that he accesses while in the depression state versus the excitement state.

We explain this in NLP by saying that our learning, memory, perception, communication, and behavior (LMPCB) all function in a *state-dependent way*. This means that while in a state of mind-body (content and structure of our Internal Representations, IR, and condition-quality of our physiology) we tend to think, learn, remember, perceive, talk and *act according to the state*. The state governs our processing.

What can we do about all of this once we find "the structure of our subjectivity?" We can *interrupt* (disrupt, interfere with) the state and its driving factors (our internal RS and SBMD). Then we can *shift our consciousness* to redirect our brain-body toward those internal representations (IR) that enhance our state and therefore life. We do this by using modality and submodality shifts, swishing our brain to desired outcomes, the "me" for whom this or that would not function as a problem, reframing the meaning (significance) of an event, altering the triggers (anchors) that set the brain to go off in a certain direction and re-anchor ourselves to new directions, etc.

In a word, NLP addresses the subject of how to *"run our own brain"* so that we can take charge of the cognitive-behavioral mechanisms that control subjectivity. And what **mechanisms** control subjectivity? Namely IR (modalities and submodalities that code ideas, understandings, beliefs, values, decisions) and *physiology* (quality and use of our body and nervous system). To facilitate this, NLP has invented and discovered numerous techniques (human technologies) and methods that provide us with specific patterns (programs) that enable us to manage our subjectivity (our states) with much greater ease and effectiveness.

The Meta-Move: Meta-Levels/ Meta-States

Numerous models of logical levels occur in NLP, from Bateson's (1972) logical levels of learning, to the meta-outcome model, meta-programs, and more recently meta-states (Hall, 1995, 1996, 1997). For a set of distinctions or levels to operate in a "logical" relationship to each other, the higher level must encompass the lower level as a class encompasses its members. A higher level also relates to and functions as the context *about* the lower.

Chunking up from a primary sensory-based level to a meta-level involves what we call "going meta" or making a meta-move (taking a meta-position). This involves abstracting from the lower level and generating a higher order of abstraction or conception. Later in this work, we will introduce a model about "time" using a logical levels model (Chapter 11).

NLP Technologies

Accordingly, in NLP you will find **technologies** for doing many things that improve the quality of life:

1.   Engaging and *connecting* with another person's subjectivity (pacing or matching, detecting neurological functioning via eye accessing cues, predicates, body types, etc.).

2. *Managing subjective* states via anchoring, reanchoring, collapsing anchors (a user-friendly version of Pavlovian conditioning).

3.   *Altering the way we use our brain* (RS, modalities, submodalities, strategies) so as to create new, different and better subjective experiences—making us more resourceful (strategy transformation patterns).

4.   *Altering the meanings* that we give to words, events, persons, situations, etc., (framing, reframing, preframing, deframing, outframing) so that we initiate a new meaning, world or dimension within which we live.

5.   *Altering the beliefs, values,* and decisions that in-form our lives (belief change patterns, V-K dissociation pattern, Value Hierarchy Alteration Pattern etc.).

6.   *Re-languaging.* Linguistic understanding and analysis of the modeling processes by which we create our mental/conceptual maps about the territory, the criteria that distinguishes between well-formed maps and ill-formed maps, the meta-model of language for questioning ill-formedness and transforming a person's language so that they develop richer and less impoverished maps.

Time-line Processes

In this work we have focused on just one of the human technologies in NLP that effect change of state, personality, values, beliefs etc.—time-lines. Herein you will learn about the *nominalization* **"time"** (a verb describing a process turned into a static noun). In so using this term, we treat this term as a thing, yet, such misdefines it. What then do we refer to, and mean, when we use this term? What process does it reference?

As "time" creatures—with "time" seemingly built into the very structure of our "minds" (Immanuel Kant labeled this *a priori category*), we all process "time." We have an innate awareness of events past, present, and future—and this operates to our glory and our agony because we can psychologically *live* in any one of those "time" categories, or zones, and we inevitably (and inescapably) constantly engage in "time" travel between those zones.

We have devoted this entire volume to exploring this somewhat mysterious, yet ever-present phenomenon of "time" and how we code time via our representations and submodalities and support them with our beliefs and values, and then access various "time" states and "time" experiences so much so that it begins to form and make us various "time" persons in our very personality.

Re-Discovering General-Semantics

A person can't get very far into the domain of NLP without coming across "the map/territory" distinction as proposed by Alfred Korzybski (1941/1994) in his classic work, *Science and Sanity.* To even mention "Neuro-Linguistic Programming" (NLP) alludes to Korzybski's 1941 "Introduction" where he first introduced the term neuro-linguistic. At that time, he conducted training seminars for *"neuro-linguistic training."*

As you read this work, you will note that we have used several other linguistic **"extensional devices for sanity"** that came originally from the field of general semantics (GS) and we do it intentionally as a way of re-discovering the NLP roots in this field. Here we want to alert you to some of them inasmuch as it gives the following text a unique format.

Quotes (" ") indicate a word that we should handle with very special care. For instance, "time." It looks like a noun. It sounds like a noun. If you could smell it... But it does not exist as a true noun. Someone long ago distorted it into the form of a *nominalization*, reified to suggest a static thing, all "false-to-fact" encoding.

Hyphens (-) as in "Neuro-Linguistic Programming" reunites the world torn apart into elements that do not, and cannot, stand alone. General semantics uses hyphens to re-address the elementalism and dualism that has so afflicted the West. "Mind" and "body" references nothing real, only a linguistic fiction, and so with "time" and "space." These cannot exist apart. In reality, we only find "space-time" and "mind-body."

Etc. Used here not as a trite over-used term due to bad habit, but intentionally and on purpose because in the infinite world of the territory, no map we can create can say it all. To remind ourselves of this non-allness in the world, we use "etc." It indicates our awareness of our own limitations as we articulate about a subject.

E-Prime—the priming of English of all "is" words (the "to be" verbs: is, am, be, being, been, was, were, etc.). This enables us to specially eliminate the "is" of identity ("He is selfish") and the "is" of predication ("That chair is red"). These "ises" map out more false-to-fact representations that, in turn, misrepresent the territory and create problems for sanity and for adjusting ourselves effectively to the territory. While the auxiliary "is" provides no problems in that way ("he is coming from Texas") nor does the "is" of existence ("that chair exists"), all of the "to be" verbs tend to express actions in a very passive form and leave out any accurate description of what we would see, hear, or feel occurring.

Process language—since reality as we now know it via physics exists as "a dance of electrons" and sub-atomic parts, **"thing" language** most inadequately describes reality. We need more of a **process language** since everything always changes. Here verbs, movement, function, process, etc. more accurately maps reality. In NLP we stress this in two ways, first by *asking for see-hear-feel (VAK) descriptions.* This makes language more dynamic, empirical, sensory-based, and indexed to time-space, person, event, etc. We do it secondly, by *de-nominalizing the nominalizations* (verbs turned into nouns) that dominate English. Accordingly you will find some strange uses of "time" such as "time" as a verb, "timing," "time-lining," etc.

When you come across a row of dots...within a quotation, that indicates we cut off the quote in the middle of a sentence. When you find such dots in a set of instructions for experimenting with some form of subjectivity, that indicates "stop, go inside to your own unique "library of references" and experience this referent." If you get lost, we have added some appendices to help, a glossary, and index.

Chapter 1

"Time"
A Conceptual Semantic State

"What is time?
The shadow of the dial, the striking of the clock, the running of the sand, day
and night, summer and winter, months, years, centuries—these are but
arbitrary and outward signs, the measure of Time, not Time itself.
Time is the life of the soul."
Longfellow

What does the word "time" refer to? **What** do we refer to and mean when we use this term? Long ago, Augustine gave his hand to explaining "time:"

> "What, then, is time? If no one asks me, I know; if I want to explain it to someone who does ask me, I do not know. Yet I state confidently that I know this: if nothing were passing away, there would be no past time, and if nothing were coming, there would be no future time. And if nothing existed there would be no present time. How, then, can these two kinds of time, the past and the future, be, when the past no longer is and the future as yet does not be? But if the present were always present, and would not pass into the past, it would no longer be time, but eternity. Therefore, if the present, so as to be time, must be so constituted that it passes into the past, how can we say that it is, since the cause of its being is the fact that it will cease to be? Does it not follow that we can truly say that it is time, only because it ends toward non-being?" (Ryan, 1960, p.287-288).

Part of Augustine's difficulty here arose from his use of language about "time"—rather than the referent itself. Augustine knew that *events change*, but he then confused, or didn't know, the level at which our term "time" operates on. He seemed to confuse levels. On the primary sensory-based, empirical level, events change. But on a conceptual level, a level meta to the primary level, we measure, mark, and relate the changingness of events by our term "time."

"Time" as a noun seemed to have thrown Augustine into a quandary as it continues to this day to throw most of us. For we too tend to predominately use it as a noun as if it stood for a *thing*.

"I don't have enough time."
"I have too much time on my hands."
"When will I ever get enough time to build that shed?"

Such use of language utilizes a noun form, grammatically, so no wonder we think of "time" as a "thing."

Yet, we have a *nominalization* in the word "time." We have a verb (designating a process) which someone has erroneously turned into a static, non-moving noun. Underlying the noun-form of the term we do not have anything that we can put in a wheelbarrow (the NLP test for a nominalization). We have nothing we can see, hear, smell, touch, or taste. What does "time" smell like? Does it have temperature?

What we have in the word "time" lies in the realm of an action. First we have *events happening* then we have our *mental thinking and conceiving* (another process) about those events which involve our understanding of the relationship between events occurring. So, **"time" does not have an external referent**. It refers to nothing in the empirical world. It exists as something *invisible*—something in the mind, an abstraction of a higher logical level than "things." Emmanuel Kant (1787) three centuries ago, postulated that "time" exists solely as an *a priori category* in the mind. He thought of this mental concept and evaluation as existing innately within consciousness, much as Chomsky (1957) later argued and demonstrated that language capacity exists genetically inherent within the brain. Scientist Joost Meerloo (1970) has noted,

"It was Kant who brought the concept of time (and space) completely around to the subjective, to the idea that it belonged inside man's thoughts and inner sense, and did not exist independently." (p. 8).

Koheleth (Hebrew for "Ecclesiastes" which refers to a philosopher or speaker) attributed this a priori category to our original design.

> "I have seen the business that God has given the sons of men to be busy with. He has made everything beautiful in its time; also he has put *eternity* into man's mind, yet so that he cannot find out what God has done from the beginning to the end..." (Eccl. 3:10-11).

Some translations translate *'olam* (the Hebrew word) as *"a sense of time past, present, and future"* (New English Bible).

"Time" then exists as a **conceptual reality,** an understanding of the relationship between events—and not anything actual or literal beyond our nervous system. For some, this high level abstraction about an abstraction (understanding of "time") takes a while to get used to. We have talked about "time" as a thing and treated it as external and confused it with "the clock." This will also challenge those who operate from a more literal frame of mind and who might not progress much beyond what we call "the concrete thinking" stage.

In NLP, when we discover an ill-formed map in the form of a nominalization, to recover and understand our meaning, we *de-nominalize* it. We put the static term back into a process or verb form. So what verb effectively describes the action inside of "time?" When we denominalize "relationship" we have relating. In "motivation" we have having motives and moving. In "hypnosis" we have "going to sleep to the external world as we highly focus on the internal world." But what process do we have inside of "time?"

The Shortness of "Time"

Gregory Bateson (1972) warned about "short" words. He warned that certain short nominalizations especially tend to get us to thinking erroneously about things because they trigger us to create **misplaced concreteness.** He specifically made this complaint against Freud's invention of such short nominalized words as "ego," "id," etc. We here bring the same Batesonian complaint against "time."

What verb or process lies hidden within this short term? At the most fundamental and primary level we use the term "time" to refer to our cognizing or mental recognition of events happening. When we make a distinction between an event happening, and then later happening, we create the concept of "the distance" between those events." Consider the relationship between the earth spinning on its axis. We say that the "time" it takes to complete one revolution of that process represents a "day." So we sub-measure it into 24 hours and each hour into 60 minutes, etc.

This leads us to two of the most basic kinds of time, *physical time* and *mathematical time*. Thus when we *"time"* a runner racing around a quarter mile track we correlate that event by measuring it up against the event of the earth turning. We make this comparison using a stop-watch and thereby measure chronological time. Here we use the term "time" as a verb, we "timed" him or her. This "timing" speaks about our recognition of the relationship between two events; starting to run and reaching a certain point.

In addition to "time" first referencing events and then our conceptualization of the order, sequence, distance, etc. of those events up against other events, we also use the term "time" to reference *rhythms*. Hence we might describe the rhythm of the earth's movement as it spins, or its movement around the sun, or through the universe. We may refer to the rhythms within physiology that create the events of waking and sleeping, that involve diurnal cycles, lunar cycles, bio-rhythmic cycles, etc.

NLP on "Time"

NLP addresses "time" by first (as noted) describing the term itself as a nominalization, rather than a true noun. This empowers us to look not at things, but processes in our search for understanding of "time." It warns us to take care in talking about it as a thing. NLP next inquires about how we *internally* represent it. This then leads to asking numerous structural questions:

- How do we *code* this concept of "time" in our minds-and-bodies?
- How do other people *represent* "time?"
- Does everybody use similar patterns for coding "time?"
- What differences do we find in people in how they think about this concept?
- Can we code the past, present, and future in ways that do us harm?
- Can we change our "time" codings so that they will serve us well?
- How can we alter our "time" representations?
- What determines how we represent "time"—genetics or nature?
- Does birth into a given culture fate us to a certain way to experience "time?"
- How much does experience play a role in our experience of "time?"
- Can we change "the past?"
- What effect does our "time" coding have on our "personalities?"
- What effect does "time" and our representations have on our emotions?
- *Past experiences* profoundly influence today's present state, but how much?
- What do we need to do to transform our memories of the past?

In the pages that follow we acknowledge the extent to which we have developed into the person we know ourselves today in our thinking, emoting, behaving, etc. due to the influence of past experiences. We moved through such experiences and as we did we created many representations, ideas, beliefs, and values about "time." These have become our "programs" for thinking, believing, feeling, valuing, functioning, etc.

We also acknowledge the changeability of "time." As a mental construct and neuro-linguistic representation, NLP offers many patterns and processes for transforming our experience of "time," how we represent it, the meanings we give to it, and therefore our "time" personality. Repeatedly we highlight the outrageousness of Richard Bandler's statement that "It's never too late to have a happy childhood." The techniques of time-line processes that follow will allow you to de-energize old hurtful memories, various malalignments to "time," and to access numerous resources for adventuring more joyfully and lovingly through "time."

General-Semantics on "Time"

"At what level does the term 'time' refer?"

The domain of general semantics offers yet another analysis of the term "time." This domain views the word "time" as a **multi-ordinal word.** Korzybski defined multiordinality as words so generalized (similar to nominalizations) that they can and do function at many different levels of abstraction. Yet at each level wherein we abstract our understandings, the word carries *different meanings* and associations. When this happens, we have to exercise extreme care with regard to the word to index at *what level we use the word.* If we don't, we *confuse levels,* identify processes or phenomena at different levels and end in a variety of pathologies: identification, confusion, non-sense, creating non-referential terms, misplaced concreteness (reification), etc.

In other words physical "time" as rhythm differs radically from psychological "time" (fast and slow "time"), historical "time," linguistic "time," etc. Later (Chapter 11) we have devoted an entire chapter to presenting a mode of "time" in terms of its logical levels. Until we get to that point, we will only remark that there exists many kinds of "time" and that these kinds of "time" operate on various levels. This directs us to identify *how the term operates multiordinally on various levels* and not to take the word "time" as always meaning the same thing. Doing this will protect us from identifying *the concept "time"* from the physical referent on the primary level of "time" —events occurring and changing. And this, in turn, will protect us from uttering all kinds of non-sense in terms of "time."

Ultimately you'll discover that "time," as a concept (conceptual "time"), emerges from the way we represent happenings and events in the world, and then develop abstract understandings **about** the relationship between those events. This calls upon us to language "time" as a concept about events, and also as a concept about other concepts. When our map of some process in the territory does not fit with the territory, we can confuse ourselves endlessly. Therefore much of the task of any science involves the task of getting a decent fit between map and territory. We seek to do that here by de-nominalizing the term.

The Languaged Phenomenon of "Time"

Every day we turn our minds toward "time"—*toward our sense of time*, time past, present, and future. Why do we do this? We do it because we have a very special kind of consciousness. We have a "time" consciousness that preeminently processes the multiple levels of "time." And as we develop our "time" consciousness, it orders and structures our experiences (emotions, neurology, rhythms, etc.) thereby creating various "personality" structures.

At the primary level of empirical experience, we measure "time" by days, months, and years. This enables us to chronicle the **quantitative amount of "time"** we have lived. Yet, daily we also make a meta-move to a higher level as we turn inward and reflect upon the quality of life that we have lived within those "time" periods. We also then go meta again to our sense of "time" itself to thereby create psychological "time."

The Greeks had different words for these facets of "time." They designated the first by the term *chronos,* and the second by *kairos.* These two Greek words for "time" distinguish external and internal "time." *Chronos* comes into English as chronology, chronicle, chronogram, chronograph, chronologist, chronometer, and even chronic (marked by long duration, always presenting, constantly vexing or troubling) etc. This refers to *quantative "time"* the numbers and measures we use to mark off distance between events.

We don't have any direct words to translate *kairos* in English. In translating the word, we use such terms as "opportunity, opportune, timely, season," etc. By these we convey its qualitative significance. This refers to *qualitative time* or psychological time, the quality of the experience or event as felt, understood, and valued from the inside, hence, subjective time.

As each of us came into the world, our mothers experienced a merging of *chronos* and *kairos*. For when her "time" came to deliver us, that "timely moment" (*kairos*) involved her qualitative experience—whether positive or negative, an unforgettable moment of time(!). As such, her "time" refers to what happened and how it happened—her story in time. Yet externally, the "time" (*chronos*) that the doctor or nurse recorded on the birth certificate specified the hour, day, and year regarding when that special event occurred—"objective" time.

What "Time" Do You Have?

As creatures with a **time-consciousness**, the phenomenon of "time" plays a dominant role in our lives. At the primary level we experience "time" pressures, problems with "time" schedules, etc. Many times a day we check about the "time" or ask someone, "What time do you have?" We do this to orient ourselves in "time."

Then we jump logical levels and inquire, "Where does all the time go?" And more times than we like to count, we complain or hear the complaint, "There's just not enough time in a day!" "I need more time." Suddenly we have moved into psychological "time." To such "time" problems, we or others offer various "time" advice (perhaps not in a "timely" manner), "Why don't you take a time-management class?" "You need to manage your time better."

How different this is to our childhood experiences of "time." Then "time" moved so slowly. It took fooorrreeevvver. And we got bored so often and so quickly. So, we complained, "There's nothing to do." We waited for summer vacation and Christmas which seemed to take its sweet "time" to come. We thought we would never turn sixteen and get to drive.

But now "time" seems to have sped up. It moves at greater speeds. The days, months, years, and even decades seem to go faster and faster. "Where did last summer go; it just zoomed by!" "It seems like we just took down the Christmas tree." "Your seventh birthday—why I remember when we went to the hospital to see you, it seems like just yesterday."

In these ways, and numerous other ways, we experience *psychological time* within our minds-bodies to our glory and to our misery. But what do we mean by "time" in the first place? What kind of "thing" do we have reference to?

The Non-Thingness of "Time"

Since "time" does not refer to a **thing,** we erroneously mis-speak when we so talk about "time." Yet we do it constantly. We assume that it exists externally apart from our mind-body, from our neuro-linguistics, as if you could see, hear, or feel "time" empirically. "Time" does **not** exist in that dimension of reality, it rather exists in the realm of "mind." It refers to a conceptual way of marking out a **process** as events transpire and between events that occur.

With "time" as our awareness of *ongoing movements* that occur in between reference points that we mark out, this corresponds to Webster's definition. "The measured or measurable period during which an action, process, or condition exists or continues, duration; the point or period when something occurs."

To punctuate "time," we use events like the movement of the rotation of the earth and the movement of earth around the sun. As a concept and mental representations of the concept, the term "time" stands for a *complex abstraction* which we use in living. As a consciousness of an abstraction, we then develop beliefs about "time," values (or disvalues) about it, decisions about it, feelings of it, etc. These **semantical features of "time"** as a construct generates our phenomenological experience of time. M. Stuart in *The Psychology of Time* wrote,

> "We do not perceive time directly. We cannot taste it like sugar or smell it as we smell some gases. The only thing we are aware of is that *things change*, that it is getting later. This is our nearest approach to a person perception of time."

In the term "time" we refer to a conceptual understanding. Yet given the nature of our language, we find it very difficult to even talk about "time" (there we go again) without nominalizing it as a thing! Though we use a word that looks like and sounds like a noun, we must continually remind ourselves that "time" does **not** refer to any "person, place or thing."

It refers to a **process**—our mental conceiving (abstracting) of previous events, current events, and future events. So in treating it as an *ongoing process of events*, we typically need to use verbs. If then the *ongoing movements* that occur in between marked out reference points comprise the essence of our concept of "time," then we process "time" by mentally thinking about and referencing such processes (e.g. the planet making one rotation on its axis). So a day stands for one unit of that process. From our point-of-view, a "day" comprises the "time" that we perceive the sun as rising, moving across the sky, setting, our world's baptism in darkness, and then the rising of the sun. We *conceptually punctuate the "time"* of a day using these events. How do we measure a "year?" We measure it as the process of the earth making one complete revolution around the sun, a process that takes 365.25 days. We measure these "time" units in terms of how long it takes some other **processes** to occur.

Treating "time" as a thing endangers of *reifying* this construct. When we turn our understanding of this concept into a thing, an entity apart from the conceptualizer, we give it "a misplaced concreteness" (Whitehead). Here then we deal with a high level abstraction. We should not let the tiny little word "time" fool us. The size of words don't always accord to the level of complexity or conceptualization within them. So with "time."

This non-thingness of "time" exists so intimately in our consciousness that it seems "real" in an external way. Yet this seeming reality of "time" plays out deceptively. It does **not** exist externally at all. We can't see it, hear it, or feel it. It exists solely and entirely as a subjective, psychological *abstraction*. So this "mind"-thing of "time" refers to how we *think about, represent, and code* movement and changes of our experiences of events and **between** events. To denominalize this noun ("time"), I like to sometimes use the word in verb form, tim-ing.

At the micro-level of reality, **everything exists as processes**—as ongoing, never-ending *change* as sub-atomic particles dance around in a wild and chaotic way. As this changing-ness goes on and on and on, we represent it as "time." We recognize that some events as having already occurred ("past" time), some occurring now (present time) and some that we anticipate will occur ("future" time).

"Time" refers to our understanding of **processes** in various stages of development. General-semantist Robert Pula describes the sub-microscopic level as a place there we do not find *"things" changing* as much as *change thinging.*

> "We call this the sub-microscopic level where whirls of what we call electrons, protons, quarks, etc. and a whole 'zoo' of sub-atomic entities relate in various ways to make the basis of what we experience as a desk, a chair, an apple, you and us." (Kodish and Kodish, 1993, 37).

"Time" Consciousness

The importance of "time" lies in that human consciousness exists as a *"time"* consciousness. That makes us "time" creatures. Whether you believe with Emmanuel Kant (1787) that "time" exists as one of those Kantian *a priori* categories, or with Alfred Korzybski (1941) that we create our sense of "time" within our "mind" as we abstract from our experiences in the world and thereby create "time" as one of our mental constructs, or go with the old Ecclesiastes writer who asserted that God has put "eternity" ("a sense of time past and present") into our minds (Eccl. 3:11)—ultimately we recognize that **"time"** *intimately, intrinsically, and inescapably forms and structures our consciousness about ourselves, others, life, history, the future, etc.*

Conceptualizing "time" as we do makes us **"time" creatures**. It endows us with a sense of transcendence regarding "time." Though we live in "time," we conceptualize things beyond "time."

We also *bind "time."* Korzybski (1921) added another facet to this analysis of "time" when he defined humans as "the 'time' binding class of life." This refers to how we can utilize the learnings, developments, and progress of those who lived in previous times and by the means of symbols, symbolization, and language, we do not have to start over with each generation as animals do. We can build upon ("bind" to ourselves) the previous learnings. We can carry the benefits of "time" via our ability to symbolize in language. (We will develop this understanding further in Chapter 10).

We also *travel through "time."* We do not only exist as a "time" binding class of life, but in our everyday experiences, we demonstrate ourselves as a **"time" traveling class of life.** This refers to how we can mentally (conceptually) make "time" trips backwards and forwards on our "time-lines." And this can, and does, create for many of us various "time" problems (and resources). This can challenge us about even living in our *psychological present.* Those who can't often end up missing the "here and now" as they lose sensory awareness of today. They live too much in the "past" or in the "future." Therefore, as a way to stay in the present—we have to develop awareness of all of our mental trips to the "past" and the "future" so that we don't get lost in those "time" zones and miss the here-and-now present.

Those who get lost in the past "time" zone can get so stuck there in the places of the "past," that they can't (psychologically) come into the *Now.* What causes this? - usually an unresolved traumatic event which the person has not "come to terms with" (conceptually). As a result, that person just keeps playing their memories and representations as an old "B"-rated movie over and over inside their head. As they do, it fills up consciousness and torments them with images, sounds, words, and feelings of pain and distress. And this, in turn, induces them into very unresourceful states. Obviously, the "past" does not represent any place to live—to visit for a little while, yes, to take little day trips to for the sake of nostalgia, perhaps, but not to live.

To get **un-stuck** from the places of the past necessitates exploring how we have "the past" coded in our minds, *and recoding it* in order that we develop enough mental flexibility that we no longer feel stuck. We have identified the specific time-line processes (Chapters 3-6) to accomplish that very thing. There we look at the ways you may have coded the experiences of your "past" that do not work very well for you. There we look at processes for reframing the old meanings and beliefs that create our "trauma map" which keeps inducing us into ongoing traumatization.

We can similarly get "stuck" in the future. We can over-focus on the non-existent "future" by accessing too negative imaginings about worrisome and fretful movies of the future. Or, we can overwhelm ourselves by building as too large future pictures.

Either way, we can live so much in that "time" zone that we miss the **Now.** Given the danger of these "time" problems, time-line processes enable us to learn new and efficient ways to creatively and effectively use, and adventure into, our past and future "time" zones.

One of the overall "time" skills we need to develop involves a kind of *flexibility of consciousness* that allows us to move through the "time" zones in such a way that we integrate and use the wisdom obtained from each "time" perspective without getting stuck or caught in any dimension to the exclusion of the others.

We can derive **wisdom** from our adventures through the "time" zones. For going in-and-out of those "time" zones we can make valuable learnings from the "past." We can also learn to do more consequential thinking about where current actions will take us in the "future." The resulting wisdom empowers us to take more effective action in the here-and-now to create well-formed outcomes that we desire and which will pull us into a positive and glorious future.

Conclusion

With Augustine we also sometimes feel, "What, then, is time? If no one asks me, I know; if I want to explain it to someone who does ask me, I do not know." Yet now with the linguistic analyses available in Neuro-Linguistic Programming and general semantics we have the tools for discovering this category of the mind. We can do more. We can work with our construct to form and reformat it as a mental map that has a better fit with the territory. We can also adjust poor and inadequate maps that we have made in our journey through "time," as we do what no other creature can do—"time" travel. Tighten your seat-belts, the journey now begins!

Part II

Time-Line Patterns
& Processes

Chapter 2

Time-Lines

The Basics About Our Coding of "Time"

How Does the Brain Tell "Time"?

As the Greek word *chronos* describes linear time, it means a span of time. We measure *chronos* as distance or motion like the hands on a clock face, or dates on a calendar, hence chronology. Beyond *chronos* we have *kairos*—a time of opportunity. You can't see *kairos* on the hands of a clock. The emphasis in *kairos* focuses on quality, not quantity. In time-line processes we make changes in relation to our *chronos*, which then creates a new *kairos* for us.

Since NLP focuses on process rather than content, let's ask the process question: *How* does our brain record, code, and measure "time?" What goes on, mentally, that enables us to know the difference between the past, present, and future? How do we know the order of events? The brain does something to create this distinction. If it didn't we would not have the ability to distinguish between events. A clue lies in some of the sayings we use about "time:" "I see it in front of me." "I feel stuck back there, and can't get out." "I look forward to seeing you." Such sayings indicate that we code events in the way we locate those events; visually, auditorially, and kinesthetically.

Eliciting Your Coding of "Time"

Try an experiment. Think of something you do on a regular basis like driving to work, brushing your teeth, dressing, or something else. Remember doing this five years ago. If you can't find a specific time, then recall it generally. Next, recall doing it two years ago, once you remember that, recall doing it last week. You did it this morning, think about that... and you know you'll do it next week—imagine that, and again, in two years... and then five years from now.

As you recall and imagine this event, most people do so using a series of pictures or visual images in some way. Now, as you look at those pictures again, what differences exist in the submodalities? Check your pictures for the following distinctions:

In color or black-and-white
A movie or still picture
3D or flat
See your younger/older self or looking out from your eyes
Framed or panoramic
Bright or dim
Close or far
In focus or blurred
Location of picture in field of vision

Take a moment now to identify your coding of these "time" zones. By means of this coding you signal your brain to distinguish between events of the past, the present, and the future. These distinctions enable you to recognize the events as memories of the past, current representations, or future ones. We do this process unconsciously, mind remembers the location of your memories. Tad James asks a question to underscore the importance of our "time" memories,

> *"When you woke up this morning,*
> *how did you know to be you?"*

Consider that. Do we not know ourselves because we use our collection of memories for our self-definition and identity? This makes our sense of our identity highly dependent upon our "time" codings, does it not?

We can break the sub-qualities of our **modes of awareness** (the sensory modalities) into two basic formats: those that enable us to represent as either-or and those that enables us to represent along a *continuum*. The first case of either-or coding we call **digital** to indicate, like a digital watch, on-off distinctions. We see our pictures as a snapshot or a movie, we see them either as bordered or panoramic. The second case of *continuum coding* we call analogical to indicate that we can record *a range of responses and distinctions*. Thus in terms of submodalities, location probably gives the most clarity of representation (close to far) for a set of continuum distinctions. Although, we can also use dim to bright (image intensity), slow to quick (speed of movement), blur to clear (clarity of representation), low to high (volume), small to large (size), etc.

Thus in time-line processes, we generally find that the *location* of our images and pictures of past events usually serves as the most crucial factor. Most people store their concept of "time" sequentially and linearly. In listing the submodalities of your time-line, did you notice the importance of location?

The on-off distinctions of the digital submodalities do not tend to work very well for representing sequential time. Color or black-and-white represents one digital submodality, frame or panoramic another. Such submodalities do not allow for variation along a continuum. And yet a sequence of events, and our ability to note relationships between these events, requires variation. Therefore, our brains tend to primarily use analogue submodalities as the basis for our coding of these variations.

The brain primarily uses the visual submodality of **location** to store and represent "time" for the very reason that location functions as an analogue submodality. Thus location permits us to distinguish and access sequential events—events that occur one after another. Brightness and focus lack enough variation to represent "time." So most people, in most cultures, rely on *size, distance, and location* for representing this concept of time. This enables us to store our "time" in various places around, behind, before, above, and below us (various locations at varying distances). Further, if we step back to get an image of the overall configuration of this "time" representation, we usually have a line, a shape of some sort, picture... Thus, the origin of the term, "time-line."

Nor do auditory submodalities allow for simultaneous access of memories. Kinesthetic submodalities tend to lack the imprecision of the visual system (although we have a kinesthetic time-line process, Dilts, 1990, Hall, 1996). Thus, we tend to rely primarily on the visual system to represent the long and detailed continuum of our experiences over "time." The visual system can contain far more information simultaneously than can the auditory or kinesthetic representation systems.

Each of us has his or her own way of storing time. No single style serves as "the correct way" in contradistinction to the incorrect way. They just differ. Yet, *how* we store "time" does lead to various consequences in experiences, emotions, and behaviors. For example, suppose you coded your "past" directly in front of you. Would you not feel more driven by your memories? Would they not seem more "in your face" and more difficult to "get away from?"

The Significance of Our "Time" Codings

Bill came to me (BB) in a state of depression. One year earlier his girl friend dumped him. As I worked with Bill, I discovered that he pictured her leaving him and put this picture—directly in front of his face. Not a wise choice! So I used several interventions with Bill. The major change resulted when Bill moved the image from in front of his face to behind his head. I had him "put his past behind him"!

Suppose you have your vision of your future behind you! Do you think that would help you to feel driven to attain that vision? No. Your motivation would drop to the floor. Nothing would pull you forward. Conversely, what would you give your chances of attaining your goals if you had your visions for yourself in front of you and coded as big and bright pictures? Well, if you use bigness and brightness as some of your critical (driving) submodalities, you will probably feel pulled into your future! An old Jewish proverb says, "Where there is no vision, the people perish."

Figure 2.1

| Birth | "Past Events" | The Present | Future Events |

Anglo-European and Arabic Time

Which attracts more of your attention, what happens now or what will happen in the future? Do you even feel concerned about the future?

I (BB) used to live in frustration with those people who lived only for the moment. How could they not "count the cost?" At the same time, I felt envious of them. They appeared to enjoy the present moment with much more gusto than I did. After learning the NLP model about "time" coding and how people take different points of view about time, I now adopt an entirely different outlook on things. The problem lies in how a person mentally maps their concept of "time."

James and Woodsmall (1988) describe the difference between Anglo-European time and Arabic time (p. 17ff). They assert that Anglo-European time grew as the result of the Industrial Revolution due to the fact that assembly line work requires workers to get to work "on time." The assembly line required people to think and structure "time" more linearly. At each successive stage of construction, the worker placed a specific part on the equipment. Anglo-European time describes "time" in terms of one event happening after another. It sees "time" as linear and the events stretching out like an assembly line.

Arabic time describes an entirely different approach. A person characterized by the Anglo-European concept of time will seek to arrive "on time." However, a person driven by the Arabic concept of time will rarely arrive in such a timely manner. People from the Islamic countries and areas of the world with warm climates live primarily in Arabic time. They live *for the moment*. "Time" happens now, and not at their next appointment. These people can handle several matters simultaneously; they process "time" information more randomly.

A few years ago my wife and I (BB) visited a missionary friend of ours in Martinique, a French Island in the Southern Caribbean area. You may begin a committee meeting one hour after the scheduled time. If someone told you that they would arrive at your home at 3:00 p.m., they may arrive by 5:00 p.m. I experienced cultural shock with this! A person who thinks this way will rarely plan beyond two weeks. Only those forced to plan ahead will stand out as the exceptions to this. They may do it, but they won't like it.

Time-Lining

We find in the United States both the Anglo-European and the Arabic understandings of "time." Frequently, a husband will operate in the Anglo-European mode while the wife operates in the Arabic mode. Should we then wonder that conflict will arise between them? The husband wants to save money for the *future* while the wife wants to spend it now!

Discerning These "Time" Modes

How can we discern our primary time frame? Your internal codings of "time" determine which "time" frame you operate from.

Pause for a moment and do the following: Recall an event that happened to you six months or a year ago. Pay particular attention to **which direction** the image of the memory comes to you. The image may lie inside or outside your head. You may point in the direction of the image. Do the same thing for the future. Imagine something that will happen in the next six months, then a year from now. Pay particular attention to which direction you sense that image from yourself. Now point in that direction. This image lies in a different place than your past image, doesn't it? Usually, our future lies in the opposite direction from our past. If it lies in the same direction, what *other distinctions* enable you to tell the difference? It may lie in the same direction, but at a different distance, the images may differ in brightness, the sounds in volume, etc.

You may need to close your eyes to do this. Get an image in your mind of your current experience in the here-and-now, the present. Where do you locate the present? Notice where each image lies, its location, kind, and quality of representations. Notice the difference between the direction for the past and the future and imagine a line between where you locate this representation.

Through Time and In Time

Another important distinction about "time" involves whether you code it as *outside of you or inside?* When we traced out our "line" or other configuration, did you represent the images (sounds, sensations) as *out in front of you?* If so, NLP designates this as a *"Through Time"* coding. In this format, the time-line will typically stretch from right to left, but could go from left to right, up to down, down to up, etc. But regardless of the shape and location, it will occur in front of you and therefore outside of your body. If I (MH) had labeled this, I would have called it *out-of-time.* "Through time" and "Out-of-Time" people correspond to the Anglo-European mode of "time" processing.

If, on the other hand, your images, sounds or sensations do not lie out beyond you, but lie behind your field of vision, and move through you or in you, then you operate from the Arabic mode of "time" processing. We designate a person who has a portion of their time-line **inside** their body or behind their field of vision as an "In Time" person.

Re-Positioning "In Time" and "Through Time" Distinctions

By using the model of "time" levels (Figure 11.2) and so distinguishing these various kinds of conceptual time and separating them from physical "times," this not only helps to denominalize "time," it also enables us to re-position the meta-program distinctions in how people sort time that we have called "in time" and "through time."

"In time" people actually live as "in times" (plural) people; they live at the primary level of events, happenings, etc. and so get caught up in that moment, and have no consciousness, no awareness of sequencing time (a meta-level phenomenon). So "in times" people may not notice "time" as a concept at all. The "timelessness" at that level means that their focus has gone entirely to the details and content of what they experience.

By way of contrast, *"through"* or *"out-of"* time people, actually experience this because they have moved to a meta-level and notice the relationship between events that have occurred, those now occurring and those that will occur. Actually, we could call them *"meta"* time people. This explains why they do not get lost in the moment, lost to the details and content of the experience. They have a representation of "time" itself, so they live more "time"-conscious as they live out of primary time.

As you can see from the *"Time"* Levels chart (Figure 11.2)— the kind of "timelessness" that exists for "in times" (plural) people differs radically from the kind of "timelessness" that exists at a high meta-meta level where meanings transcend the concept of time. In the first case, the person just doesn't process time as a concept, in the latter, they have processed it as such, and then transcended that level.

Difficulty Eliciting the Time-Line

Usually the process of asking a person to point in the direction of their "past" and "future" will elicit their time-line configuration. Did you find yours? Other people, do not so easily discover their structure of "time." Several "problems" may arise with regard to this.

1. *Poor quality pictures or unconscious about visualizing.* Since most people operate from a "favorite representational system" (Bandler and Grinder, 1976), those who operate most by the auditory, kinesthetic, or auditory-digital systems may not visualize very well. When a person over-relies on one of these systems, they have indeed no consciousness of internal images.

As others attempt to recall a regularly repeated event, they may see "pictures," but also notice that these internal images do not seem as clear as their external visual pictures. So consequently, they will judge their internal pictures (visual images) as inadequate. Some people will even conclude that they do not make internal pictures.

Actually, most people have this experience. The majority of people report a lower quality of detail in their *internal* pictures compared to *external* seeing. This suggests that we should not expect our internal images to have the same kind of clarity as those we see in "real time."

Most people also report that their internal pictures do not "hold" or sustain themselves as do external images. Indeed, except for artists and others especially trained or skilled in holding their internal images, most of us experience our visual pictures flashing in and out very rapidly. Some people, in fact, will need to train their ability to *catch* these pictures flashing in and out.

Another complicating factor involves the possibility of a person having two or more time-lines. Use this same technique of elicitation and notice if different contexts (recreation, work, home life, vocations, etc.) may elicit a secondary time-line. Recall a series of events, at various ages, .to elicit more information about other potential ways that you have of coding "time." Recall happy events over a period of years and notice their locations... We view these "secondary" time-lines as entirely context dependent phenomenon—in other words, dependent entirely upon the context.

2. *Unable to Identify Time-line.* Suppose you still don't know the location or structure of your time-line? Then take a moment and *pretend that you do...* Just suppose you did know the location of your time-line... Go with that thought and as you relax, ask your unconscious mind to move your finger. After all, your unconscious mind knows which finger on which hand to point in the direction of your "past." If you knew where you stored your "past," what direction would it lie in? As your unconscious mind points, thank it, and ask this inner mind of yours in which direction you store your sense of the future, allowing it to point your finger in that direction.

If that doesn't elicit the information, it only speaks of just how much this information lies outside of your awareness—it means nothing more than that. Some people have some very strange ways of coding "time," some use very unusual metaphors and as with any awareness that we take for granted, we don't pay attention to its structure or form, but to the content inside it.

3. *Elicit a Kinesthetic Time-line.* Inasmuch as we elicit time-lines regularly from clients and workshop participants, we find that most people responded quickly and easily to the elicitation.

I (BB) have only had one person who did not respond to a visual elicitation. Randy had difficulty making internal pictures and having awareness of them. Randy processed primarily as a "kino" (kinesthetically). So, I had Randy place his time-line on the floor. I simply asked Randy to imagine his time-line on the floor covering ten or fifteen feet. Starting from "now" (today), Randy moved backward to the place where he had his memories. He identified his "past" and then his "future." Next I asked Randy to walk on this kinesthetic time-line.

Now while I prefer working with a visual representation (my favorite sensory system), if a person codes it primarily in the kinesthetic system, then I use that. Here, walking your time-line offers a better option than visualizing it.

One problem that may arise from using a kinesthetic time-line involves more difficulty dissociating from negative emotion. I (BB) have found that people who kinesthetically walk their time-line will find it more difficult to dissociate, because they seem to more easily associate into their memory. Yet because the dissociation process from a traumatic memory empowers a person to let go of the emotional hurt, this plays an important role. For me, walking the time-line increases the likelihood of the client's re-associating into the memory.

Taking these things into consideration, we therefore recommend the process of having the person practice *stepping off* their kinesthetic time-line, taking a **meta-position** to it, and then looking and talking about it. This will enable them to experience the dissociation kinesthetically in preparation for change work. (For more about a kinesthetic time-line, see Hall, 1996, and Dilts, 1990.)

4) *Stress Process.* As you elicit time-lines, *emphasize process*. Ask questions about the structure of the memory rather than the content. When people start describing the meaning and emotions of the memory, they have moved into the content, rather than the structure or form of the memory. Lead them to focus on the memory's structure in term of the quality of its image, sounds, sensations...

Many people have lots of auditory representations within their time-line. Some may even store and code their memories as sounds rather than pictures. Again, this carries no inherent meaning, it simply indicates how one makes distinctions about "time." The important thing in all of this simply involves discovering that structure and checking it to determine how well it works for you (the ecology check).

- Do you hear the sounds and words of an event?
- Where do you locate the source of those sounds?
- How loud or quiet? .
- What tone of voice?
- Any rhythm to it?
- Whose voice?
- How do these qualities differ in something you heard five years ago, one year ago, today, what you will hear tomorrow, next week, next year, in five years?

Parts—Other Facets of Our Thoughts-and-Feelings About "Time"

One other possible source, or cause, of difficulty in discovering and working with our "time" representations (whether a "line," circle, spiral, roll-a-dex, etc.) lies in our *beliefs* about such. What do you believe about your internal mental constructions of the idea of time? (Here we moved to a higher logical level, as we think about our thoughts-and-feelings about "time." This represents not merely a state, but a meta-state. See Appendix A).

People who frequently can't see, hear or feel their time-line have one or more internal "parts" that object. Assume that this part does this to protect you from something i.e. a painful memory, a trauma, too much introspection, etc. Regrettably, many people have experienced very difficult childhoods loaded with painful memories that they have sought to escape from and which may have become buried, over the years, deep in their unconscious mind. Consequently, people can develop various protective parts to keep these memories hidden and away from the view of the conscious mind. The memories give them too much pain, they induce desperate states.

In such cases, begin by thanking that part! Thank that part of you for protecting you from overwhelmingly negative emotions swamping you. Assure and inform that part of you with the realization that you have grown up and matured so that now you have enough information, skills, and wisdom to protect yourself in new and different ways than denial and avoidance.

As you tell this part that you have other ways of protecting yourself, assure it that mere *"information"* from the past can't hurt or destroy you. Assure it that such past memories no longer exist—except in our mind and in the way you represent it.

> "When those events originally occurred, I didn't have the mental knowledge or personal skills to cope with such. But now I can. At that time, you protected me from such painful awareness, and, did you also seek to do anything else of positive value for me that I need to know?"

Here we ask that part about its intent. When you get an answer, explore specifically what it sought to do of positive value by its actions. Continue asking this question until you get a meta-level positive intent. When you do, you then will have its permission to go clean up the old memories.

Time-lines and "Personality"

James and Woodsmall (1988) have used NLP time-lines to identify the processes by which our coding of "time" affects, determines, and interacts with our "personality." For instance, a time-line may move out in any direction and may take all kinds of forms and shapes: as a straight line, a spiral, a loop, a lily-pad, a boomerang, etc. The line may dissect your body ("in time") or move around outside your body ("through time" or "out of time"). Through time people usually dissociate from their memories and so see themselves in their memories. Because their time-line lies out in front of them, they tend to like "time," have a friendly relationship to it, view "time" as money, don't "waste time," and seek to get their money's worth.

A *through time* person corresponds to the judger in the Myers-Briggs type indicator. A *through time* judger organizes things and people and likes to do things step by step procedurally. Such a person has much consciousness about "time" and so values it and values arriving at places "on time." They tend to carry pocket calendars, daytimers, etc. A *through time* person operates in a goal oriented way, likes (even needs) closure, says things like, "Let's decide now." This paces their concept of "time" and "timeliness." Because *through time* persons see the "past" out in front of them (usually off to a side), past memories may haunt them a lot.

How different the life of an *in time* person. This person functions more as the perceiver on Myers-Briggs. An *in time* person will more likely have their "past" behind them, although actually any part of their time-line may lie behind them. Now because *in time* people associate inside of "time," they can get "lost in the eternal now," and have no idea "what time it is." This association may also cause them to have difficulty in letting go of past emotions.

As the *in time* person associates in his or her memories, this person will look out from his or her own eyes as if still in the past experience. And this way of coding and representing past "time" will lead the person to feel the "past" as if it now continues to occur. For this reason, time-line processes sometimes come as a true God-send for those who get so caught up in past hurts that they drag them along with them into the present and seem "stuck" in the past. The time-line processes can now enable them to develop a better "relationship" to "time" and to past painful memories. Via these time-line processes, a person can learn how to dissociate from old hurts and let old dated emotions go.

In Myers-Briggs, the *in time* person shows up as a perceiver. Here organizing and organization does not characterize this kind of person. A perceiver lives in the now, and enjoys the moment. Inasmuch as *in time* people live in the now, they make great lovers. After all, they do not give a lot of importance to "time." By way of contrast, a *through time* person usually has much difficulty living in the now.

An *in time* person enjoys the present and may have difficulty projecting ideas, plans, processes into the future. Such people will tend to believe, "Be here now!" Yet living in a constant state of association, *in time* people may feel more troubled by the events that come their way and have a different problem each week.

A strength for *in time* people lies in how they can often recall and re-experience any memory or state at will. As they think of an experience—they go back into that state! A weakness for them involves punching a time clock and needing to show up "on time" for appointments. Because they live so much in the moment they tend to inevitably come late! They may just forget their next appointment. As for pocket calendars and "to do" lists, *in time* people don't like them! If they have learned to use them, they still probably don't like them. As perceivers, they differ from judgers in that they don't care so much about immediate closure. They may care more about keeping their options open.

Could a person have both *through time* and *in time* characteristics? Yes! This may exist as context dependent responses (BB). Or, you may have actually created two separate time-lines, as I (MH) have done for myself and for numerous clients. The one may display behavior of both, and have a *through time* time-line while at work and shift to an *in time* time-line at home, in personal relationships, doing hobbies, recreational activities, etc. As always, in NLP we seek primarily to understand the structure of our internal experiences and to then increase our choices and abilities. And because some people operate healthily in both modes of time.

Conclusion

You now know your **representational coding for "time"** and how to find such "time" codings in others. Take a few days to continue to experiment and to experience your own personal and unique ways of representing "time." As you feel more and more comfortable with this, begin to inquire of others about prior events, present events, and future events and notice their non-verbal gestures and indicators as to where they store "time." Train your ear also to pick up on more and more temporal (time) words in your own language behavior and that of others. Like us you'll probably feel amazed at how frequently you will hear such.

Chapter 3

Time-Lining Human Distresses

Using Time-Line Processes Therapeutically
For Dealing With Negative Emotions

"It's never to late to have a happy childhood."
(Richard Bandler)

With the NLP "time-line" model as a model for the way that we typically think, represent, and relate to "time," we now want to offer some practical applications. What good-news that we no longer need to get stuck with our time-line constructions! After all, we constructed them—so we can **re-construct** them! You didn't write them in stone, you wrote them in the most plastic and moldable of substances, the neuro-pathways of your nervous system.

This concept of relating to "time" via acknowledging and working with our "time" configurations, namely, our *time-line(s)* enables us to effectively deal with those awarenesses of **the events** that have occurred or we anticipate will occur that keep inducing us into unresourceful states. It enables us to deal with old hurtful and ugly memories of such events that may still bother us. Knowing how we code the concept of "time" itself, and how we code our experience of "moving through time" from past events to the now and onto future events, gives us the ability to "travel" backwards or forwards in "time" to make changes.

Richard Bandler grabs attention by brashly asserting, *"It's never to late to have a happy childhood!"* This conviction in NLP arises because if our subjectivity arises from our construction of our memories, concepts, and representations, then as we change those internal representations, we change our "reality" structure. We do this in order to construct a map that will serve us well, instead of one that undermines our resourcefulness.

Chapter Overview

In this chapter we describe the use that we all make of "time" and our time-line constructions in building various *gestalts of under-standings*. This can work to our benefit or detriment. By under-standing the gestalting of our memories and how we use them to build meta-level constructions like beliefs, identity, decisions, and strategies for all kinds of things, we can discover the key for elimi-nating and/or transforming those that do us harm.

Here, also we present the basic NLP **V/K Dissociation Pattern** that will enable you to change, alter, erase and even eliminate any nagging memory of any kind of hurt or pain (trauma) that you feel you no longer need in your head. In the chapter that follows we will apply this *time-lining* process to specific negative emotions such as grief, guilt, fear, etc., along with other negative experiences like bad decisions, stupid conclusions and beliefs... to such pieces of subjectivity that function as limitations and sabotages to effec-tiveness, happiness, and self-mastery. We can now **time-line** ourselves into *resourcefulness!*

The Gestalting of Memories

We do not consciously remember everything. Of course not! As we move on through the events of days and weeks and months and years, events tend to mesh together in our mind and merge into various gestalts. We collect our memories together into various classifications; thoughts-and-emotions I've experienced at work and about work, thoughts-and-feelings I experienced with Mary and about Mary, thoughts-and-feelings around school, etc.

Try to recall what happened on any given day that carries no specific meaning for you, March 29, April 7, August 12. Remember that date from last year, the year before, three years ago, five, seven, etc.

This explains why most people find it difficult to access single specific memories. "Think about a time when you felt confident..." "Remember a time when you felt really empowered..." "Recall a moment when you asserted yourself effectively..." When we invite this kind of **accessing of a state or a resource**, most people's mind will bounce around from this time to that occasion and may have a mixture of events from numerous times, or find it difficult to locate the memory specifically. We can expect this of human consciousness.

To further complicate this, if a person thinks primarily in terms of "the big picture" (hence, a global thinker), then he or she will have coded and stored their memories together in a global way from the beginning. They will represent and connect memories which they evaluate as close in content or similar in emotions.

Consider thinking about a time when you met someone new who seemed very familiar—who might have reminded you of someone else. Now even though you knew that they differed from the other person, sometimes even a single cue in the stranger (his voice, her mannerisms, words they use, etc.) will *remind* you so much of the other person that it will fire off a whole gestalt of a memory. Suddenly you leave that present-moment time zone. We have "zoned out." You take a TDS inside yourself to your library of references. This may induce you into a pleasant and resourceful state, or it may invite you into a place of pain and distress.

Now because our "memories" (internal storage of past events) work this way in our mind and neurology, this process of moving back and forth on our time-line offers us a way to deal with problems in our time-line that keep old hurts or traumas alive in us.

We all naturally gestalt our memories. For something to **stand out** in a memorable way, something out of the ordinary, unusual, exceptional, greatly desired, greatly despised or regretted, etc. must *mark* that experience so that we set it apart, in our minds. Then it serves as a category or frame that we use for possibly collecting other instances of the same. Of course, "sameness" does not actually exist at the primary, sensory-based level of reality, only differences. *"Same"* speaks about a *higher logical level*—a linguistic level of generalizing to create categories, classes, and classifications.

Memories result from having some history with a person, event, or subject. Most negative gestalting (collecting of memories) begins from *significant emotional experience of pain and distress* (SEEP). To cope with, and come to terms with, these negative experiences, we develop beliefs and understandings as we draw conclusions and give various meanings to the experience. We develop decisions, scripts, identity selves, and choices ("parts") in order to cope, etc.

In time-line processes, we use this SEEP model to understand that our emotions gestalt (or connect) our memories to build *a large level understanding* (a mental construct at a higher logical level) **about** things (about self, others, the world, God, etc.). In this way we begin to build our own personal references, categories, classes, etc. Thereafter, any stimulus (or anchor) that fires off one memory will also fire off the entire gestalt so that typically we re-experience the emotions connected with that gestalt. In other words, our thoughts-emotions from the SEEP move us to reflexively think-and-feel intensely *about* that primary experience *in terms of meanings.* It thereby induces a neuro-semantic state.

Chart 3:1
The Gestalting of Memories

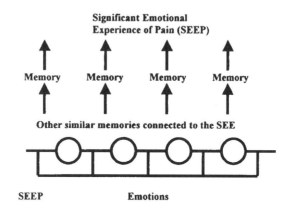

Have you ever had the experience of meeting someone who, from the start, just didn't like you? Or, conversely, someone who you (from the start) just didn't like? Why? If they didn't know you and had no experience with you then they, undoubtedly, experienced some gestalt of memories working within them that fired off connections between some hurtful person and yourself. Your voice, tone, tempo, gestures, eye movements, breathing... almost anything could have set off the connection.

If it happened to you, it may have both felt confusing and hurt your feelings. "What did I do?" you may have asked. Well, you triggered some stimuli, for that person, that carried all kinds of loaded meanings and emotions—and so they left the present moment as they went inside and took a "time" journey to another time and place. They, like us, can even do this with no awareness of doing so. When such occurs, outside of conscious awareness, it feels like "suddenly I had this feeling or this sense."

A gestalt of old pains, hurts, traumas, or negative experiences always operates by the firing of some trigger. Whenever we see, hear or feel something that has some similarity (an isomorphic structure) to the original trigger, the entire gestalt can fire. Obviously, this puts us in a reactive mode to the world and to the stimuli that can occur.

To address this using the NLP time-line processes, we will aim primarily to remove the emotional part of the gestalt by defusing the trigger. When we do that, the person's entire mental-and-emotional strategy will change.

What does the line between the beads of memories contain? It represents the *emotions* that tie the memories or the gestalt together. The emotional content serves *as the glue* that binds the memories together. The circles represent the memories (see Figure 3:1) and within those memories lie our encoded emotions. These emotions also reach beyond the memory and link one memory with another.

The emotional distress that we experience does not lie in the gestalting process itself, but in the content of the linkage. So in time-line processes we do not concern ourselves about the linkage itself. Rather, we seek to assist a person in letting go of the emotional content *within* the memory that doesn't serve them well. Doing this breaks the linkage of those memories so that the memories remain, but they will lack the negative emotional impact. The pearls stay in memory. By using the time-line process, we pull out the string of emotions. And having done this for several years, I (BB) continue to feel amazed at the results.

Both *through time* and *in time* people arrange their memories in gestalts. And inasmuch as *through time* people arrange their memories in front of them, the gestalt will tend to influence them more than an *in time* person. *Through time* people also gestalt their memories more readily than do *in time* people. When you ask a *through time* person to access a particular memory, he or she may have difficulty separating the facets of the gestalt. Instead of seeing one memory, they may see several. When this happens, ask the person to imagine their memories as if in a photo album. Then have them turn the pages back. This will help them access individual memories.

Developmental Periods

In time-line processes, we focus on doing change work around primarily the *Significant Emotional Experience of Pain* (SEEP) and the gestalt of memories. Critical to this work lies the process of locating the root cause of a negative state. Where does the root cause of the first SEEP lie? Once we locate this first SEEP, we can use time-line processes to remove the negative emotion from the entire gestalt.

The sociologist Morris Massey identified three major developmental stages through which we all pass: the Imprint Period (0-7), the Modeling Period (8-13), and the Socialization Period (14-21). We here summarize these periods as a way to locate and clean up the SEEP.

Imprint Period

The child functions like a sponge during the Imprint Period (0 to 7). At this age, the child has not yet developed mental filters. Everything the child hears and experiences tends to go straight into the mind which primarily operates unconsciously. This makes most of the learnings during this period unconscious, and so many of the memories will lie outside of conscious awareness.

During this imprint period, a child's concept of God develops, and, guess who they model their first conceptual understanding of God from? Right—father, mother and other authority figures. If the father acts in a loving and caring way, the child will grow up finding it easy to believe in a loving and caring God and a loving and caring world. If the father acts harshly and abusively, the child will tend to believe in a harsh and abusive God and world. What a handicap to begin life with! For this reason, we appreciate the usefulness of time-line processes in re-imprinting such memories. Much work with time-line processes around SEEP will focus on happenings that occurred during the Imprint Period of life. Though, not all SEEP's arise from the Imprint Period.

Modeling Period

During the Modeling Period (8 to 13) a child, both consciously and unconsciously, begins to model the behaviors of people around them. Until around the age of seven, most children do not distinguish well between self and parents. However, around eight the child begins to notice the differences between self and parents. He or she develops awareness of other people. He begins to model the behavior of heroes. Individual values begin to form at this age.

Massey says that our major values form during this period. Age ten plays a crucial period during this time. Consider what things occurred in your world about that time. Massey asserts that your world at age ten primarily shapes your values today. When dealing with people who have problems with values, look for trouble during the Modeling Period.

Socialization Period

From fourteen to twenty-one we experience the Socialization Period. During this stage the developing person begins to interact with other persons. Relationships and social values form, and these relationships and social values usually last throughout life. Via the time-line processes, we can alter these values if we desire. If a client has difficulty in the social areas of life, look for possible root causes in this period.

From "Presenting Problem" To the "Time" Gestalt to Limiting Beliefs

Counselors know that clients typically do not begin therapeutic work by freely and openly announcing "the real problem" when they first come in. Most people, even if they know the larger level problem, need to "test the waters" first to see how the therapist will respond. Will he or she respond with understanding, compassion, grace, wisdom, insight, etc.? Or will this person respond with judgments, superiority, accusation, etc?

Further, a great many people do not even know how to formulate or articulate *the larger level problem*—only the lower level symptoms and problematic thoughts-and-feelings that they don't like and want to get rid of. So how do we move from the presenting problem to the over-arching construction of the person's mental map that they created out of the gestalting of memories of hurt and pain?

Memories of Abandonment

Sue came to me (BB) distressed because her doctor had discontinued her anti-depressant medication. What factors contributed to her "depression?" Six years earlier, Sue's husband had left her, and since that time, she had grown dependent on medication to keep her feeling okay. "How could I live without the medicine?" So this was her presenting problem; her husband left her and she needed that medication!

As we talked and I gently explored through empathic questioning, a greater problem began to surface. Her mother had died from cancer during her time as a child and the memory of that death gestalted with the memory of the earlier divorce of her parents.

So the emotions surrounding the divorce of her husband gestated with the emotions of her mother's death and the earlier divorce. Thus, the divorce with her husband only served as an example of a greater emotional distress; feelings of abandonment (a SEEP).

In an effort to find and bring healing to this, I worked with Sue to take her back to the root cause (in her mind) that I knew had become a mental map. The root cause now comprised *the emotional state and meanings* that she built when she learned about her mother and father separating, and continue to maintain today.

Her own divorce simply served as another example of the same "problem" that had haunted her all her life (her "real" emotional distress). The divorce functioned as just one of the last beads on a long string of pearls. In questioning Sue, she related the great difficulty she had with discovering that her mother had terminal cancer. For the effect of time-line processes to last, we had to clear up the greater emotional distress and limiting belief that she had constructed from the SEEP of the root cause. We had to find the meta-level mental maps that she had built from that experience and transform her thinking-and-feeling on that level. Once we did that, and deleted the emotions that had lead to her meta-frames of reference, the other associated problems dissolved as well (Figure 3:2). Though the client may not have awareness of their existence, the time-line process will clean up the negative emotions from all the gestalt.

Figure 3:2
The Greater Problem

————————————————The Problem Frame————————————————
(Beliefs, Understandings, Decisions, Identity formation, etc.)

————————————————Memory of the SEEP————————————————
(Gestalts of Pain including the Original & Subsequent ones)

Person in Today —— Offering a presenting problem to a therapist

We experience our **identity** as the product of our memories. For we develop and form our self-definitions as a result of the thoughts-and-feelings we entertain in event after event after event over the years of our lives. From those experiences we draw conclusions about our Self, a high level meta-construction, a belief *about* our identity.

Consequently, as we alter and work with time-line processes, we inevitably operate directly on the *identity-forming memories*. The entire gestalt and the strategies associated with it change as a result of the process. After all, strategies form and come to operate over time. In this way, by working with "time" via our time-line constructions, we can remove entire strategies that we have not found very resourceful.

How does this work? By working directly on the *memories* that we have used as the "raw data" to create our meta-level understandings and beliefs (our strategies). In this connection, I discovered that Sue had a strategy for depression and a dandy one at that! She over-focused on the painful traumatic events, read them in a personalizing way so that she empowered them to take away her value, worth, loveability, hope for someone who would support her, etc. By enabling her to move through her constructions of "time" and altering her coding of those "times of pain," the therapy blew the limiting strategy out. It prevented her mind from swishing to those which she had used for *self-definition*. Sue could not run the strategy any more. When Sue could not run the strategy for depression in the old limiting way she had, I knew we had completed the therapeutic process.

Once Sue identified the structure of her time-line, I asked her to float above that time-line and float back to those previous memories where she constructed her meaning "programs." From there, I asked her to let the sights and sounds down there on the time-line reflect up to a screen above. And above her time-line, she could watch comfortably as a spectator the scenes of distress that showed her younger self going through some emotional hells.

Once she had viewed the old movie, I asked that she see that younger self later when the distress had passed, when she felt okay, to find a scene of comfort that she could rediscover from her past. As she did, I invited her to step into the movie at that point and re-experience that event of her younger self having a sense of comfort, pleasure, and okayness.

I then mentioned to her that movies can go backwards. Perhaps she herself had seen an eight-millimeter movie rewind and rewind at a very fast speed. Yes, she had. "So you know about how movies can rewind?" As she fully associated into that good memory, I asked her to let her B-rated movie rewind—*while living inside the movie*—and to rewind very quickly, in a second or two.

What an altered state! A back-to-the-past experience in the mind. We did that several more times letting the brain's newly developed skill of running films backward go faster and faster. After that, no more automatic and immediate emotional pain whenever Sue would just "think" about such things.

The V/K Dissociation Pattern

Since our very identity arises as a product of our memories (our representations of past events and the meanings we attribute to those events), sometimes this construction would better serve us if we deleted some of our negative memories. To do that we use a basic NLP process known *as the fast phobia cure or more technically, the Visual-Kinesthetic Dissociation Pattern.*

Richard Bandler (1985) described the fast phobia cure in *Using Your Brain For A Change.* He noted the general neuro-linguistic representational principle that when we process our memories associatedly, we re-experience the emotions associated with that experience. On the other hand, when we *dissociate* from the memory, this usually removes us from the emotions of that memory. Similarly, when we float *above* our time-line, this dissociates us from re-experiencing our memories and re-living the emotions.

While you can learn to self-administer this procedure, we recommend that you first have someone walk you through the steps so that they can measure and mark your experiences for you while you give yourself completely to the internal experiencing and restructuring. This procedure will work with most people. Those who have difficulty visualizing may encounter difficulty with it. You will find this procedure useful in erasing the neuro-semantic reactivity of a phobia. You can use it to rid yourself of any unwanted memory that serves no useful purpose. We find it most useful in removing the images from sexual, physical, and emotional abuse that torment a person.

The Process

1. **Establish a resource anchor.** In dealing with painful memories, the person may possibly associate back into the very painful memory and get into a very unresourceful state, thereby making things worse. To prevent this, establish a *resource anchor* as you begin. By doing so, we can then pull the person out of a bad experience if they happen to collapse into it. If that happens, at least they don't have to stay there! Simply invite the person to

> "... associate back into a time when you felt really safe and secure... and access that memory fully and completely... And as you get into it, gauge the intensity of your feelings of feeling safety and security. And what would you need to do with your sights, sounds, or sensations to *increase this feeling of security?*"

When they have a strong and intense state, anchor it kinesthetically. Afterwards, test to make sure you have a good state anchored.

Since such anchoring enables us to manage our states and experiences, get into the habit of establishing resource anchors. If a person associates into a bad memory, interrupt that state: get them to stand up and walk around, or shout something totally ridiculous at them. Surprise them with a non-sequitur. Give yourself permission to do anything that breaks the strategy of their emotional experience. Then, fire their resource anchor so that they can manage their own subjectivity by getting to a place of resourcefulness.

2. **Acknowledge one time learnings.** In NLP we frame a phobia as representing *an amazing achievement.* After all, people with phobias *never forget* to have the phobic reaction! Do they? They behave so regularly and so methodically! Hurts developed from strong *Significant Emotional Events of Pain* (SEEP) operate similarly. When the trigger fires, the person immediately goes into feeling hurt or some unresourceful state.

Acknowledge, validate, and appreciate this ability. "How amazing that you *always remember* to feel afraid, or hurt, when you think of that bad memory. I can't even remember to take out the garbage. And yet you have this marvelous ability to remember, and to remember every single time without fail, to feel phobic (afraid or hurt) and to recall the memory. Don't you find that simply amazing? Wouldn't you want to use this mechanism to remember something more useful—more enhancing?" "Because if you can learn to feel phobic or hurt from a one time experience, you can unlearn to feel phobic or hurt from another one time experience, right? Or you can learn to feel relaxed and resourceful from a one time learning, right?"

3. **Float up above your time-line and go back to the earliest recollection of the event.** As you float above the time-line, take care that you remain *above* your time-line and to *not* associate into it. Continue to stay above the time-line... and as you allow yourself to begin to float back... back... to the earliest memory you have of this and as you do, remain above your time-line so that you see the memory below you.

4. **Imagine an imaginary movie screen above the unwanted memory on the time-line.** Once you see the imaginary movie screen, allow yourself to place a black and white photograph of a snapshot of yourself upon the screen. As you look at this older photograph, you can see your younger self as you looked just prior to the onset of the bad memory and you can see yourself looking and feeling safe at that point.

Now allow yourself to dissociate once more, this time, imagining that you float out of your current body above your time-line and move into an imaginary projection booth where you see yourself seeing your younger self. You will now have a perception from out of the projection booth seeing yourself above your time-line, seeing yourself in the photo on the movie screen.

5.   **From this perceptual position run a black and white movie of the memory or phobia.** Run it all the way through to the end of the event. Doing this, you experience a double dissociation from the memory. You watch yourself watching the movie of your previous experience. This reduces the traumatic emotions from the event and allows you to bring to bear other thoughts-and-emotions about it.

If you still experience deep emotion by watching the movie, then either (1) send the screen farther away so that you get more "distance" from it, or (2) watch yourself watching that younger you [thereby reminding them to double-dissociate], you can notice the thoughts-and-emotions that you have *about* both yourself and that older memory," or (3) fire your resource anchor of safety and security saying, "And you can feel *this* as you watch *that* with a growing sense of comfort, because you can, *now.*"

Figure 3:3
Visual-Kinesthetic Dissociation Pattern
(Fast Phobia Cure)

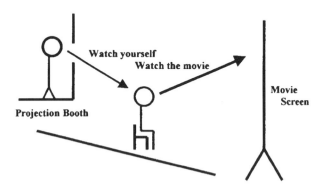

On one occasion I (BB) had a client cut off the bottom half of their body before running the movie. This client's father had raped her during her tenth year, so she felt that she needed to remove the abused part of her body from her sight. So we did it that way. We ran the phobia model on just the upper part of her body. Afterwards she attached the bottom half to herself(!) (in her internal representation), and ran the movie. This worked out beautifully. I once heard Tad James tell about having to take one lady out into the ticket booth (in her mind) before she could run the movie! The general rule we follow in NLP around such processes goes: do what it takes to succeed in giving a person more resources, more options, and more management over their own experiences. Believe in the plasticity of the human mind and nervous system and create a program that allows the person to experience a victory over old hurts.

6. **Freeze frame the last scene at a scene of comfort.** Once you have run the movie to the end, freeze frame that scene. If you like, you may ask them to white-out the movie entirely. Doing that brings a halt to the person's remembering and so breaks the state. Then ask them to see a scene of comfort. Or just have them continue to see the movie and have them see their younger self in a scene of comfort—in a time and place where they felt a sense of pleasure and delight, felt okay about themselves. They may have to fast forward the film until they come to such a scene.

7. **Associate into the scene of comfort.** Next ask them to associate into the scene of comfort at the end of the film.

> "And now you can leave the projection booth and enter your body up there above your time-line so that you enter the movie and associate into that image of the younger you up on the screen in that scene of comfort. So as you float back up into that younger you in the scene, you can see what you saw in that comfort, hear what you heard, and feel those feelings of comfort and delight..."

[This language carefully calibrates to make sure the person will dissociate through the viewing and observing of the scenes of pain and distress *and* associate into the scene of comfort at the end.]

> "And now as you have stepped into the image of that younger you in that comfort scene, you can allow yourself to fully notice what you see that helps you feel comfort, and what you hear, and what you feel that allows you to know this as comfort..."

8. **While associated, rewind the movie.** Run the same movie backwards, see it in color, and fully associated. As you have seen movies run backwards, you can now rewind this one ... in just a moment when you know yourself as fully associated in this movie in that scene of comfort. And you will notice all of the color and three-dimensional nature of this place ... Now run this movie backwards, and do so in *fast rewind*. Do it in one or two seconds. Now!

9. **Clear the screen and repeat five times.** When you get back to the beginning of the film, stop, think of the color blue. Multiply five times six. Interrupt your state. Clear the screen of your mind.

Then repeat. Begin with the scene of comfort and once in that place fully and completely, let your brain rewind that old movie even faster than it did before. Zooooommm! Back to the past! Back to the beginning. Clear the screen and do it again. Do this five times.

By repeating the backward rewinding process five times, the "information" in that old B-rated movie of your memory will grow weaker and weaker. If you desire to lose your memory of it entirely (all of the visual-auditory components of the memory), then repeat the process until the image disappears (usually this takes 15 to 20 rewinds). Removing the image completely also removes all of the kinesthetics and even recall of the event itself. In other words—amnesia! It will give you amnesia of the event. Now after your kinesthetic sensations of the memory disappear and before you have the image itself disappear, you will get a sense of the image but without the emotions.

[A caveat: After the person runs the movie backwards, take care to make sure that the person does *not* then go to the end of the movie associated. At that point ask them to open their eyes, shake their head, interrupt their state, take a break... Otherwise they will re-install the phobia or trauma!]

Then, you can allow yourself to *find yourself back* at the end of the movie in that scene of comfort all of a sudden and ready to **rewind even faster than before.** The reason for this precision lies in preventing oneself from moviong through the movie asssociated.

That would re-install the phobia "Just imagine yourself at the end again and feeling O.K. See what you saw and hear what you heard... Now, run the same movie backwards, hearing and seeing things in color, going backwards."

10. **Run an ecology check.**

"Now, when you think of this old event that used to cause you so much difficulty, emotionally, how does it feel when you experience it in this new way...? Would you like to live your life from this day forward with it coded like this? Quiet yourself on the inside and pay attention to any sight, sound, or sensation that may occur".

Now, you have come to a choice point. When you remove a memory, you may want to replace the memory with a new and more highly desired memory. You can create this by saying, "For a minute, imagine how you would have liked it to have played out if you had operated from a fully resourceful and empowered position..." Or, you can use the *Swish Pattern* to install "the you for whom none of that would have offered you a problem." (See Swish Pattern that follows in Chapter five).

Tad James has said:

"When you keep people up above their Time Line and run the double dissociated Phobia Model where they're outside their bodies watching the event, it will change the entire gestalt."

All of the associated events from that single event will change as we change that one SEEP. Time-line processes, such as this, provide us with a means to change our memories and all of the neuro-physiological responses that result from those memories. Few, if any, single therapy procedures exist that more effectively enable us to detach troubling and dysfunctional emotions from past events than such time-line processes.

Conclusion

We do **not** have to carry around *"bad"* memories if those memories tear us up, lead us to drawing negative and limiting conclusions, put us into unresourceful states, and generally make life a living hell. In NLP we say, *"Once was enough!"* To which, after we run the V/K Dissociation pattern, we can follow with, "And never again...forever..."

Floating back on your time-line and *editing your own personal films* in such a way that you drain them of the negative emotions via this dissociation process, empowers you to **change your past!** You can then either leave it as a *de-energized memory* or, outrageously, even go so far as to replace it with a new and invigorating memory! (The subject, by the way, of Chapter 5).

Either way, you do not have to live with even "accurate," but hellish codings of your past. If you don't want to, you don't have to! You can use your past for something other than pain—namely, for learning! Or, for resourcefulness. Imagine the possibilities!

Chapter 4

Updating "Time"
With Better Memories

"The past that you remember—never happened anyway!"

*"Life can only be understood backward,
but it must be lived forward" (Kierkegaard)*

Can we change *"time?"* You bet! We have already described the process for changing our basic coding of sequential time (our "time-line"). *Can we change our memories of events that occurred in "time?"* Again, yes!

After all, our own personal histories never occurred precisely the way we remembered them. For that matter, we do not even record accurately and precisely our current perceptions of "reality" as it occurs in the here-and-now of this moment. We can't. We *selectively attend* to information and stimuli as we delete certain things and as we generalize other things. These mapping or modeling functions of our nervous system means that whatever **constructed internal representations** we entertain in our head arise through a variety of meta-level mechanisms, e.g. values, beliefs, purposes and intentions, habits and familiarity, etc.

Should we change "time" or our memories of such? Yes, if we want to live in a resourceful way. We inevitably will anyway. After all, given the forgetting process, whatever we don't attend to, invest interest in, recall, refresh, etc. will eventually lose its representational and semantic power. This describes the power of forgetting. We lose interest. We learn other things, new things, things of much more interest, and so eventually old memories and interests suffer a de-energization of thought-and-emotion. As we do these things, we inevitably change our memories, often by outright forgetting. With other memories, we blow things out of proportion or shrink them down in size.

Listen to any two siblings, or friends, who grew up together reminiscence if you don't believe that we all don't inevitably change our memories anyway! The more important question that we should entertain asks, " Should we change our memories of time so that we will develop more resourcefulness or to suffer more limitations and stuckness?"

Invested "Time"

A strange thing happens sometimes in human "personality" — people develop vested interests in *keeping pain* with them. It may involve the investment that they have made in their *identity defin-itions.* "I am an adult child of an alcoholic." "I am a rape victim." "I am a Vietnam Vet." "I am a Holocaust survivor." "I am..." So to give up that horror, that set of B-rated films of chaos and distress, those internal movies of victimhood, etc. would demand a total change of identity. And "Who would I be if I changed all of that?"

Thus the investment of familiarity arises. "At least I know that demon...!" The investment of familiarity gives us a kind of comfort and regularity. It gives us, at least, a known world so that we don't have to exercise thought-emotion, speech and behavior to learn new skills, and new ways to adapt. This familiarity provides the vested interest of the secure and a path of ease.

Other vested interests arise when people begin to contemplate **changing their personal history.** This may involve the investment they have in *life-long beliefs, understandings, models of the world, decisions, life scripts, values, emotions, etc.* Though they may feel painful and limiting, they at least give them an orientation in life. They may also save them from "the work" and responsibility of developing a whole new list of beliefs, understandings, decisions, identity, values, emotions, and states.

So while we all *can* potentially **update our memories and change "time"**—we all also have a price to pay for doing so. What price will you pay? Which of your beliefs would such a change make totally irrelevant? What identities would no longer fit? Who would no longer know or accept you if you didn't use your painful past to define or experience yourself?

How much willingness to explore the possibilities of changing your past would you commit yourself to giving and investing? How surprised would you feel if you found yourself excited to experience a new you and willing to pay the price of letting old beliefs and values and scripts and states go...?

Holes in Your "Time" Head, or "Defrag-ers"

Sometimes we will want to *invent and install a new memory* once we have removed a memory from our time-line. Removing a memory fragments our "mind" and leaves a hole in our head. Some people do this naturally anyway. When they de-energize a memory or blow it out of the water (send it to the sun and let it blow up there), their brain just naturally regenerates another memory to fill in that gap.

But problems may arise with this. Suppose that they have the equivalent of a Monster-Program in their head—ready to generate a Stephen King quality of Monsters!? If they had that kind of strategy already internalized, then they would find that every memory they remove, their program would come up with uglier, nastier, and more dysfunctional pictures, sounds, words, ideas, etc. to replace the deleted memory.

This reminds me of the parable in the gospels of the unclean spirit who left a man, but after leaving and roaming around, the spirit could find no resting place. So, he returned. And upon returning, he discovered the inner house empty! So, the unclean spirit found "seven other spirits more wicked than himself, and they enter in and dwell there: and the last state of the man is worse than the first" (Matthew 12:43-45 KJV). The moral? After he swept his internal house clean, he should have filled it up with some good spirits.

If the "nature of our mind does not tolerate a vacuum" then like that guy in the parable, we need to replace "bad" memories with "good" ones—memories that will enable us to learn, to feel empowered, that access resources, etc.

Other people won't need this. When you remove a memory from them, they have a "Defrag" command in their minds that restructures their sense of "time" and leaves no gap that needs filling. The "Defrag" command in DOS means "de-fragmenting." When you run it, your computer will reorganize the "space" on its memory chips that it created when it deleted documents over a period of weeks or months. The de-fragmentation program compresses the space in the hard drive so that it leaves no gaping hole that needs filling. (Given this, I suppose we could divide people into those with "Defrag" meta-programs and those with "Empty Space" meta-programs.)

The Process for Inventing and Installing New Memories

The NLP Swish Pattern provides a tool to directionalize the brain so that we can "manage our mind" in terms of **where** it goes and the resultant **states** it creates. This process enables us to provide our brains with a set of images (a new internal movie) that it will enjoy processing. And in the process of doing that, it activates all kinds of resources in our mind-body state. As such, it offers an excellent tool for exchanging monster memories or deleted memories with life enhancing memories.

The Swish Pattern operates by using submodality drivers to bring about powerful changes in how we respond to things. Bandler (1985) designed a procedure for the purpose of working on specific behaviors that a person may not want anymore. This pattern works powerfully, especially with unconscious habits. The procedure, in effect generates a *new direction* for our mind-body to go.

After we present the outline of this model, we will offer a description for the use of the swish in replacing memories on one's timeline.

Swishing Your Brain

1. **Identify a specific behavior you wish to change.** This procedure works well with nail biting, overeating, smoking, etc It works best with changing minor habits. If you would like to respond differently to someone than how you presently respond, then *the Swish Pattern* enables you to generate a new way of thinking-feeling and responding.

2. **Determine a definite cue that triggers the unwanted response.** How do you know when to do the behavior that you do not want? What tells you to "Do it now!" Do you have some sight, sound, sensation, or word that triggers the process? Suppose you wanted to teach someone *how to do this*. What specifically would you tell them to do? What to hear? What to see? What to notice? What to say to yourself?

If you have an external cue, notice exactly the image of what you see that sets off the response. Associate into the experience. If it involves biting your nails, you may see your hand moving up to your mouth. As with most NLP techniques, we present the Swish Pattern first using the visual modality. Auditory and kinesthetic cues also fit into this model. Discover the submodalities of the cue.

3. **Identify the critical submodalities.** Experiment with size and brightness first. Stimuli cues will typically utilize *size and brightness*. If you don't find that these factors drive the response, try *distance.* The swish works best with analog submodalities. In fact, I (BB) have not found that it works well, if at all with digital submodalities. Since I (MH) have had some success with that, I tend to use them from time to time. As noted in chapter three, digital submodalities operate as either/or qualities like frame/panoramic and color/black-and-white while analog submodalities vary over a range like size, brightness and distance.

4. **Form an image of your ideal self.** How would you see yourself with the desired change? What would you look like if you did not bite your nails? If you did not smoke? If you responded to criticism with soft eyes, calm breathing, and a thoughtful state of mind? How would you look if you had obtained your desired weight? Make a dissociated picture of the *you* with these desired traits and qualities.

The process here works from an associated state (the problem) to the dissociated desired state (the solution). In an associated picture you already have the feeling of accomplishing your desired outcome and so associated pictures do not provide a lot of motivation. With such, you send the message to your brain, "I already have this." So you end up with no stress, no tension, no directionality, no "eye of the tiger" motivation. So picture "the me for whom this will offer no problem," as a highly compelling, desirable, and dissociated outcome. We want it to pull on us. So make *this ideal you* desirable, compelling, attractive. If you begin to drool as you look at it (hear it, sense it)—you've got a good one!

5. **Check to see if the desired state functions ecologically.** Let's now run this desired self through the well-formed outcome model.

- Have you contextualized this ideal image?
- Have you affirmed what qualities you want?
- Have you coded it in V.A.K. terms?
- Can you see or hear the small chunk steps and stages in moving toward it?
- What will you lose when you actualize this image?
- How will this affect your relationships?
- Does any part of you object to moving in this direction to actualizing this self?

6. **Swish.** Using size and brightness (or your driving submodalities), swish from the cue picture of unresourcefulness to the end picture of *"the Resourceful You."* Begin with the cue picture, seeing-hearing-and feeling it as bright and large. See what you see when you associate into that cue picture. Then, in one of the lower corners of the cue picture, shrink down the outcome picture of your Ideal Self into a small, dark, and dissociated picture the size of a dot and put it in a corner.

Now, let this large bright cue picture *quickly* shrink down. Let it shrink down into a dot at lightning speed while *simultaneously* the small dot that contains your desired image suddenly grows so large and bright that it completely fills the screen of your mind... Do this very quickly.

Brains learn fast. When you use this pattern with someone, make a swiiissshhhing sound to assist the quick swish from old picture to new one. Then clear the mind's screen. Break state for a moment. Then repeat this procedure five times.

7. **Future pace.** To test the results of this procedure, we future pace. Think of the cue that used to trigger the undesired behavior. What happens? If it produces the new image, you have succeeded in re-directionalizing that old brain of yours! You have finished the work of "telling that brain where to go" for more resourcefulness. If it doesn't, go to the next step.

Figure 4:3
The Swish Pattern

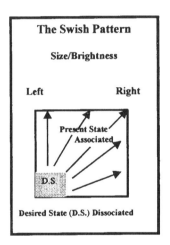

8. **Swishing the images using distance.** If size and brightness do not do the job, then use distance as a possible driver. Test to check this out. Follow the same procedure using the small dark picture in the person's lower left corner, except this time, swish from a distance. Take the cue picture of the unwanted behavior and zoom it out on the horizon until it becomes a black dot. Out there also the person has put their desired self/behavior as a small, dark, and dissociated picture. So as the cue picture zooms out—*simultaneously and quickly,* let them **zoom in** the desired behavior from the horizon so that it pops in on the screen of their mind—completely filing up the screen. Again, speed makes this work much better. Repeat five times, and test.

Figure 4.4
The Swish Pattern

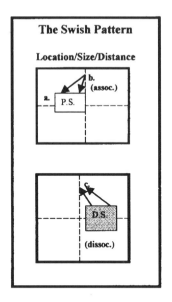

Replacing Memories Using The Swish Pattern

Now that we have all the pieces, let's combine the time-line process with the Swish Pattern to replace memories and/or build in new and better ones. If, after using the phobia cure (V-K Dissociation pattern), and having erased the image of a memory so that you have a blanked-out area, use this process to fill it in with something very good and very powerful.

First, form an associated picture of the blanked out area. Should some of the picture still remain, simply form an associated picture of whatever remains. Swish this associated picture with a dissociated picture of a pleasant and resourceful memory which you choose as a replacement of the old memory. The following steps (which come from the work of Bandler and James) describe how to lead someone in the actual therapeutic process.

The Replacing Memories Pattern

1. **Establish rapport.** Before any therapeutic intervention, always establish rapport with the person. Test for rapport before moving on.

2. **Gather structural information about how the process works** to re-access the process. The experience of inappropriate emotional distress from dated emotions involves having built certain kinds of mental maps about *meaning and causation* that no longer serves one well. This means that the person now operates from a program that says, "feel bad" on cue to some action, thought, memory, etc. The program says, "This event causes me to feel bad because it means..."

Since we work (using the NLP model) primarily at the process level, we don't need a lot of content. When a person says, "I'm depressed!" move them from the content of that emotional *effect* (labeled "depression") to cause by asking, *"How* do you do that?" At first, this usually evokes confusion and lack of understanding, "What do you mean, 'How do I do that'?" We can then frame our question as an exploration for the process, "I want to know what goes on inside you that enables you to create this depression."

Since "depression" represents a nominalization, linguistically, and because most people bring their problems coded as nominalizations, this starts the *de-nominalizing process.* If we can't put the hurt in a wheelbarrow (i.e. guilt, anxiety, fear, shame, etc.), then we only have *nominalized effects*, not *causes* or *processes.*

Asking, **"How do you do that?"** de-nominalizes as it inquires about the process itself. It also works well with mind-reading and cause-effect statements. By asking, "How do you do that?" we invite the person to associate into the problem process. Usually, they have to run the strategy of the problem that generates it in the first place. As long as the difficulty does not consist of a phobia or intense trauma, invite them to run their activating strategy. You can then calibrate the state of the problem. We do this so that you will know, upon completion, whether the process has worked. If they cannot run the strategy again, presto!

The "how" question effectively works with nominalizations, mind-reading, cause-effect, and association. Accordingly, this question (as a language pattern) functions at a level above the Meta-Model inasmuch as by it you *chunk up*. The Meta-Model itself, by examining the structure of the language of the problem, works a level above the problem. Thus, in asking the "how" question you have moved two levels above the problem—at the structure of its process. Knowing this enables us to effect change in a *content free* way. In other words, we can work with a problem without needing to know much about the content of the problem. Neat, don't you think?

3. **Dissociate from the problem.** After the person associates into the problem in response to *"How do you do that?"* dissociate them from the problem by asking, "How do I do that?" If they need help in processing this, use the *Temporary Employment Agency Frame.* "Imagine that I have come from a temporary agency to fill in for you today. You get a day off if you just show me how to have your problem. Wouldn't you like a day off from your depression? Good. Then as I fill in for you, *how* should I do what you did to experience the kind of depression you felt?"

In this way, we can learn their strategy for how they generate their problem experiences. Asking the question in this way (with past tense verbs) gets them to explain what they do inside their head to run the problematic process. And, in so explaining the problem, they have to dissociate from the problem as they take a more objective point of view. This question functions at a level above the previous "how" question.

Recently a neighbor of mine (BB), Diane, who had serious health problems called for help, as if that didn't give Diane enough to cope with, her mother had recently attempted suicide, and almost succeeded. Diane spent most of the day in bed, crying.

I asked, "How do you get yourself into this state where you cry all day?" Diane said, "I see myself over mother's casket."

"So, if I wanted to experience what you have experienced all day, I simply make a picture in my head of me standing over my mother's casket? Yes, I think that could make me cry."

Then I began exploring the qualities of her internal images. "Diane, when you look at that picture you have, how close or far do you have the picture?" "Close, very close."

"And if you send it far off, would it still work to produce the crying?" "Yes." "Where do you have it located? Up high or low? To your right or left?"

"I see it low and down to my right."

"If you move it up to your left would it still work?"

Diane struggled with that shift. "It still hurts, but not nearly as bad."

4. **Scramble The Strategy**. What happened in that exchange with Diane? Her strategy for crying involved first seeing a picture from the associating standpoint just over the casket of her mother. Distance did not drive her experience. However, when she moved the image from down to the right (kinesthetic) to up and to the left (visual recall), her emotions changed. Remembered painful images belong in visual recall, and not in kinesthetic.

This process essentially *scrambled the strategy* of her emotional distress. It interrupted the strategy so that it could not work as it had. How did that occur? We simply took the image of the problem, found the submodalities, tested for drivers, experimented with the flexibility of the strategy, and found out the limits of the submodalities on the experience.

When we tell someone, "Send it far off. Does it still work?" They have to try this process "on for size." And, pushing submodalities out to their limit (the structure of the process we call "Compulsion Blow Out") it tends to blow experiences out of the water. If we stumble accidentally upon the submodality driver that makes the problem strategy work, the person typically annihilates the old unuseful strategy.

In the above example, distance served as the driver, so she sent the picture off to the point where it simply disappeared. The internal representation, literally, exploded in her mind. We describe this process as "going over a threshold." When this happens, one typically will no longer run the strategy. At times, just using this series of questions will initiate the necessary change. At best, it scrambles their strategy.

5. **Discover the original trigger.** The above process often enables a person to identify the root cause of the emotional distress strategy. However, more typically, the process only prepares one's unconscious mind for discovering that root cause. To accomplish this, time-line processes provide us with an ingenious question to get to the root cause. You might just want to memorize it. Upon completing step four, ask,

> "What serves as the root cause of this problem, which, when you disconnect from it, will cause the problem itself to disappear? ...If you should come to know this answer...would it have occurred before, during, or after your birth?"

And, as usual, you can expect many to reply, "I don't know." Validate that, "I appreciate that you think you don't know that you know, but *just suppose* you did... it would have occurred...?"

If the person answers, "After my birth," affirm and inquire, "Good, and what year?" If they say, "Before," affirm, "Good, did it happen in the womb or before?" If they say, "In the womb," affirm, "Good, and during what month?"

Frequently I (BB) have had clients go back into the womb in identifying the source of their distress. For me, this makes sense inasmuch as the questioning of time-line processes addresses the unconscious mind more than the conscious mind.

When I first started this, I saw the wife of a minister friend. With her I asked, "If you knew the root cause of your problem, which when you disconnect from it, will cause the problem to disappear, when would it have occurred—before, during or after your birth?" Immediately Sandra replied, "Before birth."

I affirmed her response, "Good, did it occur in the womb or before?" She said "In the womb." "Good, during what month?" She said, "The fourth month."

It seemed at that moment that astonishment shone all over her face, and mine. Then she said, "I heard mother say, 'My God, the last thing I need is another child.'" As the fifth child in her family, she grew up feeling unwanted. The root cause of her distresses had occurred that far back—while she grew in her mother's womb.

Far-fetched? Perhaps. Although, modern medical science has demonstrated that a fetus does respond to outside stimuli. So today both fathers and mothers speak to their children—while in the womb, talking to the yet-to-be-born child through the mother's abdomen. When couples do this, the new born child will respond to dad's voice, and not to another man's. Studies indicate conclusively that the baby in the womb hears, feels and learns. These early experiences in the womb begin to shape attitudes and expectations about himself.

In the Hebrew Bible, we see God calling various prophets from the womb,

> "Listen to Me, O islands, and pay attention, you peoples from afar. The Lord called Me from the womb; From the body of My mother He named Me" (Isaiah 49:1). "Before I formed you in the womb I knew you, and before you were born I consecrated you; I have appointed you a prophet to the nations" (Jeremiah 1:5).

In response to the question, "In the womb or before?" what options arise if the person says, "Before?" Occasionally, we receive that response. In the NLP time-line processes we typically respond, "Did it occur in a past life or passed down to you genealogically?"

Now, folks from the Judeo-Christian traditions (Jews and Christians, and probably Moslems) as well as others will not buy into beliefs about past lives. Though as a Christian, I (BB) do not believe in past lives, if my client does, I match their "model of the world" and continue on with the therapy. At that moment, I serve as a therapist, not as a judge of their ideas!

How then can we address this? Do the Judeo-Christian beliefs match the concept of problems being rooted generationally? I think so especially given the fact that various texts do speak of "problems" (or "sins") passing on down the generations from father to son (Exodus 20:5, Deuteronomy 32:7).

Conclusion

With this neuro-linguistic technology we now have all the resources for experiencing that happy childhood we missed! We can update other memories that may no longer serve our peace of mind or add to the kind of self-image that we want to live from. Beginning with the understanding that we "think" in sensory modalities with the qualities of those representation systems functioning as key signals to punch into our bio-computer, we now have identified some other NLP patterns for updating our "personality" programs. Moving back and forth along our time-line(s) and altering the inadequate maps that locked us into pain and trauma can empower us to use our past for learning rather than re-traumatization.

Installing today's learnings and resources *back* in the past and informing our brain-neurology to treat it as "real"—and therefore *realize* it in today's "personality" invites our mind-body system to do some very creative and resourceful things! You can swish your mind to the You for whom various trials would provide you "no problem." You can also swish your "past" mind (your memory) to do the same! No "mind" police will ever stop you. So, **go for it**!

Chapter 5

Time-Lining
Old Dated Negative Emotions

Getting Unstuck From Old Dated Emotions
That Hold You Back

Negative emotions from previous experiences can feel as if we have a millstone hanging around our necks and weighing us down. Not a fun way to live! Not a construction that makes for vitality, courage, commitment, etc. Such negative emotions of the past can rob us of energy that we could more productively devote to other pursuits.

Psycho-physically, *negative* emotions function in our body and "personality" as do the brakes on a car, stopping or inhibiting, etc. Whereas *positive* emotions function like a car's accelerator— moving us forward, giving us energy and fuel, propelling us into our futures. Thus, joy, happiness, contentment, pleasure, calmness, humor, relaxation, love, excitement, etc. (the positive emotions) propel us forward on the highway of life. They provide us with the mental-emotional energy to get things done.

Fear, anger, dread, disgust, sadness, upsetness, frustration, guilt, shame, timidity, etc. (the negative emotions) slam on the brakes in our "personality." They inhibit action so that (ideally) we will, "Stop, Look, and Listen". They give us the motivation to gather information about how our values feel violated or threatened.

Normally, these **go** and **stop** signals and emoting processes work well and to our benefit. But sometimes, instead of using our negative emotions to "Stop, Look, and Listen," and take effective action to transform things, we build programs out of them. We incorporate them as "the meaning of our life," or as some program that defines our ongoing reality. Not wise! Because in doing this, we then misuse our emotions and try to *"live in"* our negative emotions.

Yet we don't *live* well in negative emotions—they don't work well for such use. Positive emotions we can live in, but not the negative ones. They work best for braking purposes. Yet when we begin to use our negative emotions to "live in," we create a program of *dated emotions* (emotions not current to today's events) and begin to drag them with us.

To change all of this and resolve the negative effects of negative emotions rapidly and effectively, we can use the time-line processes. Accordingly, the following procedures will work with any negative dated emotion (depression, guilt, shame, fear, grief, sadness, etc.).

Letting Go Of Negative Emotions

Since one of the best ways to thoroughly learn processes as these time-line patterns involves experiencing them through specific applications, we have designed this chapter as one of application. Now that you have identified and experienced your time-line, the V-K dissociation pattern to de-energize emotional reactions and a process for memory replacement, the following exercise will give you experience in letting go of negative dated emotions that hold you back or weigh you down.

Before you begin this exercise, carefully examine Figure 5:1. If you let this diagram represent your time-line, then the line above the time-line illustrates *dissociating above* it. The numbers indicate four key positions involved in this process. Mentally picture in your mind these four positions in relation to the time-line.

Figure 5:1

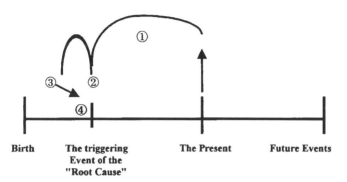

Position 1: Position above the time-line, your state just prior to going to the
   root cause
Position 2: Position directly above the root cause
Position 3: Fifteen minutes before the root cause
Position 4: Association into the event

| Birth | The triggering Event of the "Root Cause" | The Present | Future Events |

To experiment with this, select some experience in your life that
has created a minor negative emotion for you. Someone could
have hurt your feelings, or perhaps you did something that
continues to cause you to feel bad in some way. Choose a *minor*
negative emotion that you would like to *let go*. For now, do not
select a trauma and never associate into position #4 with regard to
a trauma. Get into your favorite place and position of relaxation.
You may wish to have some relaxing music playing in the
background. With awareness of the memory, float up above your
time-line (to a meta-line), and allow yourself to travel back in your
mind along "time," until you pass over the event (#2) and go back
in time 15 minutes further (position #1). From this position you
see the "root cause" of the original event below you and in front of
you.

From position #1 move forward in time to position #2, where you
can rest comfortably in a position directly *above* the original situation. From here take a good look at that experience, the you in that
event, and other factors within that situation—just observing.

Now, float down *into* the event. **Associate into** the event of the
root cause totally as you see what you saw, hear what you heard,
and feel what you felt at the creation of that initial emotion.

Next, *disconnect* from those emotions and float back up to position #2. From this position, just float back comfortably to position #3, fifteen minutes prior to when the root cause arose. Drop down into position #3 so that you can then turn and look forward— toward the present. You will see the event from which the negative dated emotion arose. Question. "Where is the negative emotion?" At this *point in time* it does not yet exist! So you won't see it. And, further you can notice that it and all other negative emotions from that experience have simply disappeared from sight, have they not? So enjoy this perspective... fully.

[If after looking toward the present you still experience any negative feelings, remain in position #3 and let those negative emotions *flow out of you*. Remain there until all the emotions flow out completely. Should you not let the emotions go completely, you undoubtedly have a part that you need to reframe. The section *"When the Emotions Won't Let Go"* will provide you with specific Parts Reframes for letting go of emotions from position #4.]

Using This Time-line Process To Release Negative Emotions

1. **Access your time-line and float above it.** Utilize what you have learned about time-line processes to empower yourself to access and use this model.

2. **Seed the representation of release**. Ask yourself,

   "If I knew the root cause of the negative emotion, which when I disconnect from it, will cause the negative emotion to disappear, when would that have occurred—before, during or after my birth?"

3. **Discover the original source ("root cause").** Once you identify *when* you think the root cause occurred, gently float up above your time-line and go back into the past towards the root cause of the negative emotion experience. Ask your unconscious mind, or inner spirit, or God's Spirit to allow you to go back to the original event of this negative emotion. Float on past it on your meta-line so that you float back, remaining above your time-line (position #1).

4. **On your meta-line, float directly above the event.** Now move forward until you arrive at a position directly over the event (position #2). Once you have moved directly over the event, take a moment to look at it from this perspective,

Then *float down* into the event and **associate** into your body at that event. You can now look out through your own eyes, hearing what you heard during that experience, and feeling what you felt during that time. And as you do, allow yourself to notice the emotions you feel there and to calibrate to them. As you do this, make a list of all emotions you experience.

[When you later test, you will want to use this list to make sure all the emotions have become "flat." Why do we ask people to float down into position #4? Why have them associate back into the experience? We get better results if we experience these emotions just before we disconnect from them. One moment we experience all the pain and hurt from the root cause of the negative experience, then the next moment those emotions disappear. This helps to ratify the change to the conscious mind.]

[A Caveat: Do not use Position #4 for trauma. **Never** associate yourself or another into a traumatic experience! This includes phobias, memories of severe abusive episodes, or any intensely negative emotion that "wipes a person out." For "trauma," use the V-K Dissociation model (Chapter 4) to neutralize the extreme emotional and neuro-semantic reactivity.]

5. **Float up to preserve learnings**. Now float up, out of position #4, and back up above your time-line (position #2). From here take a moment to preserve what you have learned from that experience. Because you have learned something of importance from that experience, haven't you? As you identify some things that you have learned, then in that special place in your mind where you preserve such learnings, preserve what you have learned from this experience.

Whether you had a special place in the mind to preserve your learnings or not prior to this doesn't really matter. In so languaging this (if it fits) you there create such a place— another one of the marvelous creative things that we can do with language! Why preserve learnings? Because even in the most severe trauma or abuse, we can learn things of value and importance.

Suppose a person has suffered as a victim of rape. Preserving learnings might enable her to guard herself better if she experiences a future threatening situation. We wouldn't want her to have to go through rape again to learn the signs of someone possibly threatening to rape her.

[If you use this pattern with someone, check to preserve learnings. "Have you gained some knowledge or learning that you would like to preserve? Then in that special place in your mind where you preserve such learnings, I want you to preserve what you have learned from this experience. And you can do that... now."]

6. **Float back 15 minutes prior to the Event**. And as you rest comfortably there above your time-line, you can now float back fifteen minutes (position #3) and look down on your state of 15 minutes prior to that event.

If you use this pattern with another person, calibrate to their eyes and facial expressions to learn to tell when they have moved into position #3. "And do you now see the event below and in front of you? ... And what has happened to all those emotions? Have they all disappeared as well?"

On occasion you may need to give the person time to *let the emotions go*. With particularly heavy or intense emotions, once the person has assumed position #3, "Now you can let those emotions *flow right out of you.*" Pace them by repeating the phrase, "Let the emotions go." Repeat these words each time the person breathes out. As the client releases the emotions, you will literally watch a life change in front of you.

7. **Test from Position #2.** As you float forward again to position #2, test by associating again into position #4. "Now from this position, do you experience any of those old negative emotions at all?" The emotions should have gone flat. If you find yourself unable to experience any negative emotions, you have completed the process. If any of the emotions remain, see the section, "When the Emotions Won't Let Go."

8. **Return to the present.** Float out of the original event (position #4) and above the time-line and come forward to the present. And you can come forward above your time-line only as fast as you can allow all the other events between then and now with similar emotions to *release them fully* so that you find them *gone completely* as you *let them go* fully and completely. And you pay particular attention to these events. And, just before you get to them, should you experience any negative emotions from that experience, you can just *let them go* as you float along above those events. And take your time, as your unconscious mind can take all the time it needs to *complete a full release.*

9. **Future Pace.** Imagine moving into tomorrow with this new sense of release from those old dated emotions.... and you may even think of a future time when some trigger may occur that would have previously invited you to have those old emotions and notice now, how they have vanished completely.

Using Time-line Processes to Release Guilt

Working with people inevitably involves addressing the sense of guilt, pseudo-guilt, and "heavy loads of guilt." Psychotherapists, like pastors, often work with people in hearing confessions of errors and sins, acknowledgments of having taken a wrong road, and a passionate search for forgiveness. People from all religious traditions, and those from none, often seek forgiveness. Yet sometimes they report that they just cannot experience the forgiveness they desire. As a result they live with a "load of guilt weighing them down." In this way guilt as a dated emotion can operate to cripple the person. It begins to cling to them as an inner uneasiness that doesn't go away and that ruins their joy in living.

Let's then apply the time-line processes to empower ourselves to forgive ourselves and others. The time-line processes works very well with guilt, as with other dated emotions because we experience and create "guilt" in time.

Before we do this, lets first distinguish several forms of guilt.

a. *Theological guilt.* Feeling guilty due to having violated a divine law. Here we feel "guilty" or "in the wrong" over a moral issue because we recognize that we have violated some divine law. To resolve this kind of guilt, one must "change the mind" (*metanoia*) and take the necessary actions of acknowledgement and amendment of wrongs.

b. *Psychological guilt.* Feeling "guilty" when we actually should only feel "bad" in some lesser way because the "wrong" involved no moral issue, but some lesser violation of some value. Here we should rather feel discouraged, frustrated, ashamed, embarrassed, fearful, self-conscious, etc.

Consider John. As his mother went into a hospital in her last days of her long struggle with cancer, he found himself living a hundred miles from that hospital. After several days at her bedside, John left the hospital for home to get some clean clothes. While away on that business, his mother died. John felt guilty about this. He felt that he "should have been there for her." He felt that he "let his mother die alone and let her down." Yet what law did John break? What "wrong" did he commit? He certainly did not break any divine law, yet, he felt guilty. He had violated either his own law (rule), his mother's (perhaps), or those of some friend, or his culture's.

This *psychological guilt* feels just the same as the theological guilt. The two differ in *whose law* we feel that we have violated. We may also distinguish between *realistic and unrealistic guilt.* In realistic guilt, we truly have to do a wrong according to some standard— some value. In unrealistic guilt, we have not. To "feel guilty" for "being imperfect," for instance, represents a *totally unrealistic standard*, yet the "guilt" feelings from that pseudo-guilt, once coded and represented mentally, sends messages of "condemnation, rejection, needing punishment, etc." in the nervous system. This form of guilt (unrealistic pseudo-guilt) can operate in a devastating way in one's personality if not addressed properly and quickly.

With *realistic guilt,* whether one evaluates that he or she has violated a divine command or a human command (rule), one must still take *effective action.* This may involve acknowledgement, confession, apology, change-of-mind, the making of amends, etc. Many spiritual persons who have a belief system that acknowledges God's forgiveness, "intellectually" knows that God has forgiven them, but they may not have forgiven themselves.

Some people with a highly developed conscience operate in such a "morally sensitive" way to doing wrong, violating any rule, "should," expectation, etc. that they go into a "guilty state" over anything that triggers a negative emotion. They can't feel embarrassed without also feeling guilty. They can't feel shame without turning it into guilt. They can't feel discouraged or upset or stressed or frustrated in not living up to some other person's standards without feeling guilty about it. These represent more illustrations of *pseudo-guilt*. In all of these cases, the time-lines processes can offer a new lease on life—freedom from all forms of guilt.

Releasing Guilt

1. **Determine the kind of guilt/guilting**. First, run a well-formed outcome process about your experience of guilt. Sometimes this emotion provides a check that keeps us from engaging in negative, hurtful, or immoral behaviors. For ecology, we don't want to eliminate our legitimate moral and ethical standards or value criteria. "What part of me values and wants this feeling as a warning and aversion from engaging in that behavior?" If you respond, "My conscience part, my moral part, my ethical part," etc. then validate it and the emotion, as a learning.

If you respond, "My relationship part, my wanting a good image in the community part," etc. then reframe your part so that you can learn to experience "bad" (negative, unpleasant) emotions (sadness, shame, embarrassment, disappointment, etc.) *without* going into the guilt state (feeling condemned and needing punishment). Do you have any other parts that can and will perform the same function (keeping them living within the rules of their family, society, job, etc.) *without* the guilt. Access the part that runs your "good behavior." Ask that part if it will take control of your behaviors.

If you feel that you need your guilt, then access your meta-outcome in maintaining that feeling. "And what will having these guilt feelings do for me?" Once you find that, then ask, "If I could design and install a part in myself that will accomplish these meta-outcomes without all of these negative guilt feelings, will all of my parts agree to allow that part to take charge of things?"

2. **Repeat the processes for accessing and using the person's time-line codings.** Have them access their sense of "time," gain some flexibility in moving above their time-line and moving forward and backward in "time."

3. **Discover the root cause of your guilt.** "If I knew the root cause of my guilt, which, when I disconnect from it, will cause the guilt to disappear, when would that have occurred—before, during or after my birth?

4. **Float back to that event.** Once you identify the root cause, float up above your time-line and to go back into the "past" toward the original source of this. "And I can allow myself to float back on my meta-line comfortably to the original source of this root cause of my guilt... and go back even further as I float back, while remaining above my time-line to 15 minutes prior to the event (position #1).

5. **Come forward in time and associate.** Comfortably move forward until you come to a place directly over the event (position #2). Once directly over the event, float down into the event and associate into your body. "And I can now look out through my own eyes as if in that situation again, seeing what I saw, hearing what I heard during that experience... and I feel what I felt then and as I do I can notice and identify the emotions I feel..."

6. **Float back up**. Float out of this experience (position #4) and above your time-line. "I have learned something from this experience, have I not?" "In that special place in my mind where I preserve such learnings, I can preserve what I have learned from this experience."

7. **Go back 15 minutes**. "And as I float above my time-line, I can float back fifteen minutes before that event ever took place (position #3) and direct my attention forward... to the present...." Pause and then process this experience.

"And as I now see the event below and in front of me and knowing that I have acknowledged the wrong, changed my mind about those actions, have cultivated the willingness to apologize and make amends, I can now give myself permission to *fully let the guilt go, now!* Because I can just let that guilt flow out of my body."

When I (BB) met Charles, he daily lived in intense guilt. Guilt had made itself his constant companion since 1981. Charles, while married, had succumbed to temptation through sexual involvement with a married woman. This lead to two families breaking up. Charles' guilt stemmed from a gestalt of three memories. The first arose from when he started flirting with the woman. The second from his first sexual encounter and the third from his awareness of his wrongdoing after the affair.

From the perspective of 15 minutes prior to the event—on his meta-line (position #3), Charles saw all three events *below* and in front of him. As the guilt flowed out of him, he said, "It is all turning milky white." I inquired, "What do you see as milky white, Charles?" "All of those images!" "And what does this white signify to you, Charles?" "Purity!" he said.

8. **Test**. Float forward to position #2 and then associate into position #4 again. "Do I experience any of those former feelings of guilt at this point?" At this stage in the process make sure that the emotions have flattened out and de-energized.

9. **Zoom the release through time**. If the guilt has roots in more than one event, as you go forward in time above your time-line, let go of all of the similar emotions that followed from the original cause.

10. **Future pace.** Associate into a future experience in which you would formerly have re-triggered your guilt. Test to make sure that you don't drag along the old "dated emotions" any longer.

Reclaiming Old Resources

Sometimes people may simply *forget* their forgiveness, acceptance, appreciation, love, peacefulness (or other resources). In other words, they may, at a meta-level, experience a *forgetfulness* **about** some resource thereby eliminating that resource. They may have resolved a misbehavior or problem, but then later recall it in such a way as to "bring it back" as a guilt rather than as a forgiven guilt (for such describes the power of "mental" representation!).

Since we may want to keep and use such memories in "time," we can use our time-line process to recover these resources and stop the self-torment of too vividly re-representing old problems.

I (BB) did this once with a lady who had gotten herself into some very negative guilt states. Since a significant part of her self-definition involved her Christian faith, I used her *positive* SEEP to enable her to go back to the time when she first accepted her faith to re-experience it again. As she re-associated with herself as a ten year old girl (position #4), she saw the little church. "And as you float down into your body and fully re-experience that re-living as that little ten year old again, you can see what you saw then, and hear the sounds of the music, and the preacher's voice, and you can also feel what you felt at that time."

"Oh, yes." she said. "I remember it well. And it feels so good, again... to feel totally forgiven.... I had forgotten..."

> [For people from the Christian tradition, we refer to Dr. Bodenhamer's short monogram entitled, *"Taking a Bitter Root to Jesus"* as an NLP process for releasing guilt and gaining a sense of freedom using the resources within that frame-of-reference.]

Using Time-lines to Let Go of Grief

Grief represents a universal experience that we all experience when we lose someone or something of significance to us. And as such, grief offers us a marvelous way to let go, thereby freeing us up to create new space inside for new connections, relationships, meanings.

Yet many people cannot grief directly and forthrightly. Old dated emotions of grief prevent them. So when they grieve for a new loss, they not only grief for that loss, but a whole gestalt of griefs come rushing in—and overwhelming them. This makes the normal and healing process of "grieving a loss" impossible.

When "unfinished" gestalts of grief arising from dated emotions stored as belief, understanding, and decision programs occur, we complicate today's emotional difficulties with other *significant losses* that we have suffered. These dated emotions of loss and grief may have arisen from the death of a significant person, from a separation, divorce, abandonment, firing, the loss of employment, loss of prestige, an amputation, a mastectomy, a loss of a home to fire, etc. Grief itself originates *when* we *lose anything* or *anyone* that we value and love. Dated grief occurs when we take those experiences with the thoughts-and-emotions that drive them and install them as beliefs, understandings, and decisions.

When this happens, instead of "doing our grief work" and finishing it, we perpetuate it. We keep it inside as an unfinished program. Then that dated grief magnetizes other emotions to come along for the ride—emptiness, loneliness, futility, self-pity, self-contempt, etc. These other thoughts-feelings often complicate matters making it difficult for us to process through the grief and bring it to a healthy resolution ("good grief"). Generally, we process through current and appropriate grief in various emotional stages: shock, denial, guilt, hostility, depression. But when we install the grief as our identity program—we not only *live in it*, but these other emotions as well.

Normally, when the loss first occurs, we experience shock and denial. "This can't be happening!" Sometimes in our grief reaction, our denial may last for weeks, and even stretch into months. Some people *guilt* themselves as part of their grief, thinking about all the ways and times they let the person down or blame themselves for something. When we lose a significant loved one, we frequently feel guilty, if for no other reason than that we live on while the other did not.

Hostility frequently shows up in grief. We feel anger—at ourselves for the loss, at the person for dying(!), at God for letting it happen, at "reality" for "being this way." Grieving minds go into all kinds of irrationalities and cognitive distortions, "What have I done to deserve this?" "God, why did you take my husband?" "Why didn't you take that S.O.B. that lives next door?!" Etc.

Bewilderment also comes. We feel confused and unsure about things. We lose our "grip on reality" —our reality strategy often fails us when a loved one dies. "What am I going to do? How can I make it on my own?" This induces stress. Many women have gone from wealth to poverty upon the death of a husband or father. And so they connect that meaning to the experience of "grief."

King David felt the deep, dark agony of shock, anger, guilt, bewilderment, regret, etc. when his son died a violent death. His words of loss ring out illustrating the complicating emotions of grief.

> "O my son Absalom, my son, my son Absalom! Would I had died instead of you, O Absalom, my son, my son."

We need not think that the experience of grief or grieving as "bad" in itself. Grief actually comes to help us de-invest from what we have lost as we re-define ourselves. Then we can move on. A normal and healthy grief reaction usually involves all of these kinds of emotions. Such "emotions" reflect our "thinking" (internal representations) as we "come to terms" with reality, adjust our perceptual and conceptual maps, and reframe the meanings in our journey through life. The sign that we have appropriately and graciously *accepted the loss* is when we can shortly thereafter "get on with life." This means not carrying along the baggage of the overwhelming grief emotions by programming them as beliefs.

Discovering the Structure of Grief

How do you represent your loss? As you notice your pictures, words, and sensations (VAK modalities), elicit fully your modalities and submodalities by which you code the "loss." Check the visual and auditory systems for both real and symbolic pictures. Then do a contrastive analysis with a dated grief by asking for how you represent *"beyond grief and back to normal and feeling good."* What submodality differences exist between the two?

If you have difficulty with this then think about someone or some thing that you have lost, but regarding which you no longer grieve. What loss have you experienced that you now have fond memories of? Elicit the submodalities of this representation.

Andreas and Andreas (1989) have created a Grief Resolution procedure using submodalities. It works by mapping the submodalities of the loss over onto the submodalities of the *fond memory* so that you code your current loss as you code your "fond memory."

Time-lining grief enables us to address all of the concomitant emotions that frequently go along with it. When you associate back into the memory of the original experience (position #4), list all of the additional emotions present. This can provide insight about the kind of limiting learnings you might have made with that original grief.

Then use *the Swish Pattern* to imagine "the You for whom this offers no problem." Bring all the resources to bear that you need as you re-define yourself. It usually helps to identify all of the rich resources that this person or experience provided you so that you can take those resources with you into your future. In this way, you can have fond memories in spite of the loss, because out of the experience, it enriched you. Here, too, resources of acceptance, spiritual faith, wisdom, appreciation of the person, etc., help us to see "the me who can move on in life."

One particular vicious way of thinking-and-feeling about things gets us stuck in grief so that it becomes a dated emotion forever dragging us down, namely, over-identifying our value, worth, self, and future with the object of our loss. Do that and you not only grieve the loss/death of that object, but of *yourself* as well. Linguistically we code this non-sense in such statements as, "That was the death of me." "It ended my world." "I'll never get over his death." "When she left me, I knew I would never love again."

Such constructions need reframing so that we give new, different, and better meanings to our experiences. Here separating person and behavior comes in as an enhancing perspective. It allows us to recognize that we exist as more than our experiences. It empowers us to recognize that regardless of our situation, we always have choice of our responses and the way we think-and-feel.

When dealing with grief, future pacing also provides another important tool. Go into an imaginary future event where you would have re-experienced the grief. From there language yourself to *"fully let go of this grief* in the full realization that I can now move on with my life as I go into my future *remembering that loss with fond memories.* And as I do, I can *make an image* of the values and resources that this person has bequeathed to me. And as I look out into the future I can *see myself drawing on these resources* and thanking that person for them because they now enrich my life... and I can keep these resources with me for the rest of my life and no one can take them from me."

Letting Go of Fear and Anxiety

While out for a walk, Wayne, Sheila, and Brenda stopped by. Actually, Sheila had an important, reason for stopping by. She wanted to talk with me (BB) about her anxiety. In two weeks she would have a hysterectomy. Her fear about this brought her quickly to the point of tears. Knowing the power of using her time-line, she asked if it could help now.

"Could you help me with this fear?" I assured her that I could. "I don't understand, how can you help me? I haven't had the surgery, yet?" "No you haven't. But, you know what? Women have hysterectomies all the time and *do well with it.* My wife here had a hysterectomy and she *did very well.*" And so she confirmed that.

I then said, "You see, Sheila, women do have hysterectomies and do very well just like you will do well, won't you?"

"Yes, I guess so." she said. "I just feel so scared of the surgery."

"Then can you allow *yourself* to see yourself after the successful surgery *doing well...* and know that you can feel *safe....*"

"Now allow yourself to float up above that time-line in your mind... and now float out over your future until you come to two weeks from now when you will have the surgery. ... and as you see the hospital below and yourself receiving the surgery ...and seeing everything going well... then you can float out another couple of days and down onto your hospital bed when everything has worked out successfully and enjoy *feeling the good feelings of that success...*"

I paused a moment. "And now, you can—from that position, float back up and turn around going forward to after the surgery and from there look backwards toward this present moment. And as you do, you know that you can just let go of whatever fear and anxiety you had at that present, because you can do it just as you have let go of other negative emotions before, now."

When she had processed this, she said, "Yes, I can feel those negative emotions flowing out of me. It works! It really works. How amazing!"

This led her anxiety to disappear from her "future." Thereafter Sheila did well both during and after the surgery.

To work with fear and anxiety using time-lines, simply follow the same procedures as with negative emotions and end by having them float into their future. Anxiety and fear, like guilt, have no meaning outside of time.

Using Time-lines for Undoing Limiting Decisions

Frequently, out of life's events, and especially in times of stress, trouble and strong negative emotions, we *make limiting decisions* about some aspect of ourselves, the world, others, etc. Yet in "making a limiting decision" we limit ourselves, although we seldom do this consciously.

I (BB) once met with an old friend who came for a visit. As we talked, I inquired about her health. Ann had experienced an aneurism in her head plus a heart attack. Eventually I asked, "Ann, didn't your mother die of an aneurism at an early age?" "Yes," she said, "She was forty-seven and I was just sixteen."

As she spoke of her mother's death, she shed some tears. "And, how old were you when you had the aneurism?" "I was forty-nine." "And how old were you when you had your heart attack?" "I was fifty-one."

Then, I asked, as a matter of curiosity, "Do you think those events are connected?" She thought about it. "I knew a lady who had a heart attack at forty-seven and I found out that her mother died of a heart attack at forty-seven. She had always dreaded turning forty-seven for that very reason. Today she feels fine and has completely recovered."

At that Ann acknowledged, "I too have always dreaded reaching my forties."

"You seemed to have felt a lot of strong emotion when you thought, a moment ago, about your mother. Many years have passed and yet, you seem to still grieve over her..." "Yes, I do still miss her very much."

Did Ann *choose* to get seriously ill when she reached her late forties? Considering that as a possibility, I treated her situation as a case of living, unconsciously, by the frame of a *limiting decision*. I then used the time-line processes to help her clean up her "dated emotions" of grief and eliminate the limited decision about an early death. By clearing that out of the way this created a brighter future for herself. Today, she lives like a new person.

How many illnesses result from such limiting decisions? How much human misery and unresourcefulness? What decisions have you made that continue to limit you? And how pleased would you feel if you eliminated those limiting decisions and replaced them with empowering decisions... now?

We treat a limiting decision by following the same steps that we used in eliminating a negative emotional pattern. As you seek to discover the root cause, inquire,

"If I knew when the event occurred that triggered me to choose the limitation, when would that have occurred — before, during or after my birth?"

This question emphasizes *the event* that prompted us to create the limiting decision in the first place, rather than the choice itself. While we assume a person as the agent, we here place emphasis on **the event** rather than the decision to by-pass the conscious mind.

After identifying the first triggering event, associate into it and ask, "What emotions do I feel as I see what I saw, hear what I heard and feel what I felt during that event?" These emotions play an important role along with the limiting decision. After experiencing them, float out of the experience and back 15 minutes prior to this decision (Position #3 on the time-line). When you get to this place, ask, "Where have those emotions disappeared to? Where has that decision gone?" From that perspective—*they do not yet exist.* So now allow yourself to fully experience this *void of the not-yet...* wondering what enhancing decision you would like to come into it in order to have a space to put in something much better.

As you cannot recall a decision from that point of view, feel free to insert a new more empowering one. Because now you can make new *enhancing decisions* about how you can orient yourself, that will bring out your best. Then, take the decision and insert it into your time-line. You may also want to imagine *the you* who makes this more enhancing decision and swish your brain from the old stimuli and cues to this more resourceful identity.

Afterward float up to your meta-line (position #1) and then forward 15 minutes. When you move there, notice all the changes down there on the time-line and then float down into that old event (position #4). Do this to make sure that the old dated emotions have gone flat. Then, with your new empowering decision go forward in "time" and notice how the new decision reorganizes your memories and feelings as you move through time bringing with you new understandings about yourself and your world.

Using Time-lines to Address Trauma and Abuse

When we use these time-line processes to address the after-effects of trauma, we essentially do the same things. The "bad," hurtful, and negative emotions that result from a major and out-of-the-ordinary negative experience (rape, robbery, kidnapping, natural disasters, war, hostage, etc.) involve the same kind of intense negative emotions (stress, anxiety, fear, anger, guilt, resentment, disgust, etc.) only in extreme forms.

These SEEP contexts of trauma (the original events) generally evoke such strong, chronic, and intense emotions that it can easily re-evoke the trauma. We call this Post Traumatic Stress Disorder (PTSD) and it indeed offers a challenge. Yet with these processes we can effectively deal with such traumatized emotions.

When working with trauma thoughts-and-emotions, **do not attempt this on your own.** Get someone to work with you so that the other person can set up "bail out" anchors (anchors of relaxation, comfort, okayness, unconditional dignity, etc.) or anchors of interruption, uptime or disruption, etc. In the previous processes a person can move in and out from experiencing to thinking about the process and then back to experiencing, etc. The intensity of trauma emotions makes this very difficult. Accordingly, having someone else to mark and measure the handling of the processes frees a person to work in a more protected environment. Further, with traumatized emotions, we will want to secure a second level of dissociation so that we don't step back in before we de-energize the trauma memory and create new resources.

With *trauma* other considerations arise. Sometimes in trauma, people will dissociate and block things out and do so to such an extent that they will experience no memories of the trauma at all. In such situations, people will notice "dark" or "blank" spots in their time-lines and not have a clue as to what happened during that time. Later, they may experience the return of those memories and rediscover them.

Does that mean all rediscovered memories actually occurred? By no means! It may, it may not. The mere occurrence of a memory of abuse, rape, etc. has nothing *in itself* to do with what actually happened. We can, and do, have lots and lots of false memories. Intense representing of anything, especially while in a highly suggestible state (watching a horror movie, experiencing a nightmare, etc.) can install that information in our psycho-neurology.

What signs or cues might lead us to suspect abuse? I (BB) believe that ideally we will find the quality of brightness very similar in our representations of the past, present, and future on our timeline. However, abused and traumatized victims will tend to have dark areas, or at least, a darker quality to it.

Once Joe floated above his time-line, I asked him to compare the brightness of the past with his present and future. He said, "There is no comparison. The past is much darker than my present and future." For me then, dark areas, dark spots, or gaps in time-lines can possibly alert us to the possibility of abuse. And true to form, Joe had suffered abuse as a child and again traumatized in both Korea and Vietnam.

When a person has such dark areas or gaps, provide them with instruction about how to adjust the submodalities of their memories. Use an unimportant memory and direct the person to adjust the brightness and darkness. The person will thereby learn the process. Once they do, ask them to brighten the dark area. Frequently, they will find this difficult if not impossible. Proceed with caution, as I take it that the inability to brighten up an area *may* indicate a trauma or abuse, but it does not necessarily indicate such. At such points we must take care not to install such a memory through our suggestions or implications.

As a counterbalance, I (MH) tend to not view gaps or dark spots, etc. as indicators of abuse at all. I take it that many people do not remember, and so have dark memories, because they simply didn't pay much attention to things in the first place. Or they processed information globally and so overlooked details, and/or just didn't give much significance or importance to various happenings. Or they may have a "darker" (pessimistic) attitude about a particular past. Coming from a cognitive-behavioral background and knowing about the most fallible and constructivist nature of "memory," I take reports of abuse with great caution. All of us have invented false memories inasmuch as even our memories exist as constructions. And the danger of installing false memories strikes me as a very real danger.

Time-line processes offer a major benefit here because, by definition, one experiences a trance state via the very process of floating above one's time-line. As soon as we dissociate above our time-line to our meta-line, we enter into a mild trance.

Then, when we use Milton Model language patterns, we intensify the resulting trance experience. Consider the hypnotic nature of the question that we have repeatedly used, "If you knew the root cause of your problem which, when you disconnect from it, will cause the problem to disappear, when would that have occurred—before, during or after your birth?" As this question focuses attention on the problem, it creates a more intense focus.

As a person floats above the time-line and back into their past toward the memories in the dark areas, sometimes just asking them to brighten up those areas will uncover a memory. Often, however, it requires more digging. Frequently the person has gestated the memory of the abuse to similar memories so as the person begins to uncover less painful memories from the gestalt, he or she may find more emerging.

Some people will begin to describe the house where the abuse happened and discover rooms inside that they do not want to enter. Gradually they will enter into the "bad rooms." When they do, have them dissociated above the time-line.

Sandra had tried hypnotherapy, psychotherapy and many forms of drug treatment; she had seen therapists from California to North Carolina and yet her hurt remained. All of her therapists suspected abuse, but none could get to the source. Sandra drove from a distant city in a last ditch effort to obtain help through the new procedures of time-line processes.

After three and one-half hours, the memory surfaced. At five years of age, her mother's boyfriend raped her. Though she had repressed this painful memory, the memories continued to work havoc in her. Sandra could not function sexually and remained in a constant state of depression; signs that something significant ate at her on the inside. Through using her time-line, she moved with little distress back over the house and the room where the rape occurred. From that meta-position and in that dissociated state, she vividly saw his face. Now she knew the cause of her internal pain—and knowing, she could begin to deal with it and finish that gestalt.

Using the time-line processes we removed the negative kines-thetics that had worked such havoc in her life using the V-K Dissociation pattern, accessed lots of new resources from her present self, and updated old beliefs and decisions. Eventually Sandra forgave the man and began stepping into a place of true *freedom* from those old maps that she had carried with her and used to navigate life for so long.

Conclusion

With the processes of time-lining as we have described them, you now have the *neuro-linguistic tools* to take charge of yourself. You can now begin to "run your own brain" which thereby gives you the mechanisms for running your own emotions. You can "have your emotions" instead of letting them "have you!"

While none of us like our "negative" emotions in and of themselves, we can now learn to appreciate them for the signal value; warning us that something lurks in our environment that violates or threatens our values. Now we can welcome and fully accept our current emotions of distress (e.g. anger, fear, disgust, sadness, frustration, etc.). We can welcome them as messengers.

We can also totally release those *old dated emotions* of distress that have no signal value left. Since they referenced previous unpleasant experiences, violations or threats to values, we can travel back in time and either finish those experiences or just update our programs so that we don't have to carry them with us.

Doing this powerfully frees us to *live in the now* and to begin to build compelling and attractive futures.

Chapter 6

Trouble Shooting Skills

Time-Lining Processes

Can difficulties arise while using this basic NLP "time-line" process? Of course! To address various potential problems that may arise we have included this chapter. Here we do time-lining *trouble-shooting*.

At the end of the last chapter, as we moved from lighter emotional difficulties to heavier, we suggested that one should not attempt to use time-line processes on traumas, but should find someone to assist in the process. By having someone to facilitate the process, it provides a safety net least one collapses into a negative emotional state. It allows someone to measure and mark our progress and to pull us out if we get into trouble.

What problems can arise? We can lose rapport and need to do more pacing, people can lose track of the process and get confused. We can start to feel afraid of the process itself (a meta-state). We can fear that our memories will lead to the most unenhancing meanings, that it will "discover some dark secret of the past" and overwhelm us.

Obviously, when time-lining with others we must continue to utilize the basic NLP processes of pacing and leading, calibrating to state, checking out "message heard," and not assuming that our intent got through loud and clear. We need to maintain an awareness of the meanings generated and reframe such things as "failure," "misunderstanding," "the feeling of one's feelings" in a way that encourages a person to continue with the process.

In this chapter we want to offer some specific trouble-shooting processes and patterns.

"I Just Can't Remember!"

Sometimes people have memories which operate destructively within, and yet they lack access to them. They "can't remember." They "go blank." What then?

To have a set of representations within that seem "blocked off" from us, "out of reach," "blank," "beyond a wall of amnesia," etc. describes two parts. It describes having one **part** that knows and yet another **part** of us fears us knowing. Yet these parts lack a connection so that they can work together harmoniously. Structurally, we have an unconscious/conscious split.

When a painful existing memory exists in this fashion, but does not surface, we will first want to attempt a *"parts reframe."* Long before we ask the person to release their negative emotions and delete the memory, we **welcome** the memory back into consciousness, and before we do that (for ecology sake) we will want to preserve learnings of that memory. "And what have you learned that you want to keep with you that can protect you from this ever happening again?"

Structurally, we usually find a *part* within the person that seeks to protect them in some way. So if someone can't access the memory, we language the person with validation and protection.

> "A *part* of you objects to this memory surfacing undoubtedly because of the pain that it causes in some way. And we respect this part, and would highly appreciate it letting us know of its objection. And so you can ask that part if it will communicate its positive purpose for you in consciousness so that we can validate it and protect that positive intention fully and completely."

When the part states its purpose, we frame it in a way so it can permit the disclosure of the abuse or hurt. From a logical level perspective, consider what that piece does. Here we have welcomed our distress into consciousness—the "welcoming" state exists at a higher meta-level to the "distress" state. This counter-acts the other meta-state that the person had suffered from:

"rejecting" the "distress." Yet we have done more. We have "validated and appreciated" its "positive intention" (probably "protection") by keeping it blanked out or in amnesia. These higher levels modulate, organize, and drive the lower state.

Figure 6:1

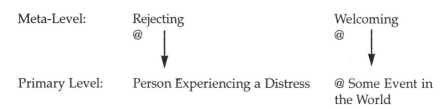

Meta-Level:	Rejecting @	Welcoming @
Primary Level:	Person Experiencing a Distress	@ Some Event in the World

"What do you do if the part doesn't communicate its positive intention?" **We assume its positive intention.** We just work from the assumption of protection and then reframe it as that.

> "A part objects to disclosing the internal pain and as we appreciate the part for so protecting you from such, let us assure that part of this—we will not do anything to interfere with it protecting you—in fact, we only want to offer it better and more adult ways to protect you. *We respect its highest intent.* At a younger age, you did not have the resources you needed to protect you as you do now and so that part protected you in the best way it could, because you have survived. So we do appreciate this part. However, now you have become older and wiser and have other resources to protect you from pain. Also, if you continue to hold down these hurtful memories that requires much energy and ultimately harms you. So we only want to offer this part newer and more adult ways to offer protection."

Next, once a painful memory has surfaced, we use the dissociation of looking and hearing it *from* the perspective of *above* the time-line so as to give the person the "wisdom" of other perspectives *about* it. Then, from there we run the V-K Dissociation Pattern to neutralize the phobic reactive emotions. This enables the person to courageously face the memory. Afterwards, we may inquire whether the person wants to delete the memory entirely. I (BB) find that most of the people I work with do. When they affirm that they do, I use the V-K Dissociation pattern to simply delete it. Then afterwards, I replace that memory with a pleasant memory of the person's choosing.

What if the Negative Emotions Don't Release?

Suppose a person does not let all the negative emotions go when they move to the 15 minutes before the source experience (position #3)? What then? Frequently, people do not let all of the emotion go. When you test, you will discover that some of the emotions have not gone flat. When this happens, we again usually assume that *some objecting part needs reframing* so that the meanings that magnetize the old hurtful emotions can shift enough to allow releasing. We have found the following reframes most helpful.

1. "As you relax comfortably, you can become aware of the part within you that somehow thinks you should have learned something else from this event. And, as we know the importance of preserving all such positive learnings in that special place you reserve for such learnings... so that you can move into your future with more safety and wisdom... And as that part now makes those learnings, it can acknowledge acceptance to that protective part to *let those negative emotions go completely... now, wouldn't it?*"

2. "And as we recognize that the highest intent of your *unconscious* mind involves preserving your body's integrity and safety, I wonder if your protective part now completely knows that when you hold on to those negative emotions it actually causes a very harmful process to occur to the body, and as a protective part it can *resist that holding on* so that that part can now give you its full permission to *let the emotion go... now*, wouldn't it?"

3. "And you can begin to attain more awareness than ever before of the intent of this protective part... and as you do, what does it seek to do for you that you would value as important? ..."

Repeat this line of questioning until you obtain its highest intent which then gives permission to release the negative emotion. You may need to find some other part to perform the same function in a less harmful way.

What if the Emotion Does Not Go Flat?

On occasion, you may encounter the negative emotion that does not go totally flat when you test for it at the end of the procedure. When this occurs, the problem will probably lie in one or more of the following areas.

1. **The person has not accessed position #3.** Make sure the person dissociates from the memory above the time-line from position #4. After that the person must not only take a position **above** the memory, but also **before** the memory. Through trial and error, we have learned that fifteen minutes before the memory works best. You will undoubtedly discover exceptions. A warning about this process: when people have lived for a long time associated into a negative memory, they will naturally and quickly re-associate into the memory. This necessitates that we watch our use of language and guide the person carefully and comfortably to position #3.

To assist the client from re-associating into the negative memory, you can ask the client to imagine having a sheet of plexiglass under them. Some people desire to imagine that they travel above their time-line riding in an airplane or in the gondola of a baloon. Others may wish to imagine that a resourceful person either human or divine travels the time-line with them. Utilize whatever works for the client.

2. **The person has not gotten to the first event or the "root cause."** When this happens, the person will still get the release of a lot of negative emotions from their SEEP. Those Significant Emotional Events of Pain you worked with may not comprise the original event. If the person reports that 90% or more of the emotion has flattened out or disappeared, we don't consider the therapy finished. We don't because even when they have just a small amount of emotion left, a total gestalt could regenerate—it could get re-anchored into existence! So we like to continue

working until all of the negative emotions disappear. Many times doing this will feel like peeling an onion. You will clean up one event only to discover another. Continue until you get the first event and the emotion flattens out.

3. **The emotions may not have flattened out because an objecting part doesn't feel ready to release the memory**. Process back to the section, about the negative emotions releasing and letting go.

What if the Person Feels Incomplete?

This suggests you should re-imprint them to undo unfinished development task development to thereby eliminate any vestiges of co-dependency and/or dysfunctionality.

In cases of trauma and abuse, people often end up having deep inner needs unmet and unfinished. Such persons usually come from co-dependent and dysfunctional families in the first place where parents made their children serve the function of supporting some "sickness" in the home whether it consist of abuse of alcohol or drugs, or emotional, sexual or physical abuse. Experientially, instead of receiving acceptance and nurture from their parent(s), the parent(s) forced the child to accept and nurture them.

These families also typically required the total obedience of the child. If the child's behavior didn't feed the family's sickness, the parent(s) forbid the child to have his or her own feelings. To survive in that climate, the child learned to dissociate and repress—to numb out.

John Bradshaw (1988) says the repression of the child's feelings leads to the destruction of the child's soul.

> "Soul-murder is the basic problem in the world today; it is the crisis in the family. We programmatically deny children their feelings, especially anger and sexual feelings. Once a person loses contact with his own feelings, he loses contact with his body. We also monitor and control our children's desires and thoughts. To have one's feelings, body, desires and thoughts controlled is to lose one's self. To lose one's self is to have one's soul murdered."

This destroying in "the child's soul" leads to the "dragon-like" emotions of pseudo-guilt and a shame-based identity. A sexually abused child inevitably thinks-feels as if *they* have done something wrong and somehow deserves the punishment.

A distraught mother called recently. She had stayed up most of the night with her ten year old daughter. The reason? Because her thirteen year old brother had exposed himself to her. And yet the little girl felt terribly guilty.

Dysfunctional families produce **shame-based personalities.** This differs from just feeling accurate and appropriate guilt which says, "I *did* something wrong." In contrast, shame says, "*I am* wrong." So whereas in guilt we rightly feel, "I *made* a mistake." In shame, we falsely conclude, "*I am* a mistake." The person tends to internalize shame and make it their **identity.** This involves a misbelief due to personalizing about one's identity or self.

In addition to these consequences, the child also fails to develop developmentally and to progress through many of the psychosocial stages of development (Erickson). This means that developmentally, the person may think-and-feel as a ten-year old even though actually forty or sixty years old. They have not yet negotiated the developmental stages.

Figure 6:2

Eric Erickson's Developmental Model
of the Psycho-Social Stages:

Trust/Mistrust of others who respond to and care for our needs
Autonomy/Shame and Doubt—Functioning as self-sufficient and exploring
Initiative/Guilt—Exploring and negotiating boundaries
Industry/Inferiority—Learning to become competent, productive in mastering skills
Identity/Role confusion—Establishing a sense of self
Intimacy/Isolation—Dealing with companionship, love, friendships
Generativity/Stagnation—Making a meaningful contribution
Integrity/Despair—Making sense of life.

Trauma often interrupts the developmental process. It blocks the normal personality development from occurring while the person stays preoccupied with surviving. Further, because of the lack of this personality development, the person often lacks the skills and resources necessary for integrating their understandings of the trauma experience in their mind and memory. Lacking the "ego strength" that they didn't get to develop in normal ways then prevents them from understanding, accepting, and accomplishing the other tasks before them.

Consequently, the trauma itself functions as "unfinished business" within. As an aftermath they miss out on some growth/development. So once we have dealt with the un-negotiated piece of trauma that has troubled and sabotaged the person, we may then need to assist them in catching up on the other developmental personality stages that they may have missed.

Most people want to understand. So the process of *connecting the events* that created the shame functions is a major way to rediscover their freedom. They learn that their thinking-feeling and behaving does not relate to them, but to what happened to them. Using the time-line provides a tool for accessing these memories and restructuring them. For shame-based identities—look at the imprint period of development for the root cause(s). Now, to remove this *map of shame* from the person, we must address the memories wherein they created the shame, removing them and re-imprinting them.

The following borrows from Dilts (1990) concept of re-imprinting and James and Woodsmall's (1988) concept of Time-Line Therapy™. I (BB) have developed this simple *re-imprinting procedure*. In doing this, merely cleaning up images and emotions of abuse does not suffice. We especially see this when the person grew up in a dysfunctional family or received abuse over a long period of time. This results because they developed without receiving the necessary love and nurture they needed to feel completely whole. So I have combined time-line work with re-imprinting to also create new more positive memories. After having cleaned up the emotions and traumatic experiences, use the following steps to build new memories.

The Re-Imprinting Process

1. **View the clean-up**. Invite the person to float above the time-line and over the memories they have cleaned up. If you used the fast phobia model, ask them to see the "times" deleted. Ask them to name the significant people in their lives during the trauma event.

2. **Identify missing resources**. Upon naming their significant people, ask, "And what did these people need for themselves as personal resources in order that they could have given you what you needed at that time in your life?"

3. **Search for resources.** "Does that person now have that needed resource?" "What would it feel like if they did?" Through questioning direct them to gain a clear representation of the needed resources. Who do they now know who has those resources? Upon naming the resource, invite them to make an image in their mind of the resource and to associate into that resource. Anchor this and then test the anchor. You will want to have a good anchor—you will use it during re-imprinting.

4. **Give the resource away.** When the person has the resource image in mind, say, "I want you to take that image of the resource and give it to the significant person (name the person) in your life at that time... and see, hear and feel them operating fully resourceful in —love, grace, calmness, gentleness, etc.

5. **Associate into the person with the resource**. After giving the significant other the resource, invite the person to associate into that person's body. "As you now step into this person's body, having all of that resource fully that you needed at that time, what would he/she say to you, having this resource, in order to give to you fully?" Give them time to express what the person would say, then have them float to position #2.

6. **Repeat.** Repeat steps 2 through 5 with each significant person in that memory.

7. Back up to before the event. "And you can now float back, back on your time-line to some time prior to the event." Then ask them to associate into their younger self before the abusive event.

8. Fire the resource anchors. As they identify with their younger self prior to the event, fire the resource anchors and have the person come forward, fully associated, through the memory. In case of deleted memories, bring them through the newly installed image drawing from the significant others the resources they needed. Hold the resource anchors. The person will re-experience the event and draw upon the *needed resources* from each significant person. Deleting the emotions, deleting the memories and re-imprinting the memories will build a totally new history for the client.

Finishing the Unfinished Business

The following pattern I (MH) put together as a process for assisting a person to catch up in their psychic development.

1. Adopt a commitment to reality. Having cleared up the hurts of the past, and having used your new understandings and "ego strength" to face those past hurts from your strengths, you have begun to "make yourself a friend to reality" rather than an enemy. Those days of feeling and thinking in an antagonistic way to reality have ended. The skill of "going meta" to the experiences that that younger you had "in" time by *floating above on your time-line* has given you the skill to look at and accept the disliked, obnoxious, dysfunction, etc. *without taking it personal*. What a skill! And you can congratulate yourself for learning to accept without confusing it with approving, validating, or endorsing what existed. You can accept what exists—what existed—and dislike it and realize fully that it only existed as an event, an experience, a set of behaviors—and that *you* exist as so much more than those experiences.

This skill signifies the adult recognition of reality as a *dispassionate fact*. How different from the way we thought-and-felt as children! Then we took events personaly. We thought in ego-centric ways, we introjected the hurtful behaviors of others, and we built disempowering beliefs about ourselves and we have now learned to do that no more.

2.   **Access a state of adult acceptance**. Think about a time or situation where you accepted something that you did not like. Pick something simple to practice identifying these representations: cleaning the bathroom and toilet, doing dishes, preparing your tax return, etc. How do you, representationally, construct this *acceptance of disliked activity?* What beliefs and values support this state. When you have it fully and resourcefully, anchor it.

3.   **Access a friendship to reality state**. Maturing, developing, and becoming fully human necessitates a commitment to what actually exists, in the place of wishful thinking, magical thinking, and regretful thinking ("oh, if only...!"). Access a time when you positively felt that kind of orientation getting your internal representation, submodalities and supporting beliefs, and anchor it.

4.   **Access the state of "finishing business"**. Identify the state of "finishing something." What project, task, relationship, etc., have you engaged in, invested yourself in, and then brought to a completion and released so that you let it come completely and thoroughly in a positive way so that you simply took the resources of that experience and moved on to the next step? Think about a grade in school that you finished, or a particular subject or skill that you learned. How did you **complete that business** with your instructor, coach, friends?

In accessing this resource state of "having positively brought something to closure" notice all of the internal representations and supporting beliefs that made this an enhancing life experience for you. You "came to terms" with the time-limited nature of the subject. You began something, and then you completed it. Anchor this.

5.   **Finish the "unfinished business" in your mind-emotions**. As you now float above your current time-line, where you live and act and feel and think today... looking down upon it and noticing how it moves back into the past, allow yourself to notice what developmental tasks (of the Erickson list, p. 98) that you did not complete; trust, autonomy, identity, etc.

From *above* your time-line move forward into the future to a time when you can imagine seeing yourself as having finished that task. Now go there. What does finishing that task look like, sound like, feel like? What supporting beliefs, values, and actions go along with it? Fire the "finishing business" and "a friend to reality" anchors as you float down into that time and fully experience it with completeness. And you can enjoy the full development...

6. **Use as a swish.** When you have fully captured the feeling and meaning of finishing that old business, return to now and look into your future at that future you, noticing the steps and stages that you will *take day by day* as you move more and more into your future... because you can.

Changing Your Time-Line

Can we actually change our time-line/s? Sure! Our time-line simply exists in our mind-body as *a coding of the concept.* And, the process of changing our internal representation of "time" can occur relatively simply. But... a warning, when you change your time-line, you may initially experience disorientation, even feel dizzy, "strange," "weird," etc. When I (BB) change my time-lines, it always blows me out! So take lots of care with this one!

If you have a *Through Time* structure, first, float up above your time-line and from there straighten your line so it runs left to right. Then, rotate your time-line ninety degrees (or rotate yourself ninety degrees), then drop down into your time-line with the realization and feeling that you now have your "past" behind you. And as you let you represent your "past" as behind your head, you can open your eyes to see the "present" directly in front of your face, while the future seems at arms length or further in front of your face. Take a moment with this... How does it feel?

If you have an *In Time* coding, float up above "time," straighten your time-line and then rotate your line ninety degrees (or rotate your body ninety degrees). Now drop *behind* your time-line so that everything lies directly in front of you. Make the images about six inches to one foot square and place "past" images an arms length to your left (if right handed). Notice that your "future" has moved to the other side. The present goes directly in front of your face about a foot out. Imagine the tops of all three images to stand at eye level. You have now taken on the codings of an ideal *Through Time* person. Take a moment with this... How does this feel?

Some people experience profound changes as they do this exercise. Others experience few changes. A few people will lack the ability to do this on their own and will need assistance from someone trained in working with time-line processes. You may wish to leave your time-line in its opposite position for a while just to experiment with it. But avoid driving when you first try on a different time-line. When you feel ready to put your time-line codings back, float up again and reverse the adjustments you made.

"Time-Lining" Structural Change

I (MH) had a client a few years back who "lived in the past." He had a tendency to think negatively and pessimistically, to see the future in dark and bleak terms, and to recall negative events from the past and to feel bad about them over and over. Obviously, he did not live very celebratively.

When I explored with him his "time-line"—guess where he had coded and stored his "past?" Right out in front of him. Not behind him. Not to the side—but right out in front of him, in color, close, and panoramic! If you want to filter everything in the present and future through a painful "past"—try that one on! It will most assuredly induce negative and gloomy feelings so that you feel powerless to change or to see brighter days.

He also had his future representations out in front of him, only the "past" pictures stood in front of the future ones. So he couldn't "see" them very well. Nor could he create visual images on the "screen of his mind" of anything even a year or two off, let alone a decade or two. He had known for years that he "didn't have the ability to 'visualize'" about future events. So he had reckoned it as some kind of learning disability(!). [A distorted map (conclusion) about his inadequate "time" map!]

With his past right in front of him and literally "in his face," this map didn't allow him much ability to live in the present. When I introduced him to the *concept of sensory awareness*—of coming into **an uptime state** with eyes, ears, and skin wide open to all of the millions of sensations impinging upon him, he didn't know quite what to make of it. My words about "coming into Uptime" seemed like foreign words of another language. And no wonder, he already had his visual, auditory, and kinesthetic channels filled with images, sounds, and sensations of "the past." Quoting Fritz Perls, I told him that he needed to "lose his mind and come to his senses!"

I asked him a series of questions to get him to step back from the way he had coded and represented "time." "Do they serve you well?" "Do they enable you to leave the past behind you and move on into your future with grace and power?" "Do they enhance your life?" "Do they limit you in any way?" Via these questions, he eventually felt a shift and began to develop more awareness of his "time"-line.

Soon he developed awareness that by investing far too much importance and energy into those past events—he had done to himself more damage and harm than **the events** themselves had. He had made them his filters and beliefs. In so doing, he had carried these negative events and feelings with him for years and had contaminated his present.

"Those simply represented **events** that *you* went through. *You* experienced those events and made some learnings from them— but you exist as so much more than those events! Further, those events do not represent the last word about *human beings or human potential*. They do not say anything about what we can legiti- mately anticipate from resourceful and conscious people—they indicate what we can expect from unresourceful, hurting, limited, and unconscious humans—the ones who inadequately parented you!; the ones who failed to show up for Parenting #101.

"So as you look back on those events, allow yourself to float above your body and look at your 'time-line' and notice how it can **straighten out** as a line and slowly move so that the past events lie to your far left and going back almost behind you while the line moves to your right into your present right in front of you and then on to your right moving upward and out into a bright future."

This brought about all kinds of shifts and changes in his physiology. "How does this kind of a 'time'-line feel to you?" "Great," he said. "How would you experience yourself, your family, your work, and other facets of your life if you moved out with this as your map of 'time' tomorrow and in the days to come?" "It would be great." "Then listen to the sound of this line snapping into place like the sound of a giant iron gate closing on a castle. As it clangs into place, you can allow this structure to solidify in your consciousness ... and you can allow your unconscious mind to take these representations and the beliefs and values that it generates and store it some place very special inside you..."

In the days that followed these conceptual alterations in his "time" coding, he found himself in a new and very different "time" frame. He said that his "past" had seemed to de-energize, more like a wisp of a wind, yet less memorable. "My future also seems brighter, more hopeful, and now I am getting a sense of what you mean by sensory awareness—it seems like I can see, and hear, and smell and feel for the first time in a very, very long time."

How Time-Line Therapy Works

How and why does time-line processes work? Throughout we have offered some of the reasoning, now we will make that reasoning more explicit.

Time-line processes work, in part, due to the effect of *dissociation*. By "going meta" to our concept of "time" (already a meta-concept), we get distance from our more immediate thoughts-and-feelings. This empowers us to think clearly, with more objectivity, and to bring other awarenesses to bear on our states. This dissociation process also enables us to know ourselves as more than our experiences in "time."

Time-line processes work by means of the submodality of location. Neurologically, as with almost all other NLP processes, the changes and transformations created by moving systematically through "time" occurs at the submodality level. And, psychologically, our emotions require "time" in order to express and create their meanings. So when you go *before* (a temporal predicate) the "root cause" of an event (the context out of which we make an un-enhancing map), we find it impossible to "reckon," "account," or represent any map that would generate any emotion. Neat!

Since our brain-body system does not know (or experience) any difference between information just imagined vividly from what we have actually experienced, when we send the messages to our brain that we do using time-line processes, the brain *represents it and the body experiences it.* And so it actualizes as "real" internally and subjectively. This explains why you can vividly imagine eating a lemon... and then your mouth begins to water. This explains why when thinking about someone's finger nails digging in and scratching on a blackboard, we cringe within our skin. Similarly, when a person imagines floating above and before an event, they cease experiencing the emotion that would have derived from the event. We've changed the context. We have outframed the old frame. The emotions just disappear. From that frame of reference the event in "time" has not yet occurred and therefore does not exist, and so the emotion can't have yet occurred.

Cartesian Logic and Time-Line Processes

From the field of neuro-physics we now offer another reason for how and why time-line processes work to bring about empowering transformations. If you have some familiarity with Cartesian Logic, then you know that in Cartesian Logic we posit a theory through four quadrants to generate four questions. In order for us to validate a theory as true, it must hold in all four quadrants

Figure 6:3
Cartesian Logic

Converse **A not B** What would happen If you didn't?	Theorem **AB** What would happen If you did?
Non-Mirror Image Reverse **Not A Not B** What wouldn't happen If you didn't?	Inverse **Not A B** What wouldn't Happen if you did?

Let's suppose you asked someone to make a presentation, but they turn you down saying, "I can't do that because I can't present in public." Now let's consider their statement as a *theorem.*

To respond to this, our inverse response would go, "What will not not happen in that situation and in your life because you can't present?" Our converse would ask, "What will not happen in that class and in your life because you cannot not present?" The *non-mirror image reverse* would go, "What will not not happen in that class and in your life because you cannot not present?" When we turn a stated problem into the non-mirror image reverse, neurologically, the stated problem reverses. The non-mirror image reverse and the Phobia Model function, neurologically, similarly. Also, Position 3 above one's time-line works as the non-mirror image reverse.

111

Figure 6:4
Cartesian Logic

Converse	Theorem
"What will not happen in that class and in your life because you cannot not present?"	"I can't do that because I can't present in public."
Non-Mirror Image Reverse	**Inverse**
"What will not not happen in that class and in your life because you cannot not present?"	"What will not not happen in that situation and in your life because you can't present?"

To appreciate the power of the non-mirror image, write down a problem that you currently have. Put it in the form of the non-mirror image reverse. What happens? When our unconscious mind processes the non-mirror image reverse, we will experience physiological changes as our brain re-codes the problem. Neurologically and psychologically, time-line processes work due to these kinds of logics and patterns that changes the way we code information about ourselves, others, "problems," "time," etc.

Overdurf and Silverthorn (1995) in **Beyond Words** utilize the conceptual basis of Cartesian Logic for explaining time-lining processes. They utilize the analogy of a glove and suggest that **the inverse** of the glove would consist of *the glove turned inside out*. The converse of the glove would comprise the other glove or its opposite.

The *non-mirror image* reverse of the glove would include every-thing else in existence other than the glove. Another way of viewing the non-mirror image reverse in the context of the theorem of a problem would involve saying that the non-mirror image reverse of the problem includes everything the problem does not consist of.

The power of this? Once we impose the non-mirror image reverse on the problem, *the problem cannot hold up*. This results because "the everything else" of the non-mirror image reverse engulfs the problem. That which defined the problem disappears.

Julia Silverthorn gives another example to provide a visual metaphor. She talks about preparing Jell-O. Consider having a Jell-O mold inside a larger and deeper pan or dish. If you poured Jell-O into the mold you would have a Jell-O form. But if upon pouring the Jell-O inside the mold, you then discover that the mold has a leak, then all of the Jell-O would first go into the mold. Then it would flow out and into the inside of the larger dish. Eventually, as the mold and the dish would both fill up, and in doing so, the Jell-O inside the larger dish would engulf the Jell-O mold. The Jell-O mold would then, in effect, disappear and essentially serve no purpose.

In the *non-mirror image* reverse pattern, the "everything else" engulfs the theorem and if the theorem holds no purpose for the individual, it would disappear as a problem.

In time-lining, we believe that position #3 both *above* and *before* the problem equates to the *non-mirror image reverse*. So when we both dissociate from a problem and in our imagination we then exist before the problem, **the problem disappears.** Why? Because that structure no longer has any function.

In the dissociated position of position #3 before the existence of the problem, we experience the "everything else" that the problem does not consist of. From this broad perspective, we have the choice to reframe the problem out of existence with the choice of creating new and more positive outcomes from what we originally perceived as a problem.

Part III

Adventuring In "Time"

Chapter 7

Adventuring In "Time"

Traveling and Balancing the "Time" Zones

As we have explored our relationship to "time," our "time" consciousness, our "time-line(s)," etc., we have noticed that we experience various "time" zones (past, present, future, eternity) and that given these "time" zones, we experience ourselves as persons who conceptually engage in "time" travel. The old biblical passage said that God put into our minds *"a sense of time past and future."* In so putting "eternity" or "consciousness of 'time'" in our minds, we now have the ability to not only live in the present, but also in the conceptual "past" and "future." We can, in fact, so transcend the now that we think-feel and respond as if living in another "time" zone.

Conceptually, and then neurologically and behaviorally, *we can send out our consciousness* to representations of events of the past or future so that we can become completely preoccupied, absorbed, and even "stuck" in those representations.

The "Past" "Time" Zone

Much of time-line work involves getting unstuck— unstuck from the places of the "past" in our minds. The psychotherapeutic work involved here addresses the danger of **coding** some past hurtful event, or series of events, in such a way that rivets it in our minds so that those memories bind us and we seem unable to "get over the past," "put the past behind us," move on and get a life today, etc.

Yet, as we have emphasized, "the past" does *not* actually or literally exist. The referents of "the past" have truly passed away. Those *events* no longer continue. If other events, similar events, continue to occur, then we speak about current or present events and not "the past."

"The past" as our memories of former events and former understandings, learnings, meanings, and representations about those events *only* exists today **in our "mind."** They only exist as mental representations (accurate and distorted) about former happenings. They only exist as conceptual understandings that we keep playing over and over on the theater of our "mind" that keeps us focused on former happenings (and that can certainly occur at an out-of-consciousness level so that we may not even have awareness of such ongoing symbolization).

Only in this way can a person "live in the past." Such does *not* describe anything literal. It describes, metaphorically, where the person sends his or her consciousness. Yet, wherever we send our "mind" and whatever representations we then entertain and process, those representations as a mental mapping do what all mental processing does; it *generates neuro-semantic states*: feelings, emotions, responses, behaviors, reactions, sensations, etc.

By contrast, *using the "past" time zone* to enrich our present describes an empowering way to live. Calling forth images, pictures, and movies from our memory banks and re-experiencing resourceful times of joy, confidence, love, excitement, passion, celebration, wonder, curiosity, learning, motivation, etc.—this offers us a marvelous pathway for greater personal empowerment.

NLP preeminently encourages this kind of use of the "past" time zone. Once we learn to "run our own brain" to so send out our consciousness to our internal "library of 'past' references" of great and wonderful times—then we can so **order our consciousness** that we need never feel desperately alone again or without resources. It provides an incredibly powerful meta-resource that enables us to retrieve thoughts, feelings, and experiences stored in your brain and neurology so that we can use them again and again.

Running our own brain in this manner enables us to use our past for literally **reaccessing positive and resourceful states** so that we can bring them with us into the "now" and into our future.

Another positive use of the "past" time zone involves pulling up old memories of painful times and *taking a spectator's position in reference to them* so that we see them, metaphorically, up on "the theater of our 'mind.'" Sitting back in a tenth or twentieth row of a theater so that we can comfortably watch an old internal movie of something that did not turn out to our liking, enables us to do two things.

First, it enables us to avoid repressing or denying the events. This prevents stuffing the hurtful events down inside, where at a deeper level of "mind" we expend psychic energy keeping it out of consciousness. Trying to push painful awarenesses out of consciousness does not work. It only lodges a toxic and poisonous piece of neuro-semantic understanding deep in our body where it will probably poison our soma (body), use up our energy, and prevent us from positively using the experience. Denying the reality of events that previously occurred does not make for sanity—or any other positive quality.

Second, it will enable us to avoid using the "past" time zone for feeling bad. Some who don't repress and deny end up with an option just as bad—they keep playing the old "B" rated movie in their head over and over and over which creates more hurt, trauma, and pain. This then programs them for, and installs in them, neuro-linguistic "buttons" that people can push that sets off the toxic neuro-semantic state. They become "sensitive," phobic, reactive, out-of-control, negative, pessimistic, cynical, and ineffective.

In other words, when we **misuse** the "past" time zone, through either repression or submersion to psycho-archeology, then our "past" "time" consciousness operates as a painful and destructive power to us. Accordingly, this highlights the value and importance of taking the representations of the "past" that we evaluate as negative, hurtful, undesired, etc. and coding them from a new perspective—a spectator's perspective so that we can think **about** them from a position or state of comfort and resourcefulness rather than thinking **of** the pain.

If representations always and inevitably induce state, but some states create much emotional distress, pain, conflict, etc. (negative semantic reactions), then we need to totally **transform some repre-**

sentations of past events. Start by shifting away from associated representations (sights, sounds and sensations that we see from out of our own person) to dissociated representations. Look at things and hear events from a third-person perspective, from a projection booth perspective, from above our time-line, or from the resourceful you perspective. We have an infinite number of positive alternatives. Often times, once we learn how to dissociate from painful memories, we automatically reframe our painful memories. It seems to occur naturally once we remove our kinesthetic distresses through the dissociation coding. This then permits the preservation of our learnings as well as permission to heal the pain.

Doing this allows us then to pick **the resourceful state** we want and need in order to look at those former events to make some new learnings, decisions, and beliefs that will serve us well. Now we can use our "past" for ongoing development and learning rather than something to avoid or to re-traumatize ourselves over.

The "Future" "Time" Zone

Just like the so-called "past," *the "future"* as a thing or reality, does **not** exist. We can't point to it. We can't walk over to it and handle it. We can't smell or taste it. The events, activities, and experiences that will occur on some coming day only exist as the "future" *in our "mind."* We symbolize those coming events by the things we see, hear, and feel via our mental representations in our nervous system. We imagine them.

As the mental phenomenon of *"memory"* codes symbols and gives us a sense of the "past," so the mental phenomenon of *"imagination"* provides us a sense of the "future." We imagine things to come. We mentally anticipate them.

Now in the "future" "time" zone, many people do themselves great neuro-linguistic harm by overwhelming themselves by imagining too much! They see *all* the things they have to, or want to do and then feel overwhelmed. Others let their imaginations go wild and fail to order their consciousness well and see or hear or feel *all* the things that could go wrong.

We call this negative anticipation of coming events *"worry,"* a word that refers to "strangling." And so it does. We absolutely waste our mental energies "worrying" about horrible, terrible and threatening things to come, who play the "what if..." tapes, strangle our neurology so that we feel like we can hardly breathe. We have, so to speak, zoomed off into the "futurist" theater of our "mind" and now, on stage, in the movie, we play out the mental representations of the bad things that might possibly come to pass and then experience them in a fully associated way. Not wise! In so doing, we cue our brain (and thereby neurology) to go into a freaked-out, panic oriented state! Those well-skilled at this can "fly into a panic" at the snap of the fingers. They can "scare the hell" out of themselves with just a quick dash to their futuristic mental theater and torture themselves in ways that would make Stephen King drool!

The Present "Time" Zone

Because we have "time" or eternity implanted in our "minds," and can "time" travel to other "time" zones, we often find it difficult living fully and completely and resourcefully *in the present*. To live in the *psychological present* in a healthy and balanced way does not mean avoiding or ignoring the other "time" zones, but *integrating "past" and "future"* with the present so that we can simultaneously live fully in the present while using the resources that we can find and create from the "past" and "future." A tall order? You bet!

When we experience the psychological present, we get a feeling of "nowness." William James (1890) wrote about this,

> "Let anyone try to attend to the present moment of time and one of the most baffling experiences occurs. Where is it, this present? It has melted in our grasp, fled ere we could touch it, gone in the instant of becoming."

Further, to live in the present *without* integrating the other "time" dimensions reduces us to living an animalistic life. We would then not use our gift of symbolism (languaging) so as to take learnings with us from the past ("time" binding) nor building learnings ahead of "time" about the future. We would live only for the now, aware of only immediate gratifications, and unable to tolerate any frustration of our desires.

By contrast *the human way* to enter into the psychological present involves utilizing "past" learnings and "future" anticipations. It involves tapping into the **wisdom** that arises from lessons learned through experiences (the proper neuro-linguistic use of the "past") and *the consequential thinking* and well-formed desired outcome building, or goal-setting, anticipated via one's imaginative skills (the proper neuro-linguistic use of the "future").

We come into this world born in present "time." But then as we develop awareness of memories of the "past" and anticipations of the "future" we create generalizations and concepts about "time." Eternity begins to come into our "mind" and we truly become creatures of "time."

At first, we have little "time" stored in our neuro-linguistics, but as events occur, we build up more and more memory banks holding our representations of past experiences. Thus our sense of "time" grows. This explains why as children, "time" seemed to take forevvveeerrr. It seemed that school would never get out. Summer vacation never seemed to come. Chores seemed to last for an eternity. A year for a five year old comprises 1/5 of his entire life (2 years of which the child had almost no linguistic codings). Psychological "time" did not seem to move quickly at all.

By the time we reach mid-life, however, "time" seemed to have sped up. A year for a forty-year old comprises but 1/40 of his life. And a year for an eighty year old but 1/80 of his life.

At first, with little ability to transcend "time" we want everything we want **now!** This impatience functions as a result of our inability to think consequently, to imagine and value a positive "future" by paying the price of holding back and waiting. To wait two years for a teenager of fourteen to drive meant to wait 1/7 of his life. To the 40 year old person, it seems much shorter, only 1/20.

The *"only* living for the present moment" person, whether a child or young adult experiences impatience, impulsiveness, reactiveness, frustration, and a "must-have-it-now" demandingness. The so-called "sense of immortality" that many teens experience wherein they feel so invulnerable and indestructible and which leads to dangerous driving, risk taking, and non-thinking decisions arises from too little of a sense of "past" and "future." The now seems all consuming to them.

A Healthy/Balanced Psychological Present

Obviously, living exclusively in the "past," "present," or "future" undermines sane human living and resourcefulness. Our adventure in "time" demands a **healthy balance** between these "time" zones and a consciousness that we can manage and order as it flexibly moves from the happenings that we represent that have happened, now occur, and may occur one of these days.

To journey healthily on your "time" adventure into the psychological present means living in the now fully engaged with the wisdom of the "past" and the thoughtful conscious preparations of the "future." This leads to several empowering states including:

- "being present" and available in the "now," focused,
- in sensory awareness, and truly experiencing today,
- experiencing immediacy in activities and relationships, and
- using our neuro-linguistic symbolic powers to keep architecting a desired future.

This stands in contrast to those **"time" problems** as described by:

- living in a mentally absent and emotionally unavailable way to people, experiences, thoughts-emotions, and events present,
- preoccupied, distracted, and unfocused in our manner of being in the world,
- experiencing ahedonia (lack of pleasure),
- feeling disconnected and out-of-touch with the present, and
- feeling bored, worried, etc.

Figure 7:1

In the Psychological Present	Problems to Psychological Present
Present	Mentally Absent
Available	Emotionally Unavailable
Focused	Preoccupied,Distracted, Unfocused
Sensory Awareness	Anhedonia
Experiencing Today	Not Experiencing the Now
Immediacy in	Disconnected/
activity/relationships	Out-of-Touch
Architecting desired future	Bored, Worried, Drifting

Having identified how the various "time" zones and living in them too much can block us from having a healthy psychological present, let's now raise the central implementation question. *How can we learn to enter into a healthy and balanced psychological present so that we don't misuse our "time" powers?*

Adventuring Into The Psychological Present

1. **Value the importance of the psychological present.** To adventure healthily into the **psychological present** we need to understand it and value it.

In recent decades numerous psychological models have recognized this and have made a valuation of the psychological present as part of its tenets. Gestalt therapy focuses on experiencing the *immediacy of this moment,* this person, this event, this learning, etc. William Glasser broke with Freud's version of psychoanalysis to create Reality Therapy because of Freud's deterministic beliefs about the all-importance of the "past." By contrast, Glasser put the emphasis on the *"now."* "What are you doing now?" He emphasized the *now* because it determines our emotions, skills, and experiences. The existentialism in Yalom's group processes takes a similar focus. "What are you now feeling?" "Now thinking?"

The Cognitive psychotherapies similarly put the emphasis on the "now." Whatever we experience (our thoughts, emotions, choices, communications, behaviors) occurs in the present. It may reference some past event or future event, but it occurs now. We do all of our experiencing in the "now." "Past" thoughts occur in the present. These in the here-and-now thoughts determine our focus, emoting, responding, etc.

2 **Practice living more fully engaged in the here-and-now**. After we raise our value and appreciation of the psychological present, we need to put that appreciation into practice. We can do this today with the simplest of activities. We can consciously slow ourselves down to notice the tastes and smells of our food, to take mental "snapshots" of the sights and sounds around us, to take consciousness of our breathing, posture, movement, muscles, muscle tension, etc.

To come into such sensory awareness of our world redirects our consciousness so that we can attend our here-and-now experiences. How often have we read a book for several paragraphs and suddenly realize that we don't remember a thing we just read? How often have we gobbled down a meal and never paid any attention to the smells and tastes of the food? How often have we interacted with someone and never noticed their state, their words, their values, etc.? This indicates that we have zoned out into another "time" zone. This challenges us to re-engage ourselves with life—with living today in the psychological present.

By using the wisdom of the past and the directionalizing hope of the future to truly live in the "now", *we greatly enhance the quality of our consciousness* and hence of our life. We can start this very day more fully experiencing the sensory qualities of our immediate experiences: the sights, sounds, sensations, smells, and tastes of our environment.

"Zoning out" has its advantages. But so does zoning back in. It grounds us in today's realities as well as the realities of our experiencing self. It can deepen our congruency, our sense of appreciation, our ability to concentrate and focus, etc.

Practicing living in the here-and-now for some people will mean *extending consciousness to the immediate feedback* around us. "When I do or say this or that, what response(s) does that evoke?" To not live in the psychological present causes us to operate as functionally blind and deaf to feedback. But when we extend consciousness to immediate feedback we increase our intelligence and our ability to adapt.

3. **Release your grip on the "past."** For some people, to value the psychological present will mean de-focusing on their "past." They will have to catch themselves sending their brains back to former events and referencing off those events too much. They will also undoubtedly need to *recode much of their "past"* so that those events, thoughts, and interactions will have less sway, less power, and less information bearing impact on today.

Would you want to do that? Then go inside right now and begin to rewire this neuro-linguistic reality. After you quiet yourself down internally, say to yourself,

> "I give myself permission to **release** the past. Those events and happenings only represent experiences I went through and I have the power to not give all my power away to them. I refuse to allow those experiences to define me, my value, my capacities and potentials, my enjoyment of life, and especially my future."

After so languaging yourself, notice how that self-communication settles. Do all of your "parts" inside feel good with that message? Do you hear some objections? How often do you need to repeat that communication until it will "take?" Do it.

For some people in order for them to release past events may necessitate that they engage in other empowering acts like *forgiving* themselves, others, the universe, or God. Remember, what you can't forgive, you not only tend to carry with you, but you also tend to transform into.

At other times, we release past happenings by developing a bigger heart—a magnanimous mind so that we don't take such a small-minded attitude toward people and events. Expanding our appreciation, enjoyment, and humor plays a key role in such magnanimity.

One very limiting belief system by which we give all of our power away involves believing that *the experiences* that we went through in the "past" **determines** life today. Many people believe such non-sense. In fact, this idea represents one of the central ways people allow themselves to get "stuck" in places of the "past."

They think (erroneously) that *the experiences* they have had completely defines them. Perhaps, like most of us, they *over-believe* in their experiences. Why do we do that? Probably because of the informational richness of experiences. After all, when you go through an experience, you see it, hear it, smell it, taste it, feel it, say words about it, etc. Direct personal experience gets its "learning power" in our "minds" and neurology because it richly impacts us in all the sensory systems. From it, we make rich and full mental maps about it.

Afterwards we draw an unfounded and erroneous conclusion that gets us to *over-believe, over-trust,* and *over-identify* with our experiences. We think that direct personal experience truly represents "reality" whereas indirect, vicarious, read-about, second-hand experiences contain less "reality." Wrong.

The "reality" beyond the nervous system in both direct personal experiences and secondary indirect experiences contains just as much of what we deem as real. They differ only in information richness, sensory awareness, representation vividness, and supporting beliefs.

The person who uses all of his or her sensory representational modalities of awareness to vividly cue the brain with the sights, sounds, smells, sensations, and words of an experience will also powerfully feel and experience that referent in the nervous system. This occurs in any rich and impactful learning experience, in hypnotic communication, in states of intense focus, and when we do it intentionally.

What does all of that have to do with "releasing the past?" Much. Part of **why** some people do not let go of the past lies in the fact that, in **over-valuing and over-believing in the painful experiences** they have suffered through, *they forget that they could have had other experiences* and if they had, they would have drawn different conclusions; conclusions that would free them up from the sabotaging and traumatizing mental maps that they did make.

Given the experiences that they did struggle through, it makes sense that they would have thoughts about some of the things that they thought. But when they began to *believe those thoughts* (a meta-state!), *trust* those thoughts, and use those thoughts as their guiding beliefs for being, relating, feeling, self-definition, etc.,then they created a dysfunctional semantic reality that will not serve to enhance their life. If they therefore want to **release the past** now, they will need to release those ideas, those semantically-loaded beliefs, and build new and better ones. This means reframing, doing belief changes, and inventing an enhancing linguistic-semantic reality.

[By the way, thinking a thought—even a poisonous, stupid, hurtful, destructive, ugly, dysfunctional, or erroneous thought will do no one long-term semantic harm. Usually it provides no harm at all. Harm results from "setting the mind" on such thoughts and repeating them. This thereby installs them and programs them into our person. Even more harm arises when we believe in them.]

4 Don't leave your consciousness too much or too often focused in the "future." In order for some people to value and experience the psychological present, they will need to de-focus on the "future." They will need to stop sending their brains out into next month, next year, and beyond. They will have to practice ordering their consciousness around events, thoughts, and awareness of today. That reminds us of an old Jewish Proverb.

"A man of understanding sets his face toward wisdom, but the eyes of a fool are *on the ends of the earth*" (Proverbs 17:24).

Fools do that—they send their eyes (and brains) to furthermost reaches of the future which, in turn, causes them to miss the wisdom of today!

Some people don't experience the immediacy of the now and can't relate to loved ones with a sense of presenting themselves as *emotionally available* to them because their brains have rushed off into some wonderful future of immense pleasures, successes, delights, etc. Their great big glorious dreams prevent them from enjoying the now. Again, not wise! When those future events occur and they get to those great big glorious dreams—they will miss them also. Why? They will not notice that present when it arrives. They will have sent their eyes to the ends of the earth again, painting even bigger and brighter pictures of even more glorious futures, and miss it all. So they end up never actually "living" but continue planning, hoping, expecting, and dreaming about living.

Of course, that, at least, represents a pleasant way for avoiding the "now." Others choose a darker road. Their loved ones also complain about their lack of emotional availability. But in their case, they have gone off into their "future" *to worry and fret their heads off* about every possible disaster they can imagine. This leaves them fretful, upset, negative, pessimistic, grouchy, etc. They have become too "future" focused and keep missing the psychological present.

5. **Develop flexibility of consciousness about "time" through some meta-awareness skills.** With a flexibility of consciousness, we can move through the "time" zones and dimensions in such a way that we can integrate and use the wisdom obtained from each "time" perspective and not get stuck in any one dimension to the exclusion of the others.

Such "mind" flexibility enables us to synergize these perspectives and balance them off against one another. It allows us to use the wisdom of past events and mindful preparation of consequential thinking for future events in such a way that moving through the events of life enables us to stay resourceful.

Mentally processing the concept of "time" puts us into a *"time" awareness state of consciousness.* In such, we experience this conceptualization and develop a "sense" of time. We do this because we engage and use this abstraction so often, we eventually habituate our learnings about "time." We habituate how we code and represent "time," we habituate our beliefs and values about "time," we habituate our decisions about "time," etc. Eventually, our "time" state habituates out of our conscious awareness. All we have left involves our *felt* sense of "time."

Then when that *felt* sense of "time" gets violated or shifted, we feel as if thrown into a "time" warp. We experience an altered state of consciousness. Suddenly we feel that "time" has sped up (fast "time") or slowed down (slow "time") (hypnotic shifts in our "time" consciousness).

Now the power of "going meta" in your mind to your state of consciousness empowers you with an expanded awareness of things as well as a sense of choice about how to experience things. We can do that with our experience of the three "time" zones, as well as other facets of this concept. After all, it exists as a neuro-abstraction that then, in turn, creates our neuro-semantic state.

Conclusion

As "time" beings, with a "time" consciousness that enables us to "time" travel (in our heads), how we integrate (or fail to integrate) the "time" zones radically effects our experiences, emotions, skills, and resourcefulness. Our ability to truly come into **the psychological present** depends on this integration. Otherwise "time" comes as an enemy to us, something we resent, fight, resist, hate, get stuck in, etc.

As a "semantic class of life" (Korzybski) who live by and in symbols, we cannot help but process, code, and represent *the abstraction of "time."* We also cannot but help live by symbolic representations of events and learnings that happened in the past or will happen in the future.

To our glory and to our agony, our *"time"* consciousness serves as the basis for our ability to transcend this place and time and to develop awareness of the spiritual dimension. Next we will explore how to manage our tomorrows so that we can today create our desired futures and begin to make them real (real-ize them).

Chapter 8

Creating A Bright Future

"Time" as a Resource For Architecting a Bright and Compelling Future

Our "time" consciousness endows us with the **power** to think ahead of "time" about what may or could or will occur, about what consequences will follow from various actions, about plans, goals, objectives, hopes, desires, and anticipations, and about direction in life. A pretty marvelous mental **power,** wouldn't you say? We live in anticipation of the "future."

As a "time" traveler, you can zoom ahead (in your mind) to the various possible futures available. *How effectively do you use this power?* Do you use it to "worry your little head off?" To keep yourself up at night tossing and turning on your bed? To play scary Stephen King-like "What if..." tapes of possible dreads and dangers? To depress yourself with problems?

Or perhaps you misuse this power in another way. Perhaps you use it to avoid the present, to escape current responsibilities, to step aside from facing today's realities, to evade taking proactive action, to eschew the work of consciousness, to avoid emotional availability with someone. Some people hide out in the "future" in such a way as to evade living responsibly. *How can we utilize this mental power in an effective and balanced way so that it empowers us in living more resourcefully?*

1. **Live Intentionally**

When we break down the old term "will" power, we have two sub-powers: **intention and attention**. *Intention* refers to our ability to choose and direct our intents. It refers to a state of mind wherein we purpose, decide, propose a plan, and set forth an objective or meaning.

When you use consciousness to identify, represent, and create your *intentions*—you begin to *directionalize* your mind-emotions, and therefore your states. What a power we have in "intention!" *Living intentionally* moves us out of the animal state of consciousness of merely having awareness of the current and immediate stimuli to the truly and unique human world of hopes and dreams, of visions and values, of transcendence and development, of actualization and eternity.

Figure 8:1:
Primary State:

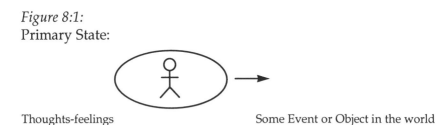

Thoughts-feelings   Some Event or Object in the world

To do this moves us out of a primary state of consciousness wherein we have thoughts-feelings about some stimuli to which we respond. It moves us into a meta-state (a state about a state) wherein we have thoughts-feelings about an abstraction; the "future," our destiny, the kind of person we want to become, the kind of experiences and achievements we want to create in that future.

Figure 8:2

Meta-State:

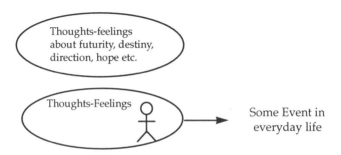

Living intentionally refers to how we can use our consciousness to direct ourselves (including our consciousness) as we move through "time" (from event to event) (another meta-level phenomenon). We do not respond merely from a primary state of consciousness caught up in the immediate thoughts-and-emotions. We respond from a meta-level awareness. We think-feel about our everyday experiences in terms of futurity:

- "Where will this lead?"
- "What direction will it put me in?"
- "What consequences will result from this?"
- "What impact will this have on my goals?"
- "What will this mean about me, about my destiny?"

To adventure into the "time" zone of the future and to effectively use our mental "time" traveling powers, we need to *intentionally decide and choose to live life intentionally.* This will entail refusing to just drift along, bouncing off the walls of events, circumstances, and stimuli. It means *deciding* to direct our thoughts-emotions, speech and behavior in such a way that we move into the future that we desire. *Intentionally* identify the kind of future we want.

All of the human psychological powers (thought-emotion, language, behavior, and self-reflexive consciousness of choice) occur automatically. We cannot not think-emote, speak, act, and choose. But the meta-level psychological power of choice, namely, **choosing to choose** does not occur automatically. It lies unused and untapped unless we activate that power. We have to consciously choose to exercise this meta-power. And when we do, we begin to truly live intentionally, consciously, and humanly.

2. With Intentionality Direct Your Mind

What "programs" (beliefs, values, visions, etc.) have you intentionally directed yourself toward since you entered into adult life? Most of us have intentionally directed our minds to very, very few conscious programs. We have simply accepted those "programs" inherited in our heads from our childhood upbringing and our adult experiences as we float and drift and bounce through life, reacting to people, events, situations, and stimuli. Such programs operate as our *default programs.* Yes, we choose them, but we do so unconsciously.

The one who lives intentionally chooses a different way of life. *To live intentionally* involves owning and assuming our proactive power of directing our brains and bodies, our thoughts-feelings, our speech and actions so that we move forward in the direction that accords with our values and visions. How do we do that? By consciously choosing what we will think-and-feel, and say and do. We consciously sit down and plan the direction of our life. Covey (1987), in *The Seven Habits of Highly Effective People*, designated this as his second habit (after proactivity). He called it, "Beginning with the end in mind," and described it as the self-leadership habit. To what destination have you decided to lead yourself? What "end" do you have in mind? What intention have you established deep inside about where you want to end up?

Take a moment now and exercise this transcendental power. Get a sheet a paper and begin to outline some of your desired outcomes.

- What kind of a person do I want to become? (Internal goals: qualities, characteristics, style, etc. i.e. caring, loving, gentle, warm, enthusiastic, optimistic, curious, spiritual, etc.)

- What kind of achievements and accomplishments do I want to make as my contribution to the world? (External goals: how best to give of yourself, your energies, your aptitudes and capabilities.)

- What kind of experiences and states do I want to accomplish? (The quality of life that you live as you achieve things and actualize your vision.)

- What kind of meanings and values do I want to create and find as I move through life? (This too lies within our power of choice. Do you want to find optimistic meanings or pessimistic meanings?)

- What kind of actions do I want to develop and take as I move through life? (i.e. to learn from defeat, to take criticism in a good spirit, to speak words of endearment to my loved ones, etc.)

If you begin a notebook (how about an "empowerment notebook"?) with a page or two devoted to each of these categories and regularly work (once a week) on updating and keeping your desired outcomes in mind, you will find yourself getting more and more "on purpose." You will experience your life as more focused, directed, and energized.

Well-Formed Outcomes

Next, to help you form and design your outcomes so that they operate in a well-formed way, use the following list from the NLP model to check-list your outcomes. This will greatly assist you so that you do smart goal-setting.

State it in the positive by describing and affirming what you want. By all means avoid writing goals that describe what you do not want. "I don't want to be judgmental." Negation ("not") in the mind always evokes what it seeks to negate. Don't think about Elvis Presley dancing with twelve wild monkeys.

State what you can do. If you write something like, "I want others to like me," you have not written anything that you can do and that *disempowers you*. State things that you can initiate and maintain, things within your response-ableness.

Contextualize. State the context within which you want your goal. Specify the specific environment, context, and situation.

State in sensory-based words. Describe specifically and precisely what someone would see, hear, and feel. Whenever you use an abstract or vague word, specify the behaviors that someone could video-tape. Not, "I want to become charismatic in relating to people." Write, "I want to smile, warmly greet people with a handshake and use their name..."

State in bite-size steps and stages. Chunk the outcomes down to the kind of size that you can do. Otherwise the goal may overwhelm. Not, "I will write a book." but "I will write four pages every day."

Load up your description with resources. What resources will you need in order to make your dream a reality? More confidence in your ability to speak in public? Then write that as a sub-goal that thereby loads up the desired outcome with a needed resource.

Check for ecology. Does this goal fit in with all of my other goals, values, and overall functioning? Do any "parts" of me object to this desired outcome?

Specify evidence for fulfillment. How will you know, in addition, to the previous criteria, when you have reached your goal? Make sure you have specific evidence for this.

As you use these criteria to quality-check your goals, you make your desired outcomes well-formed as mental maps about your "future." This enables you to do smart and wise goal-setting that will work in directionalizing your brain and creating a bright and compelling future.

3. Enrich Your "Future" With Lots of Empowering Meanings

We not only choose *what* we want to do, experience, actualize, and achieve, but *why*. Remember also that the person who has a **why** for living can endure any **what** as one develops an empowering **how** (adapted from Nietzsche and Viktor Frankl). Our self-reflexive consciousness enables us to create and/or find meanings, reasons, motives, and significances for those actions. This describes one of our drives (unique to humans); our drive for meaning.

Without rich, plentiful and significant **meaning** behind your actions, goals, and objectives, life can take on a feeling of meaning-lessness and futility. So focus on this most empowering question; **Why** do you want what you want? What will that get you? Asking **this meaning question** obviously drives us to a new and higher meta-level of awareness, to a level of transcendence. It drives us to our highest level of beliefs and values, to our *worldview* about ourselves, others, life, God, and the universe. Do you have enough **empowering beliefs** at this level (a spiritual level) to move you and invigorate you to go after those highly desired outcomes? What beliefs do you see and hear in others that seem to drive them?

Normally we do not ask *why* questions in NLP. "Why do you look so down today?" "Why did you mess that up?" *Why* only activates a person coming up with and inventing reasons, explanations, philosophies, etc. So when we ask a why question about a negative experience, this will result in the person coming up with supporting evidence for the *negative experience.*

Yet if we ask *the why question of positive experiences;* experiences that we want to perpetuate and reinforce, a person will find supporting evidence in terms of reasons, explanations, philosophies, and meanings.

This question about "the meaning of life" takes us right to the heart of *ontology*—being-ness, existence. Yet as soon as we start asking those existential questions: What meaning governs everything? Why does the universe exist as it does? Where did it come from? Where will it go? What role do we play in it? What lies beyond death? Suddenly, we have moved into theology.

Now **theology** and theologizing speaks about our understanding and wisdom of "God." A word we use to refer to the ultimate mind/power, the source, origin, and destiny of everything. Whether you think of yourself as a believer or non-believer in "God," you cannot help but *theologize*—to ask those existential questions. Our "time" consciousness so drives us. This leads us to **sacred time.**

Nor do these questions or this abstract area of transcendence play no small part in everyday living. They greatly effect everyday thinking-feeling. For as we pass through "time," our sense of the meaningfulness of life depends upon a sense of moment, a sense *that our adventure in "time" will take us somewhere,* that it exists for some reason or purpose, that this sense of "eternity" planted in our hearts does not exist as a mere illusion of some cosmic joke.

Obviously, as we find/create these ultimate meanings it provides us a reason to live, a reason to care, a reason to want to develop and actualize everything we can experience. This, in turn, provides us with *fuel* (motives) as we move into our future. This describes the healthy use of "religion," not as a crutch to avoid reality, but as an empowering belief system that gives us a reason to care. This also fits with the Judeo-Christian perspective, such biblical statements as "God has not given us the spirit of fear, but the spirit of power, love, and sound mind" (II Timothy 1:7). "I am come that they may have life and life more abundantly" (John 10:10). Living fully and authentically indicates that healthy "religion" should *add to the quality of life today and to the quality of life* as we grow. Paul described the fruit of the spirit as culminating in his marvelous list of empowering resources: love, joy, peace, patience, kindness, goodness, faithfulness, gentleness, and self-control (Galatians 5:22). How about that as a description of the kind of person to grow into? How about this as a list of experiences or states to go for?

> "Make every effort to supplement your faith with— virtue (manly courage), knowledge, self-control, steadfastness, godliness, brotherly affection and love. For if these things are yours and abound, they keep you from being ineffective or unfruitful..." (II Peter 1:5-8).

Further, we need this kind of spirituality in order to live vigorously, enthusiastically, and lovingly. We need a sense of the meaning and purpose of the universe and our place in it. Albert Day wrote,

> "The real test of the Christian faith is in its ability to call out our devotion, to mobilize our energies, to unify and enrich our personalities. If, however, Christianity leaves us soft; if it maims our personality, turns us into pallid ascetics, afraid of life and incompetent to meet the demands of human life; if it makes us dry-as-dust intellectuals or fails to evoke our highest potentials—it is a failure." Actually, we can say the same about any spirituality.

Paul described his ability for handling effectively the "time" zones when he said that he made it his intention to do "one thing...forgetting what lies behind and straining forward to what lies ahead, I press on toward the goal..." (3:13-14). So, we can easily forget the past *if we have a compelling future* that powerfully pulls on our heart strings.

Look deeply into a past-oriented person and you will find that he always and inevitably lacks a much needed resource; *a compelling future.* He will not have bright and colorful pictures in his mind about things to come. Rather, he will have, right in front of him, pictures of his past.

This writer had mapped-out for himself a big, bright "future" and thereafter talked about his hopes and dreams. And given that he wrote this from *prison,* and yet managed his adventure in "time" in that positive way, says a lot, wouldn't you say?

4. Re-Work Your Codings for Tomorrow

Earlier (Chapter 3) we described the process for discovering your coding of your time-line. This involves thinking about something that you do regularly like brushing your teeth and discovering how you represent this activity in the past, present and future and then drawing a conceptual line between your past pictures, to today's, to your future pictures.

Once you identify your time-line, then you can start noticing the qualities of that line. Where does it start and stop? A great many people experience their "line" of "time" as starting over to their left, perhaps curving from behind, coming in front of them, and then off to the right. My (MH) "time-line" has about a thirty-degree angle from my far left going up to my far right where I tend to put my future pictures and representations.

For many people their "time-line" starts directly behind them (their "past"), comes right up to them, through their body, and out immediately in front of them into their "future." Some people have a boomerang configuration. The shapes, forms, and sizes of "time-lines" vary greatly with people. Presumably, we have learned to so code "time" as a line due to our experience of growing up studying historical time-lines in history books that have this same kind of structure: left to right, past to future.

Earlier we suggested that inasmuch as the sub-qualities of our visual, auditory, and kinesthetic modalities of awareness play a central role in our coding, we should pay special attention to *location and configuration* (tilting, straight, curving, at an angle, spiraling, Y shape, pyramid shaped, etc.) as well as size. Check them for detail, transparency, brightness, focus, and color.

Most people have their very old memories coded in black-and-white silent snapshots. These pictures have little or no sound in them. More recent pictures, conversely, will have more color, sound, and movement in them. Typically, they will also seem much closer. Today's pictures (memories of this morning or imaginations about this evening), we tend to code as if living from "inside" the movie. We see them as three-dimensional, very colorful, full of movement, etc.

Then, going off into the future of tomorrow the pictures have less clarity, less color, more transparency, fewer sounds, fewer words, less "real." This increases for our pictures as we think about next year, five years, ten, twenty. The pictures get darker and less distinct.

If "time" exists as a mental construct, then this makes our representational coding of "time" critically important. So identifying and becoming aware of our coding as well as working with it, altering it gives us control over this concept so that we can frame it in ways that enhance our life. Because how we code "time" will radically affect our relationship to this construct, we can so form our constructions so that they will serve us as a false and erroneous map.

As an example, suppose someone kept all of their past pictures right in front of their face, close, associated, in 3-D, in color, vivid, full of sound and words, etc. while simultaneously coding the present and the future in small, black-and-white snapshots behind them? How would that affect one's everyday experiences? Wouldn't that make a person "past" oriented, "living in the 'past,'" unable to live in the present, unable to plan and dream, etc.?

Suppose someone coded all of their future pictures in the same qualities of images, sounds, and sensations as they code their memories? Wouldn't that cause one to feel the "future" as solid, unchangeable, fated?

Recognizing that we endow our internal representations of thoughts with these sensory system qualities, and that *these qualities drive our "time" consciousness*, we need to make sure that we have our "future" coded in a way that excites, empowers, enhances, gives us more choices, and compels us appropriately.

When you think about your future goals and desired outcomes, do you *have a "bright" future*? Do you find those future movies in your mind compelling and exciting? Do they give you enough of a sense of choice? What do you need to do to your future representations that will cause them to pull on you more and induce you into more resourceful states?

The Changeability of "Time"

Given the multitude of ways that we can alter our representations, we can change our "future" and our "past." To recall Bandler's quip, "It is never too late to have a happy childhood" we can understand such an outrageous statement precisely because our "past" only exists *in our mind*. It exists only as a mental construct and set of representations. So, when we change our representations, we change our "past."

This provides us with one way to get over our "pasts." We can simply re-code them. We can give them new representations and new meanings. This "renewing of the mind" subsequently transforms "personality."

Should we do this? Of course. We *should* do whatever makes us more resourceful and enables us to get on with tasks and challenges at hand. What value lies in sitting around whining and moping about the "past?" Or about using the "past" to constantly feel bad about?

Do we have the right to change our sense of "time?" Again, since it completely functions as a product of our brain functioning and constructing in the first place, then of course we have that right and responsibility. If I have the right to run my own brain, especially in ways that enhance my living effectively, lovingly, focused, and graciously, then, yes, of course! What value lies in keeping a hurtful, traumatic "past" coded and represented in all of its horrific pain?

141

Our "past" in no way determines or fates our "future" unless we let it do so. If we take action to alter our representations, we architect a new "future." The decisions we make today about our intentions, directions, and orientations serve as the seeds of a new "future" for us. As we make new and enhancing decisions about our identity, desired outcomes, experiences and meanings, we forge out a new destiny for ourselves.

Fine Tuning Our "Time-line(s)"

How much space or room do you have within your "time-line" for "today?" Do you want to have a greater sense of having more "time?" Then *give yourself some more "time."* Push out today a little more. Perhaps you have a sense of having too much "time" and need to condense "today."

The way we represent "time" greatly affects our sense of "reality" and how we track with it. It affects our sense of what we experience as "real." Since we have experienced events, we "know" them as real because we have coded those past representations as solid, firm,and unchangeable. Since we have not yet experienced the things that we anticipate and hope to occur, we usually create representations of possibility and potential.

If, however, we don't have enough sense of potential and possibility—we can lighten up our representations of the future, make them less solid, make them more vague and undefined and thereby open up our future for ourselves.

Personality and "Time"

What kind of a person has *"time"* made you? Since our concepts and representations of "time" at meta-levels and meta-meta-levels (Chapter 2) crucially affect our personality, values, beliefs, and relationship to "time," how we code "time" effects our personality. It can form us as a person who lives in the past, someone stuck in the past, someone who lives in the now, someone impatiently stuck in the present, someone who lives in the future, or someone who borrows miseries for themselves from the future.

We have already noticed that if "time" goes through our body, then, in terms of NLP meta-programs, this structure makes an *"in time" orientation*. We will tend to process, experience, and relate to "time" in a random way rather than sequentially. This gives us the ability to "get lost in 'time,'" to live in the "eternal now," and to have little sense of "what time it is." *"In time" orientation* moves us to live in primary and physical time.

Conversely, if our "time-line" does not go through our body, but stays outside, then we have the meta-program that makes us "through time" in our sorting, or "out of time." Since we experience "time" outside ourselves and therefore dissociated, we have moved to a meta-level of "time" (Chapter 2). By moving to a meta-level to "time," most people with a "through time" orientation have a much greater sense of clock time, and therefore process "time" sequentially. These *out-of-time* or *above-time* people can also adopt many of the other kinds of "times."

We mentioned previously that these distinctions of *"In Time"* and *"Through Time"* generate what we might call Eastern and Arabic "time" and Western or Anglo-European "time." As such they creates different kinds of personalities; Eastern and Western personalities. These differences in "time" coding put people in different worlds or on different channels.

Watch out when a person with an "in time" orientation and a person with a "through time" orientation marry. Each relates to this construct of "time" so differently. They will frequently find themselves *out of sync* with each other, and no wonder, they each operate from a different rhythm about events. The one who can get lost in time ("in time") can offer the most frustrating experiences to the "through time" person. The latter wants things "on time," and expects the other to appreciate sequential experiences as much as s/he does.

Our coding of "time" and "time-line" configuration organizes our thoughts-emotions toward this concept, it structures our beliefs and values about it, and it organizes us and our experiences as we move in "time." The random "in time" person will have more difficulty organizing, planning, scheduling, and managing him or herself through "time." Not so for the "through time" (out of "time"person). This sequential person finds it easy to plan, schedule, and manage "time." And s/he may not understand the other person very well at all.

The person who thinks in lots of specific details also differs very much from the more gestalt and general thinker. A specific thinker tends to reason from specific to general or inductively. This represents the mind of the technician, the scientist, the detective etc. A gestalt thinker tends to reason in the opposite direction, from general principle to specific application or deductively.

In processing "time," the meta-program of thinking in "specifics" will cause people to gather, store, and code memories in great detail. People who do this will have specific files, catalogues, or movies and when they pull them out of their memory banks, they will have a rich plethora of details. Thinking in gestalts, on the other hand, motivates one to gather, store, and code memories in groups or classes of similar subjects. People who do this may have difficulty thinking about a specific time, place, state, or experience since they have gestated their memories and when they recall them, they have allowed several memories to merge together to form a collage.

To what extent does "time" form and mold our "personalities?" In NLP we assume that our "personalities" reflect our memories more than our DNA and genetics. After all, our coding of "time" at primary, meta-levels and meta-meta-levels inevitably affects the rhythms within our nervous system. We therefore believe that you would find it an interesting exploration to examine your meta-level concepts of "time" in relation to its effect upon your neurology.

Conclusion

Whether we want to or not, each and every one of us creates **"tomorrow"** today. As "time" creatures with "time" consciousness, we inevitably venture forth through the "time" zones (past, present, and future) and cannot do otherwise. A balanced and flexible consciousness enables us to tap into the wisdom of yesterday's learnings and tomorrow's hopes and dreams so that we can experience the presence fully, completely, and authentically.

Our experience of "time" radically affects our psychology (our thoughts-feelings), our states and experiences, our sense of "reality," our sense of our self, and our ability to tap into our resources. Additionally, we have lots of plasticity in how we code and represent "time." Representing it so that it works for us,enables us to take this in-dwelling "eternity" in our minds, and think about it so that it serves us rather than sabotages us.

Chapter 9

Creating A "Life Well Lived"

Adventuring "Time" With Grace and Power
Developing Quality Actions To Create Quality "Time"

One overall learning we can make from these understandings about "time" involves the realization that we do not actually "manage time," but that *we manage ourselves* (including our energy, our consciousness, etc.) *through the passing of events* (which we measure by our concept of "time").

We simply use the events of our planet rotating every twenty-four hours, and moving around the sun every 365.25 days, and the sun moving through the galaxy as ways of measuring events. As the first set of events occur, so do other sets of events and by *comparing* them in our mind, we create our sense of duration, sequence, and chronological time (*chronos*).

What set of events do we compare with the moving of the planets and stars? Those human events that matter most to us; our minds-bodies age, we learn new things, we marry, give birth to children, watch them grow, change jobs, move, meet new people, experience new things, we age some more, etc. In a world of ever-changing processes, we also keep growing and progressing.

We not only change on the outside in these ways, but we also change and grow and develop on the inside; in our thinking, emoting, valuing, relating, etc. This brings to our attention *psychological time*: personal time, the *quality* of the events (*kairos*).

Kairos Time

In the last chapter we began focusing on the process and component pieces of designing *a bright and compelling future.* We continue that theme here as we add more to this all-important concern of using our "future" in such a way as to let it effectively directionalize our lives, enable us to live more fully in the "here and now," and move through "time" with such grace and power that when we come to the end of our lives, we can say, *"I have lived my life well!"*

"A life well lived." We have picked up that phrase from Benjamin Franklin who wrote so much about living life effectively and about the importance of character. George L. Rogers (1990) in writing about Franklin, collected from Franklin's volumous writings *His Formula for Successful Living* and put it in his book, *Benjamin Franklin's The Art of Virtue*.

Franklin formulated a list of twelve rungs on "the ladder of success." The twelvth and last one he designated as having experienced "a long life *lived well*." He proposed that "In the process of aging and dying, the fruits of a long life well lived" would then become "most sensibly felt." For him, this comprised part of the art of living successfully. This raises several questions:

- What does it mean to experience "life well lived?"
- How does one live well?
- What factors, components, and elements make up this art of adventuring "time" in such a way that we live well?

In answering these *how-to-live-well questions* of *kairos* time, we suggested (Chapter 9) that we need to learn how to come into the now and live in the present so that we don't miss it. This means developing a good adjustment to the various time zones ("past," present, and "future"). To do that we suggested four things:

1. **Living intentionally** so that we use our consciousness to direct ourselves as we move through "time." Then from that kind of intentional consciousness, we can...

2. **Direct our minds** in such a way that we live purposefully, "beginning with the end in mind" and charting out for ourselves the kind of values and visions that will empower us. We there suggested an exercise for identifying the kind of *person* we want to actualize the kind of *achievements* we want to accomplish, the kind of *experiences* and states we desire to have, the kind of *meanings*

and *values* that we want to live in, and the kind of actions that will enable us to make such dreams real. We also summarized a set of eight NLP criteria to enable us to make sure we have well-formed outcomes.

3. To further create tomorrow today and move through "time" effectively, we need to **enrich our "future" with empowering meanings.** This enables us to live meaningfully, rather than with futility.

4. Then we can **rework our "time" codings** so that they serve us well and enrich the quality of our sense of "time" and our time-line so that it works usefully in our mind-neurology.

All of this underscored the basic point, namely,

> "A balanced and flexible 'time' consciousness enables us to tap into the wisdom of yesterday's learnings and tomorrow's hopes and dreams so that we can experience the present fully, completely and authentically."

What else do we need in learning to move through "time" with grace and power?

1. *Using insights and wisdom,* we need to shift our focus and concern from "quality time" to thinking and acting like quality persons—persons of virtue and character. To facilitate that, we have revisited his twelve "rungs on the ladder of success" that describes what he called "the Art of Virtue."

2. *Developing high-quality consequential thinking* that enables us to move through "time" without rashness or impetuousness **and** without dullness or stagnation, but in wise decisions and commit-ments.

3. *Cultivating a high quality moral consciousness* that enables us to live with integrity, courage, affirmation, acceptance, etc. This enables us to avoid the two pitfalls of an over-strict and rigid conscience full of condemnation and hyper-sensitiveness and that of a conscience that doesn't care enough and lacks enough moral fiber to stand for something.

4. *Finally, building in the kind of passions and hopes* about things as we move through "time" so that we stay vibrant, alive, on-purpose, and loving beings.

Develop Personal Excellence

We truly mis-state things when we talk about "time" management. Regarding scheduling, we do not manage "time," we can only manage **ourselves** through "time" (the passing of events). So in the matter of learning to move through "time" with grace, excellence, and power, these qualities apply to us as *persons*, not to the conceptualization of "time."

In this sense, no such thing exists as "quality time." What does exist involves thinking, emoting, communicating, behaving, and relating *in a quality way* to other people, or failing to so relate. To relate superficially, unthinkingly, trivially, uncaringly, etc. that would describe the lack of quality relating.

To experience ourselves as persons of quality, excellence, and power necessitates making this our focus, our vision, and what we value highly. Covey (1987) described this as "the character ethic" which undergirds success. Franklin described the same process as "the art of virtue."

Benjamin Franklin however never wrote the one book that he always wanted to write on this subject, so George L. Rogers (1990) did it for him. He collected Franklin's formula for successful living from his letters, journals, and others books and articles and then edited that material into the book, *Benjamin Franklin's The Art of Virtue*. The following "directives" reformulates Franklin's concepts of virtues that make for success.

We offer them here for two purposes. First, their inherent value inasmuch as they contain a lot of common everyday wisdom from Franklin. In them we see many correspondences to aspects of NLP (the science of human excellence) and to other literature about quality. Second, they put the emphasis on what actually transpires in "time" i.e. actions, events, happenings.

1. **Clearly define your desired objectives.**

   "All human achievement rests on the establishment of clearly defined objectives."

Therefore, he said, clearly define your objectives, specify your values as well as the value that you give to things. Avoid spending too much on your whistles! Aim rather to develop a "good" character and to do the good. Make this your life mission.

2. **Create a good plan and consistently act to implement it.** The achievement of one's objectives requires two things: *a good plan and consistent effort* in working at achieving and implementing it. To put first things first one must identify the virtues that comprise the good life. Franklin identified the following thirteen virtues for himself. He then sought to develop his character around them so that he would develop into *the kind of person* indicated by these virtues.

   Temperance in eating and drinking
   Silence when speaking wouldn't benefit or just trifling
   Order to create proper sequencing of things
   Resolution to perform duties and not avoid responsibilities
   Frugality in order to waste nothing
   Industry to stay employed at useful activities
   Sincerity in seeking not to hurt or offend others
   Justice to wrong none by doing injuries
   Moderation to avoid extremes, to forbear resenting injuries even if undeserved
   Cleanliness in body, clothes, habitation
   Tranquility in taking an undisturbable attitude toward trifles, accidents, etc.
   Chastity in use of venery (sexual intercourse)
   Humility as modeled by Jesus and Socrates

A *good plan* has a strategy that describes the process for getting there. It involves the use of good thinking, by which Franklin meant: long-term thinking, chunking down the goal into small pieces, and engaging in consistent effort (very similar to the conditions of well-formedness for outcomes of Chapter 9). "Constant effort" refers to initiation, proactivity, and that glad or delightful assumption of responsibility.

What virtues or values have you selected to directionalize your mind-emotions, speech, behavior, and life toward? What criteria of values have you installed into "tomorrow" that describes the future you have begun to architect today?

Figure 9:3

#9 Run Your own Brain
Induce Happiness State
Live from within

#5	#1	Person	Desired Outcomes
Transcend	Set Clear	#2 Create Good Plan	#5 TranscendentGoals
Motives	Objectives	Consistently Implement	Public & social goals
that	that you	#4 Cultivate Good Reason	
drive	define	#6 Move forward with honesty	
goals	with precision	& integrity	
		#7 Properly acquire wealth	
		#8 Stay fit & healthy	
		#10 Get along well with people	
		#11 Get along well with family	
		#12 Live long and well	

3. **Discover values of excellence by which to govern life.** Franklin wrote, "Religion is a powerful regulator of human conduct." As we clarify our values, principles, and paradigms that comprise our world-view we thereby develop a "spiritual" perspective on life. To do so will inevitably add quality and grace to our experiences. What makes a religion true and vital arises from how it enriches our relationships and enables us to cooperate more effectively with others. "Values" said Franklin, "govern life," so choose the kind of values that you want to govern your life. Choose values that uphold human dignity and that support things like love, faith, and hope.

4. **Cultivate solid reasoning to govern good actions**. Franklin wrote a lot about good reasoning. When he wrote, "Correct action is dependent upon correct opinion," he expressed the realization that we need good accurate maps if we want to effectively navigate a territory.

He further warned about the problem that holds us back from taking correct action. It lies in accepting bad information, making poor judgments, and opting for foolish decisions. This danger challenges us to make sure that we have *valid, solid, productive, and enhancing paradigms*—a map of the world that will take us to useful places, and that we carefully and cautiously use our sense of reason.

How do we handle our "reasoning" powers more appropriately? Franklin recommended that we ask lots of questions, that we regularly doubt our reasoning (a meta-state generating a gestalt configuration of thoughtfulness and open-mindedness), that we straightforwardly admit our errors when we see them, and that we don't let our reasoning suffer contamination by self-interest or other emotions. This sounds like he anticipated the current emphasis on **critical thinking skills,** doesn't it?

Doing these things enables us to move through "time" with the power to discern the real from false images which in turn increases the quality of our discernment (wisdom), which thereby gives us the grace to act appropriately.

5. **Develop motives that transcend mere self-gratification.** For Franklin, "Motives of personal gain tend to be opposite of one's true self interest." He saw this as a danger to true success. He said that when self-gratification operates as one's primary motive, it narrows life, makes one small-minded, and leads others to not trust us.

Franklin recommended that we expand our motives and that we develop intents beyond mere self-interest. To do this enables us to live usefully, to contribute more to others, and put the public good before our own. Adler would later call this "the social interest" in others and in one's community and define it as a central facet of a mentally-emotionally healthy person.

In this Franklin saw that we *add more quality and grace to our lives* by adding bigger and broader motives to our interests. A particular **grace** that goes along with this involves adopting a more modest diffidence. Franklin essentially reframed "power" in terms of selflessness, moderation, and modesty. In so doing, he made these traits attractive so that he would move toward them.

"...I continued this method some years...retaining only the habit of expressing myself in terms of modest diffidence, never using, when I advanced any thing that may possibly be disputed, the words certainly, undoubtedly, or any others that give an air of positiveness to an opinion, but rather say, I conceive or apprehend a thing to be so and so; it appears to me, or I imagine it to be so; or it is so, if I am not mistaken."

"This habit, I believe, has been of great advantage to me when I have had occasion to inculcate my opinions, and persuade men into measures that I have from time to time engaged in promoting; and, as the chief ends of conversation are to inform or to be informed, to please or to persuade, I wish well-meaning, sensible men would not lessen their power of doing good by a positive, assuming manner, that seldom fails to disgust, tends to create opposition, and to defeat every one of those purposes for which speech was given to us, --to wit, giving or receiving information or pleasure."

"For, if you would inform, a positive and dogmatical manner in advancing your sentiments may provoke contradiction and prevent a candid attention. If you wish information and improvement from the knowledge of others, and yet at the same time express yourself firmly fixed in your present opinions, modest, sensible men, who express do not love disputation, will probably leave you undisturbed in the possession of your error. And by such a manner, you can seldom hope to recommend yourself in pleasing your hearers, or to those whose concurrence you desire." (p. 130-131).

6. **Adopt a style of honesty and integrity.** Franklin succinctly wrote, *"Without honesty, there can be no happiness."* Happiness grows and abounds where one knows him or herself as a basically honest person and holds integrity with self and others.

Franklin distinguished honesty and integrity as follows. **Honesty** refers to "being true to oneself, true to the facts, and true to reality." The honest person speaks the truth. By contrast, **integrity** refers to living in a whole or complete way so that our words perfectly correspond to our life. The person of integrity *lives* the truth.

Dishonesty undermines happiness. It does this because before we lie to others, we have to lie to ourselves, and that undermines our ability to trust ourselves, and therefore to access the power of speaking and acting with congruency. In this, Franklin recognized *the principle of living from within* as involving positing our locus of control as internal to us, rather than external. He wrote,

> "True happiness depends more on one's judgment, than on the condition of external things"

Given that definition, do you use happy judgments to guide your life?

> "I give myself as little concern about [the reports] as possible. I have often met with such treatment from people that I was all the while endeavoring to serve. At other times I have been extolled extravagantly, where I had little or no merit. These are the operations of nature. It sometimes is cloudy, it rains, it hails; again it is clear and pleasant, and the sun shines on us. Take one thing with another, and the world is a pretty good sort of world, and it is our duty to make the best of it, and to be thankful. One's true happiness depends more upon one's own judgment of one's own self, or a consciousness of rectitude in action and intention, and the approbation of those few who judge impartially, than upon the applause of the unthinking, undiscerning multitude, who are apt to cry Hosanna today, and to-morrow, Crucify him." (151).

7. **Properly acquire wealth**. Franklin wrote, "The proper acquisition and use of money may be a blessing, but the opposite is always a curse." In this we again see his practical wisdom. Franklin didn't devalue the importance of money or wealth per se. He certainly recognized the difficulty and harm that poverty creates and recognized that we don't obtain any special virtue by lacking. Simultaneously, he recognized the blessing that wealth **may** provide. He put the emphasis on the word "may."

Acquiring wealth may lead to a blessing in one's life depending on **how** we acquire and maintain money or wealth. **"How"** we grow rich and accumulate wealth, for Franklin, played a crucial factor in one's happiness and true success. In fact, for him, learning to enjoy the process meant taking less interest in the end results than in the process of how to get there.

In this regard, he preached the virtues that we most of all remember him for: industry, frugality, and significant involvement in one's work. When we do this, it endows us with a quality and grace so that moving through "time" grows into an enjoyable process in and of itself. We do what we love, as an ethical choice, and feel rewarded in the doing of it, in addition to how it enables us to make a living.

8. **Stay fit and healthy.** Franklin wrote,

> "The possession of health makes all things easier, its absence everything more difficult."

Do you not also find that marvelously, and painfully, true? When you lack physical health and fitness, everything feels more labored, difficult, problematic, negative, does it not? So we don't want to blow our health on health-sabotaging recreations or habits. We want to learn how to appreciate fully the importance of health by taking care of our body. To do that, Franklin talked about daily exercise, good nutrition, modest amounts of food, getting lots of sun and air (even today we remember Franklin for his "air baths" which he liked to take in the nude) etc. and obviously, this raises the quality of life, endowing us with power and physical grace.

9. **Run your brain to induce a state of happiness.** On the subject of experiencing a joyful state, Franklin wrote, *"Happiness springs immediately from the mind."*

Way back in the 1700s, Franklin took a cognitive-behavioral approach to mental and physical well-being. He knew that our focus or orientation of mind, what we looked for, and the attitude we adopt, play *the most important role* in our experience of happiness.

Things do not make us happy, our attitude toward things creates or destroys our happiness. In this, Franklin urged that we take full responsibility for what we think and feel. He expressed this wisdom by saying that "there are no uninteresting things, only uninteresting people." So we must take control of what happens inside of ourselves—in our consciousness. We have to accept our proactive response-ability to run our own brains and then to live consciously.

> "Many who are good and virtuous in other respects have not learned to gain sufficient control of their thoughts and feelings as to be able to experience a full enjoyment of themselves or of the world around them.... To develop a happy constitution requires a conscious effort to see the good around us, to make the best of things, to look at the bridge side. Learn to have a little fun with the problems that come our way." (203).

10. **Learn how to get along well with people**. Franklin's wisdom put it this way, "Life is immeasurably more satisfying to those who get along well with others than to those who do not."

In this, Franklin identified a chief underlying problem to so much of the unhappiness in the world today, *interpersonal conflicts*. Our sense that we lack of success so often arises from experiencing quarrels, finding fault with others, giving and receiving of criticism, conflicts over differences, etc.

His recommendation? To develop our social interests and interpersonal relationships, to adopt a modesty about how we communicate. In fact, he said that he did not allow himself the pleasure fdirectly contradicting others. How about that?

He said that he aimed rather to make others feel good in his presence. He said he sought to do them good and to oblige them to himself by doing them every form of kindness he could think of.

> "I made it a rule to forbear all direct contradiction to the sentimental of others, and all positive assertion of my own. I even forbid myself...the use of every word or expression in the language that imported a fix opinion...

"When another asserted something that I thought an error, I denied myself the pleasure of contradicting him abruptly, and of showing immediately some absurdity in his proposition; and in answering I began by observing that in certain cases or circumstances his opinion would be right [he paced and validated first], and in the present case there appeared or seemed to me some difference" [then he lead].

"I soon found the advantage in this change in my manner; the conversations I engaged in went on more pleasantly. The modest way in which I proposed my opinions procured them a readier reception and less contradiction; I had less mortification when I was found to be in the wrong, and I more easily prevailed with others to give up their mistakes and join me when I happened to be in the right. ... For these fifty years past no one has ever heard a dogmatical expression escape me." (p. 235).

11. **Learn to get along well with family.** Similar to getting along with people, Franklin talked about getting along with relatives. (The difference? You get to *choose* your friends!) "Of all human relationships, the most enduring and satisfying are those of family." So maintaining healthy family relationships became one of his focuses, a way to maintain a strong support group.

"Criticizing and censuring almost everyone you have to do with, will diminish friends, increase enemies, and thereby hurt your affairs." (247).

12. **Live long and well.** "In the process of aging and dying the fruits of a long life well lived are most sensibly felt." Here he recommended thinking throughout life about the end, and about living in and with such a good conscience of life that you could evaluate your life as "well lived." This indicates a meta-state wherein one thinks-and-feels and accesses a sense of having lived morally/ethically.

High Quality Consequential Thinking

When we think about the "future" we send our brains out into the imagined area of "things to come." When many people do this, they torment themselves with all the things that could go wrong, threaten them, endanger them, etc. This does not represent **high quality** consequential thinking. Nor does sending our brain out into the "future" and creating gigantic goals that then overwhelm us.

Fitting our desired outcome to the *conditions of well-formedness* when we think consequentially empowers us to do future-thinking with quality. Such excellence in thinking involves chunking it down to a level so that we can begin today to take effective actions in moving in that direction. Thinking conse-quently empowers us so that we do not behave rashly, impetu-ously, or reactively. We truly *think* before we act. We contemplate both our actions and the quality of thinking and emoting that we engage in. One definition for "assertiveness" summarizes this same point as "thinking and talking out our stresses rather than acting them out in fight/flight responses."

We designate this process as *"running an ecology check."* We check out whether our thinking, emoting, behaving, speaking, etc. will do us good over the long-run. Does it validate and strengthen all parts of the system of our mind-emotions, relationships, health? Does it fit with our values for what we declare important and for the visions we have for our future? Do we find any place in our life where it creates incongruity or difficulties?

Developing such high quality consequential thinking means that we learn to **live consciously,** rather than unconsciously as we move through "time."

High Quality Moral Consciousness

As you could tell from much of the Franklin information about "the Art of Virtue" that comprises the rungs on the ladder of success, **living with integrity** lies at the heart of true happiness and success. Because we exist as innately ethical/moral creatures, we cannot ignore this dimension of our existence without dire consequences. Such "spirituality" enriches our life with the very qualities that we have spoken about in moving through "time," namely, grace, excellence, and power.

What "knowing" do you have with or of yourself as an ethical person? We call this form of inner knowing our "conscience." It describes an inner *knowing* ("science") with ("con") ourselves about whether we have, and continue to, live up to our *standards and values*. When we don't, we evaluate and feel ourselves as "in the wrong," unethical, not right, etc. and this will show up emotionally in a variety of emotions: ashamed, embarrassed, guilty, afraid, angry, discouraged, sad, etc.

As a meta-state, these emotions refer to our evaluative thinking-feeling **about ourselves** as moral beings. At the primary state level, we experience some interaction wherein *we have not lived up to our values and standards (or someone else's).* To this state of "wrong," which may comprise a mistake, an error, a hurt, a violation of some law or rule, etc., we then go in and entertain thoughts-and-feelings about our self as an ethical being.

Figure 9:4
M-S:

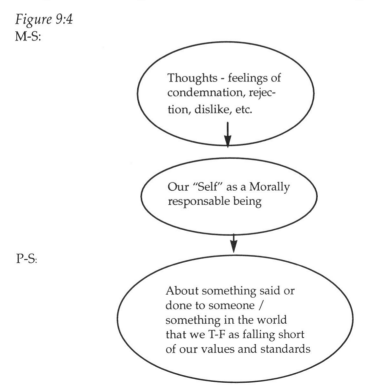

P-S:

What shall we say about all this? First I think we need to distinguish between kinds of violations. **Whose** law or rule did we violate? Our own, another individual's, society's, or God's? **How** did we violate that value or standard? Intentionally, high-handedly, accidently, out of stress, out of some limitation, unwittingly, via deception, etc.? **To what extent** and in what level of degree, did we fall short of the ideal? Just a mistake, error, severe violation with drastic consequences, etc.?

Next, we *should distinguish between different kinds of emotional upsetness about the violation.* When I violate some human value or principle (my own or another's), it seems most appropriate to feel embarrassed, ashamed, discouraged, angry, concerned, upset, etc. Such thinking-emoting can assist me in making changes, making amends, learning and not repeating the hurt, vowing such to another, etc. But if I go into "guilt," then kiss it goodbye!

Why do I say that? Because "guilt" functions as such an intense and powerful *condemning* emotion, we should reserve it only for those big moral violations. If I have only hurt someone's feelings, violated their expectations by not coming through on something, lived by a different standard, disappointed them due to some accident or fallibility, I need only enough negative emotion to become aware and alter my actions. This raises an important question.

> "Do I have the ability to appropriately and accurately feel shame, embarrassment, discouragement, fear, anger, upsetness, etc. without turning it into 'guilt?'" If you lack this ability—you will tend to live life in such a guilt-sensitive way that you will turn all kinds of little things involving basic human fallibility into some big moral issue (Hall, 1988).

We do not need "guilt" for some hurts and violations. We need a tinge of some negative feeling so that we adjust ourselves and get on with life. We see this frequently with "religious" people. It seems to arise as one of those occupational hazards of having a morally sensitive conscience. But in this case, the conscience has grown *too sensitive,* too guilt-oriented, too ready to jump on anything that goes "wrong" and make it a moral issue. "Guilt" has developed into a meta-state canopy that now "sees" and filters guilt inappropriately.

Actually, there exists lots of interactions in life that simply exist as a process of some sort that we don't need to overload and view as moral issues. Did a friend fail to show up on time for a meeting? Let it exist as just a transportation issue or "time" issue. Don't turn it into a moral issue. Did someone get hot and angry and then spew forth some strong negative words? Let it exist as a communication issue without demonizing the person! Did someone dress in a way that falls short of your standards? Let it exist as a cultural issue!

Does this entirely eliminate "guilt?" No. Guilt serves a valid role if we let it exist as *the moral violation emotion* that warns us that we have violated God's laws or some "divine" principle as exemplified in the Ten Commandments. If I kill someone, I should feel guilty. I should absolutely and totally "condemn" that behavior. The thoughts-emotions of guilt seem appropriate for those highly destructive behaviors of violating someone in physical abuse, sexual molestation, robbery, theft, etc.

Here again we speak about the need for **balance.** *Too much guilt-awareness* and we feel guilty for living, for breathing, for having desires and passions, for asserting ourselves, etc.! This leads to the neurotic disorders wherein a person feels "full of nerves" about any kind of fallibility, mistake, or error. When we have too much of this consciousness, we think-feel with too much judgment, condemnation, need for perfection, disgust for flaws, and undermines our ability to live in a happy and contented way in a world where bad and wrong things happen constantly.

Too little guilt-awareness, and we might fall off the other side into the character disorder crimes wherein we ego-centrically think that "everything goes," "whatever serves my purposes," "to hell with others," etc. Herein we don't think that anything could work as an "evil," hurtful, or ugly way of living or relating. Here we lack the moral strength to judge and condemn those things that do violate people, communities, and the human spirit.

So to move through "time" with grace, excellence, and power, we need to become conscientious about rights and wrongs so that we live respectful of the values and standards of others as well as our own. Living with integrity means living out of those values. We need to develop a high quality moral consciousness so that it enables us to respond in caring, loving, and justice seeking ways. But not so much that it turns us into Pharisees, fundamentalists, or anal retentive perfectionists! (See how we have developed this as a meta-program in *Figuring Out People*, Hall & Bodenhamer, 1997b).

High Quality Passions & Hopes

To move through "time" in a purposeful, goal-oriented way necessitates keeping our dreams and passions alive so that we have something that we hope for and long to see develop more and more reality in our lives. To lose hope invites us to depress our thinking, emoting, and behaving. And when we depress our energies, we will begin to feel depressed. Not wise.

If Viktor Frankl's work in logotherapy teaches anything, it teaches the importance of finding and creating empowering meanings in all of our circumstance! Even if we live in the hell of a concentration camp, we can open our eyes and find the beauty in nature and in people.

The old proverb says that "a desire fulfilled is a tree of life." This speaks about the sense of Eden we get, the pleasure of living in a paradise when we take effective actions so that we experience the fulfilling of our desires. Of course, this also challenges us to make sure we have appropriate and realistic hopes. "Hope deferred makes the heart sick" (Proverbs 13:12). We sicken and lose heart when we hope for that which never comes about.

We need **desires** in order to live a motivated life of passion, vitality, and hope. I (MH, 1988) wrote a chapter on "Wanting Something More Than Life" in a book about motivation (*Motivation*, Chapter 8). It focused on how to fan your passions into a flame and then direct the fire and light of that flame into constructive areas.

Time-Lining

Conclusion

One thing that you can count on in the weeks and months to come, you will move through "time." Will you so move that your movements convey power, excellence, and grace? Will you move through "time" with excitement and vitality? Will you feel empowered as you so move through "time" so that you create a life "well lived?" Will you take charge of yourself and your energies so that you will direct your mind-and-emotions toward those goals and outcomes that will enhance your life? If you so choose, you can.

164

Chapter 10

Time-Binding As A General Semanticist

Bind "Time" For Personal Excellence
Moving Beyond Real "Time" For Learning to Virtual "Time"

What kind of an adventure have you had with "time" up to this point in your life? Has your adventure in "time" felt enjoyable, empowering, effective, and humane? Or has your adventure in "time" resulted in lots of misery, pain, disempowerment, and stress? Do you experience "time" as your friend or enemy? What relationship have you developed with respect to this non-thing we call "time?"

In previous chapters, we have talked about the existence and nature of this construct of "time." We have emphasized "time" as a mental-neurological construct. Yet we so easily forget this and slip into talking about it as a real thing. Here our language itself plays a trick on us as it gives us a noun to talk about "time." In so speaking, we reify it. But no. It exists, as Kant would say, a priori in our very nature—as one of those innate categories in our brain that we use to process and experience the happenings of events.

So What?

What does all that mean? Among the most important consequences this realization include the following:

- The "past" does **not** exist apart from our thinking-feeling about it in the here-and-now as we hold various thoughts-and-feelings about various events that we remember occurring previously. Or, to drop E-priming, "There is no 'past'!" To so speak generates a "misplaced concreteness" (Whitehead) that nominalizes (names) a process as if a thing. But what does actually exist? Only our *thinking, remembering, representing, constructing, appraising, believing, etc.* the events we have experienced. The reference of "the past" exists only in our "mind."

- The "future" does **not** exist. Once again, it does not exist *apart from* our thinking-feeling about it in the here-and-now as we represent it, anticipate it, imagine it, etc. It exists only via our constructing it mentally-and-emotionally. Therefore we create many of the events that we will experience as we anticipate those emerging future events.

- These human *time zones*, in addition to the present (which does exists, and only exists), indicate that kind of consciousness that comes built into our very being—a *"time" consciousness* which enables us to conceptualize events prior to now and events that will occur subsequently. So we humans inevitably and inescapably live in "time" and travel through "time" (via consciousness). This makes us "time" travelers—those who adventure in "time."

- Therefore, we can travel these "time" zones in effective and in ineffective ways. We can get *stuck* in "time." People who tend to live a lot (even most) of their "time" in the "past" do so by *"thinking" about old events and giving them such meanings* that they get stuck in those "past" referents People who tend to live a lot (even most) of their "time" in the "future" do a similar thing. They miss the *now* by focusing, believing, hoping, representing, and constructing a "future."

- *Developing conscious awareness* of our "time" zone travels and adventures enables us to take charge of this transcendental power so that we manage the concept "time," rather than it managing us! This enables us to examine how we have coded time and change any coding that doesn't serve us well. Then we can get unstuck from the places of the past and can usefully construct a big, bright future now to use as a navigational map as each now (each day) becomes a new day and the "future" that we now anticipate.

"Time" Learnings

If you have studied the previous chapters and practiced the hands-on exercises suggested, then you have constructed for yourself some *empowering compelling outcomes* to pull you into your future. You have engaged in the process of learning to live a "life well lived" by using the habits of highly effective people (mentioned in Franklin's "rungs on the ladder of success"). So what else can we say or learn via this adventure in "time?"

Living Effectively as a Time-Binder

We mentioned earlier that general-semanticist Alfred Korzybski (1941/1994) defined human beings as a **"time binding" class of life.** What does this mean?

He said that we as "a semantic class of life" *bind "time"* as we use symbols to design, represent, and communicate conceptual meanings within ourselves and to others. He used this definition of "mankind," in fact, to create a neuro-linguistic system of sanity and effectiveness.

He noted that, as a race, we can *bind* **the accomplishments of others** who lived in previous ages to ourselves, and thereby use their learnings. In this, we can build up a "reference library" of memories within us in our nervous system, not only of our own personal and immediate experiences, but we can *learn from others*.

This means that as "time binders" we can build on the accomplishments of men and women who lived in past ages and do not have to start anew in each generation—unlike the animals.

By contrast, Korzybski described plants as functioning/existing as a "chemical binding class of life." He said animals manifest a "space binding class of life." **Plants** absorb chemicals into themselves and then transform and incorporate those chemicals into their very existence. They also transform energy from the sun chemically, storing it and using it to grow. **Animals** do the same and then go another step. They use the energy from their chemistry-binding to generate *mobility to move through space*. In this way they bind new, more and different resources from their environment which movement provides them. Thus, they exist as "space binders."

Humans do these two and go another step. We can (but do not have to) *bind the learnings of ourselves and other humans over "time."* We can take those learnings into ourselves, transform ourselves in doing so, and incorporate such symbolic learnings into our organism. This describes the meaning of "time" binding as used in general semantics. We have the ability to create symbols about our experiences in the form of pictures, numbers, and words. As we then use these symbol systems, we receive the communications, wisdom, inventions, philosophies, etc. of former generations over the ages. Korzybski (1933/1994) wrote:

> "The origin of this work was a new functional definition of 'man' ... based on an analysis of uniquely human potentialities; namely, that each generation may begin where the former left off. This characteristic I called the 'time-binding' capacity..." (page xx).

What mechanism(s) make us a "time" binding" class of life? *Language and/or symbol systems* (symbolisms). That which empowers us to bind the learnings of other humans and to benefit from their brain and nervous system consists of the unique human gift of language. Thus, as a neuro-linguistic-semantic class of life we use **symbols** to represent and communicate meanings (concepts, constructs, etc.) to each other. Such symbols also enable us to create non-existing things like concepts, abstractions, and ideas. In this way, the "ideas" of people who lived two thousand or four thousand years ago can come into our brain and nervous system, generate thoughts-and-feelings in our existence, induce us into various states, and save us the time and trouble that it took them to develop such ideas.

As a result of our symbol use, we encode, store, and retrieve the ideas and concepts of our forefathers and foremothers and keep the learnings that they made. This gives us the ability to under stand them, their life, their struggles, their understandings, etc. In this way, as "time-binders" we do not need to re-invent our culture and cultural learnings with each generation.

This gives us the power to "bind" into our own nervous system and brain the abstracts made in the nervous systems and brains of other persons—many long dead. We can bind their highest learnings and wisdom; we can also bind their blunders and madnesses.

"Time" Binding Questions

- What kind of "time" do you bind?
- What style of "time" binding do you engage in?
- How effectively or ineffectively do you bind the learnings of others over "time?"
- How much awareness do you have about your day to day "time" binding?
- What skills, processes, or techniques would you like to develop to improve your "time" binding abilities?

The Value of Developing Our Skills In "Time" Binding

1. *Time-binding save us "time" and trouble.* Consider this. Most of us still **learn** the old fashion way—via "trial and error." We dive into things, mess up, miscommunicate, misperceive, misunderstand, blunder, make mistakes, create confusion, create problems, etc. *then* we learn something from that experience! Does that describe your "strategy for learning?" How much truth does that hold with regard to your learnings?

Most people even seem to *highly value* that kind of trial and error learning(!). You can hear them value it as they talk about the ultimate importance of *"experience."* They seem to think that if someone didn't, or doesn't, experience something—they cannot possible truly "understand" it, appreciate it, "know" it, etc. "Only first-hand experience really counts!"

Now direct **experiential learning** does strike us in a most impactful way. It does give us a full sensory way of representing it (in the *sights* of images, color, closeness, 3-D, the sounds of noise and volume and tone, the *smells* of the situation, the tastes of things, the *words* spoken and inwardly heard, etc.). Yet the power of this lies **not** in the fact that "I actually experienced it!", but in the fact that we *represented it in full sensory modalities*. Those who experience similar powerful things, but don't create vivid sensory representations will not experience the "experience" as impactful. He drives too fast, has an accident, goes to jail, fails school, bankrupts relationships, and *learns nothing*! While, on the other hand, those who don't "actually" experience it in their life situation, but experience it in their imagination (via a story, a movie, a hypnotic trance, etc.) will similarly **learn** from it in an impactful way.

The key does not lie in whether we or someone else had the *experience* first-hand and personally. The key lies in *how we symbolically coded the experience*. The one who truly, deeply, and lastly **learns** does not have to go through every experience in real "time." They can do it in virtual "time." They can do it via reading, watching a movie or play, imagining with vividness, pretending with power, listen empathetically, etc.

Sometimes we meet someone, or know someone, who goes through all kinds of hellish experiences, and yet for all the pain *doesn't* seem to *learn* anything. "What has to happen to bring Jack to his senses?" we ask rhetorically. Sometimes we develop other unenhancing beliefs to explain this, "Well, he just hasn't hit bottom yet. One of these days, he will, and if it isn't too late, then he'll learn."

We don't think so. The problem does **not** lie in how much pain a person has experienced, it lies in their *strategy for learning* and style of binding (coding) their learnings over "time." Those who seem to have to "hit bottom" tend to **not** learn from the experiences of others. They tend to **not** make vivid sensory-rich representations of other people's experiences and so their "thoughts" about this do not powerfully effect them. Or, if they do—they add to it some kind of a *discounting belief* or *filter*, "Yes, I see that it happened to John, but it would never happen to me!" So it does not count in their mental world as a map to help them navigate the rough spots in life. So they move on out, mapless about that danger—the lesson not bound into consciousness.

What does all this have to do with "time" binding? Everything! For the person who does not *learn from others* does not **bind** from **the learnings** of others in "time" and so has to re-invent the wheel about how to handle alcohol, how to interact with authority figures, how to discipline their own passions, how to think consequentially, how to cope with hurts, how to get unstuck from unpleasant experiences in the "past," how to not personalize criticism, how to esteem their self, etc.

How unsane! Racially (i.e. as a human being) they function as if they exist as the first humans. These new Adams and Eves move through life as if no one else has ever traveled that road before, *as if* no one has ever created a navigational map about making that journey, *as if* the human race has just now appeared on the planet and *as if* we have to learn everything from *scratch*. In truth, many have traveled that road. In truth, many have created many helpful maps in a vast number of areas: health, relationships, attitude, conflict, business, career, finances, etc.

If only they knew how to do some good "time" binding, they could save themselves a whole lot of "time," trouble, pain, anguish, and learning.

2. *Time-binding delivers ourselves from making multitudes of mistakes.* All of us will continue to make mistakes on a daily basis. Count on it! As fallible beings in our thinking, emoting, speaking, behaving, relating, problem-solving, etc. mistakes function as our way of growing (what a reframe!). But once we learn *how to learn* from the mistakes—our own and others—then we can save ourselves from multitudes of mistakes. This saves on the wear and tear of our mind-emotions.

Where does your mind go when someone makes a *mistake*? What words come out of your mouth? How skilled would you gauge yourself in **learning** from their mistakes?

Learning from mistakes, whether our own or someone else's, involves a pretty radical shift in consciousness for most of us. If our mind and mouth does not automatically and immediately respond with,

"Great! What can I learn? How can I use this constructively?"

in response to both our mistakes and others—then we probably do not have a good strategy for *"time" binding*. You probably go through a lot of unnecessary pain in learning.

To put yourself into that kind of positive, constructive state *in response to mistakes* necessitates adopting a new set of values and beliefs about mistakes. It necessitates reframing yourself. It necessitates practicing that new mindset until you make it automatic (Yes, it demands that you *work* your consciousness!).

It also demands breaking with the old mindsets and states:

- *Blaming*: "Who made that mistake?"
- *Demandingness*: "What did you do that for?"
- *Accusations:* "What's wrong with you that you don't use your head?"
- *Insults:* "Are you stupid or something?"
- *Taboos:* "You should think before you act!"
- *Guilting:* "Shame on you! Only a bad person makes mistake!"

If your mind and/or mouth goes to any of these kinds of responses in response to a mistake (yours or another), it will effectively prevent you from the earlier reframes I mentioned. *"So what can I do about this?"*

Interrupt your mind and mouth! Create and practice some state *interrupts* that you can use to prevent your brain from going to those disempowering places and from your mouth languaging yourself and others in those dignity-denying and insulting ways.

Do you yet have an *accepting attitude* toward mistakes? What kind of a relation do you have with your own fallibility? Say, those descriptions describe not just a state, but a meta-state:

Figure 10:1

M-S:

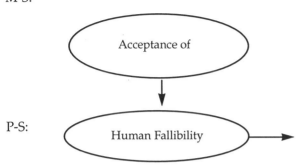

3. *Time-binding moves us into the accelerated learning experience known as modeling.* Now the empowering skill whereby we do not depend upon "trial and error" learning from personal experience shifts us into a whole new level and dimension of learning, the learning that arises from **modeling excellence.**

Herein, the NLP model truly excels. It says that all of us humans operate within, and from out of, a similar nervous system. If we can *identify the strategy components* that describe how one person uses his or her brain and nervous system in making a "model of the world" of useful learnings, then we can do the same and produce similar results.

In NLP, we call this process "the modeling of excellence." In fact, this also describes how NLP came about as a communication model and then as a set of therapy techniques. Linguistic expert Dr. John Grinder and computer programmer/mathematician Richard Bandler looked at *the structure of the subjective experiences* of several world renowned communicators and therapists such as Milton Erickson, Virginia Satir, and Fritz Perls and modeled them. They modeled their language patterns, mental sorting patterns, neurological patterns, etc. Then, out of that modeling, came models about how they so effectively accomplished their high-level skills and genius.

Now this really puts a *turbo-charger in our "time" binding* as it accelerates our learning skills so that we don't depend primarily on *error* for our learning, we can depend upon finding and following *excellence*. Now we not only learn what **not** to do, the potholes in the roads of life, but of more importance, we learn *how to take effective action*. We learn how to build enhancing and effective mental maps (models of the world) that can take us to all kinds of new and exciting places by using the learnings of others who have already made the learnings.

Bandler and Grinder noted in their first book, **The Structure of Magic**, that problems in life do not arise because we have an impoverished *reality* (territory). The problem with people who feel and think and behave in limited and "stuck" ways arises from their **map** of the territory. They suffer from a limited, disempowering, false-to-fact and/or erroneous map. "I can't stand criticism!" "I can't find someone to love me." "Nobody cares." etc.Give them a new map and watch them grow, enjoy, relate, feel great, and make enhancing choices! Give them an enhancing map about how to update and transform their maps and then really watch them zoom! This explains how many of us get stuck in the "past." We modeled someone who lived out of some very limited map. Or we created a map based on their limitations.

Time-Binding Skills

Given the importance of "time" binding, how do we develop this skill? If you read the previous pages carefully, you undoubtedly picked up on some of the most powerful and useful *"time" binding skills* available. I'll start with one of the most enhancing.

1. **Modeling excellence.** To do the best kind of "time" binding, shift your focus to that which a modeler uses. As you do that, you will train your brain to *start noticing excellence* in human behavior and responses. This will give you a compelling outcome and a target that you can begin to create today. Next, you will need to know and use the modeling process of unpacking the strategies of those models of excellence so that you can install those representational steps and states into your experience.

In NLP, this process of strategy identification, eliciting, unpacking, designing, and installing gives one the ability to **learn** at an accelerated pace. It provides us with the distinctions to make at the modality and submodality levels which create the states and meta-states for effectiveness. This "tracking with people" utilizes information about how and what the person sorts for in terms of information (the meta-programs). It also utilizes the "strategy" approach that we have often referred to and given examples of in this book (see Dilts, et al. 1980, also Hall, 1997c).

As "time" binders, we can draw on the works of Aristotle, Jesus, Shakespeare, Martin Luther King, Jr., Benjamin Franklin, and a host of others. Dilts has contributed a series on the subject of modeling geniuses. By devoting ourselves to great literature, great biographies, and great successes in human relations, we can truly live as their beneficiaries. Then we can begin to contribute to that bounty as we pass it on to the next generation.

Johnson (1946/1989), in speaking about "time" binding says,

> "Each human generation can for this reason start where the last generation left off. An American boy...can aspire to be not *like* George Washington but *better than* George Washington; he can go on from where Washington stopped. Therein lies the key to human advancement. But the fact that it can be done, that time binding is humanly possible, does not serve to guarantee that it will be done. *It is accomplished effectively only by those who are conscious of the process* by means of which it may be accomplished. The fact that a relatively conscious use of this process is an integral part of scientific method accounts for the amazing time-binding, or progress, that has been achieved in the areas in which science has been vigorously applied" 164-165, our emphasis).

2. **Making an enhancing adjustment to fallibility and mistakes.** We have already referred to the supporting belief and value about mistakes and human fallibility that enable us to attain an enhancing adjustment to this inescapable facet of life. Now we

only need to recognize our power as a meaning maker and give these external behaviors some new internal significance that will renew our thinking and thereby transform our mind (Bandler, 1985).

Kodish and Kodish (1993) speak about *personal "time" binding* as the ability to learn from ourselves and "how to make the most of our individual experiences" (157). Under this category, they appeal to Ellis' REBT model that speaks about the poor ways we use language on ourselves.

> "When we label ourselves 'stupid' or similar negative higher-order abstractions, we create a negative time-binding environment. When we make perfectionistic demands on ourselves, unconditionally, and absolutistically telling ourselves what we 'should' do ... we diminish our chances of fully realizing our potentialities." (157).

Treating ourselves decently and respectfully in how we language ourselves represents a responsible way to live. And it makes for sanity! In so doing, we can create the kind of internal state or atmosphere wherein we can even cooperate with ourself and give and take instruction from ourself well!

3. **Handling language and symbolic systems with awareness and choice.** We bind the learnings of previous "times" via language. Thereby we can transfer those learnings and make them our own. Yet all words and language expressions do not assist us in making learnings. Some terms, words, sentences, and metaphors create all kinds of mapping problems in terms of deleting important distinctions, over-generalizing distinctions, and distorting important distinctions.

In an earlier work (Hall, 1993c, 1996) we identified 20 linguistic distinctions of ill-formedness that can create all kinds of fluffy vagueness in our maps. The meta-model details other aspects of linguistic-semantic reality that can increase our resourcefulness. At the foundation, we kept emphasizing the role of words as *only symbols*, not reality. Knowing that and operating from that understanding, enables us to not take any word too seriously. This frees us up to even call in question the linguistic structure and presuppositions of our words. It also frees us from the reactivity of semantic reactions.

Korzybski complained about the Aristotelian nature of most modern languages that carry over misplaced concreteness in the way it reifies processes, over-identifies phenomena on different logical levels, and create false-to-fact structural systems as the subject-predicate sentence form. These linguistic structures make it difficult to effectively "time" bind.

What results from our "time" binding? What do we accomplish as "time" binders, build upon the contributions and learnings of others? We use language and languaging (which includes not only linguistics, but art, drama, gesture, etc.) and thereby create the human "meaning" environment, culture. Or to use the language of general semantics, *a neuro-linguistic and neuro-semantic environment. Culture* then operates as the unconscious context we live in, that meta-level frame of reference.

What importance does this have? The neuro-semantic environment or culture that results from our "time" binding then creates the climate or context within which the next generation(s) will grow up. It sets up the unconscious and presuppositional frames-of-reference and states within which they will live and grow and operate. We do our "time-binding" in human culture. Apart from culture, we can do very little "time-binding."

4. Developing communication ability. To "commune" meanings with another ("communicate"), we use *various symbolic systems* (words, mathematics, gestures, art, etc.). To the extent that we fail to effectively understand the role and nature of this and that we fail to handle the symbolic systems well, to that extent we will experience problems in communication. These will show up as miscommunication, misunderstanding, confusion, mind-reading, arguments, conflicts, hurt feelings, etc.

To receive the communication of another human being from a different "time" or "space" we have to learn effective means of handling symbol systems; indexing the person's referents, checking out understandings, empathetically listening to truly understand them, etc. If the communication takes a different medium than oral communication, then we have to adjust ourselves to that medium (art, pictures, prose, literature, letter, apocalypse, poetry, satire, etc.). Unless we do this, we will not bind the learnings they made in their "time." We will only use their communications to project *our* views and understandings.

From a "time" binding perspective, this enables us to understand meaning. What does any given word "mean"? A dictionary does not, and cannot, tell us what a word "means" now or in the future. It can only tell you the significance that former individuals and groups have given that word. "What do you mean by 'self-esteem'?" When you understand the nature of language, you realize deeply that *words do not mean anything.* **People make "meanings"** via the words they use. Kodish and Kodish (1993) wrote,

> "Communicating well involves sensitivity to our environments, internal and external, taking into consideration the multi-dimensional complexities of our neuro-linguistic, neuro-semantic environments." (153).

Then they ask, "*How* can we use general semantics to communicate in ways that encourage positive climates, help us achieve our goals and foster good relationships?" In response, they talk about:

- recognizing the assumptions, premises, and expectations that we inevitably bring to our communicational exchanges,
- recognizing individual differences in abstracting,
- recognizing the multiple "meanings" that any behavior can evoke,
- respecting the individuality of each person (cherishing their uniqueness),
- expecting differences in evaluating,
- avoiding unspecified absolutisms ("Everybody knows..." "What kind of a person would do that?"),
- seeking to understand the other's assumptions and preferences,
- developing non-verbal awareness,
- appreciating the environment context,
- distinguishing facts from inferences,
- indexing referents,

- avoiding "why" questions and replacing them with "how" questions (to shift from a blame-frame to a solution frame),
- using "etc." to remind ourselves that we can never say everything or the last word about anything (to avoid a know-it-all attitude),
- expecting misunderstandings, etc. (p. 154-156).

5. **Running meta-level ecology checks on our "time" binding skills.** Since "time" binding occurs by fallible human beings at specific "times" and places via specific communication forms and media, we need to maintain an awareness of our "time" binding. As we do, then we can "go meta" to such and run an ecology check on it.

"In receiving these ideas and learnings from this other person in a previous 'time,' does it do justice to those ideas?"

"Does this 'time' binding assist me in building a more enhancing model of the world that empowers me in living, thinking, feeling, speaking, behaving, etc.?"

"How accurate, useful, productive, etc. would another evaluate this kind of 'time' binding?"

General semantics suggests that at the heart of improving our "time" binding skills, we learn how to *effectively evaluate* what we inherit from the "past," to sort out the misinformation and unuseful parts of it, and to enrich it with our own contributions. Actually, this describes *the scientific method and attitude.* As we accumulate knowledge in science, we keep questioning it, indexing it, and revising it until we make it more and more accurate and useful.

Otherwise (and this describes one of the opposites of "time" binding) we end up *lacking the ability to learn from our experiences.* This speaks of a closed system; one not open to new information, new input, new understandings.

6. **Passing on the products of our own learning and creativity to the next generation.** If "time" binding refers to passing on our highest wisdom today through language, art, artifacts, music, mathematics, science, inventions, ethics, philosophy, etc. so that the next generation can begin their exploration where our search ended, then we can begin now to think about our contribution.

"Time" binding highlights how our survival depends on our skills of interdependence, cooperating, caring, and sharing with other people. Anything that you do that makes such inter-dependence more possible and more viable contributes to this process. What wisdom or knowledge would you like to pass on? What forms or expressions can you come up with for passing it on?

Given this definition and understanding of ourselves as a "time" binding class of life, isolationism, avoidance of social issues, non-commitment to making a positive contribution to others, etc. becomes a crime against humanity. Effective and healthy "time" binders stand up and fight **for** the contributing to the ongoing development of the human race.

The current cultural negativism, intellectual cynicism, "millennial madness" (unsanity), and television induced "news" pessimism of the race, work against "time" binding as well as the heart of the Judeo-Christian ethic of *loving our neighbors* as we love ourselves.

In what arena of concern would you like to devote your energies and make a contribution? Education? Politics? The unemployed? Domestic violence? The aged? Pick the arena.

Conclusion

Our adventure in "time" involves how we *bind* the products, experiences, and learnings that we make in "time" so that we make them resources and starting points for those who follow. Personal "time" binding means binding those learnings so that we can continue developing and don't have to start over every day! Test yourself on your "time" binding skills:

- What forms of excellence have I modelled and/or do I plan to model this year?
- How enhancing of an adjustment have I made to mistakes and to human fallibility? What reframes have I, or can I, create to enable me to accept and appreciate mistakes and failures?

- How much consciousness have I developed about my languaging of myself and others? How much flexibility in re-languaging have I developed? Does my languaging serve me well or do I talk myself into emotional dead-end states?

- What enhanced communication skills would best help me to improve my skills in handling and transmitting meanings via symbolism?

- Do I regularly run an ecology check on my "time" binding skills? How do I do that? When? With what effect?

- What products of "time" binding do I plan to pass on to others?

Part IV

"Time" In Logical Levels

Chapter 11

The Logical Levels in "Time"

You Have To Go Meta To Reach "Time"

The highly conceptual understandings and model of "time" in this chapter offers an explanation that undergirds many of the patterns that we have included in this book. "Do I have to understand this model to use the *patterns*?" No. In fact, you can even use the patterns without reference to the conceptual theorizing that you find in this chapter. We offer these high level abstractions here as an explanation, knowing that the more philosophically minded will love them. As a caveat, we do suggest that you may need to read this chapter several times to fully appreciate "time" in terms of its logical levels.

"Time" as an Abstraction at a Meta-Level

Since we do not have "time" in *the process world of events, actions, happenings, and movement* at all, we have to rise **above** that level in order to experience this conceptual reality that we call "time." When we do we can then begin "binding" "time." We do this by representing previous events and manipulating those representations so that they posit various relationships. Doing this makes us conscious of the larger context that we conceptually measure and mark and label "time."

We noted earlier (Chapter 10) that *time-binding*, from general semantics, describes the process of *binding* into our very neurology and organism the learnings, experiences, events, and abstracts made in the nervous systems of other people in other ages. This describes the essential distinguishing characteristic of humans in contradistinction to animals (space-binding creatures) and plants (chemical-binding life). We can bind into our "personality" the experiences of the past or "time." We do so by moving to meta-levels of awareness and incorporating the learnings of others into ourselves.

Gestalting the Meta-State of "Time"

So if "time" does not exist at the primary level, but only events, rhythms, activities, etc, then how do we get to "time?" As we experience events, rhythms, and activities repeatedly we come to know them as **times**, or instances, of **events**. From that awareness we then develop *a "sense" of duration* as a higher-order feeling that results from the summation (or abstraction) of many individual occurrences. This represents one meta-state of "time," namely, "a sense of duration" (an abstraction that compares and relates that configuration of events).

Then, as we talk about these "times" we begin to manipulate this symbol. We begin to number these "times," compare them, sequence them. Then we can say, "Time has elapsed," or, "it took three years to complete the project," or "in another couple of days." Yet what have we actually seen come and go? Not "time?" But events. Our abstraction of these numerous events and representation of their duration, order, sequence, etc. occurs at a higher level of abstraction.

Then we begin to use the verbal shorthand involved in the short nominalization, "time." And that leads us to begin to objectify *it* as we talk about *it* as if it had physical properties as do sensed objects. So we end up languaging ourselves by saying, "time" flows, moves, races, slows down. We then talk about wasting "time," saving it, misusing it, etc. Actually we have reference to times of something occurring somewhere, and not our concept of "time."

"Time" arises then as a *gestalt abstract awareness* that holds past, present, and future together into a structure-as-a-whole configuration, as in a time-line. "Time" emerges from our awareness of events, our sense of duration, our summation of development and growth that occurs "over time," and from our abstraction of "time" as a dimension as in the space-time continuum. When we analyze "time" (as we do other higher level abstractions, beauty, love, happiness) and find the component pieces out of which the structure-as-a-whole emerges, we do not find "time" in any of the pieces. It seems to vanish with analysis.

Meta-Time

"Time" then as a mental concept functions as one of those *a priori categories* in the mind and therefore as a meta-state itself. It operates as a state of awareness about another state.

First we experience our thoughts-and-feelings of *"time"* when we develop awareness of the relationship between events. This very awareness moves us to a high level of conceptualization because our thoughts-and-feelings do not refer to any external, empirical reality, but to *an inner "reality"* or *phenomenon*. We have now moved from what Bateson (1972) called **the Pleroma** of the see-hear-feel world into **the Creatura**; the internal world of ideas, communication, thought, information, differences, etc.

Yet, as we all know, we do not stop there. We then develop thoughts-and-feelings about those conceptual abstractions. We develop beliefs, values, feelings about "time." We love it; we hate it. We enjoy and celebrate it; we despise and regret it.

So at the primary level, "time" does not exist; at that level, only "times"—times of events occurring. When we number these elements and compare them with set standards we get what Weinberg (1959) calls "times of times" or "time." Here we compare our "feeling of an event's duration" with previous memories of the same and then as we think about this we create another meta-level awareness of "time." Thus in creating the gestalt sense of "time," we begin with our kinesthetic sensations of rhythm and rhythmic activities. To that we code and remember these repetitions of cyclical phenomena, and the repetition of occurrences generates a sense of duration—a higher-order feeling.

Figure 11:1

Meta-State:

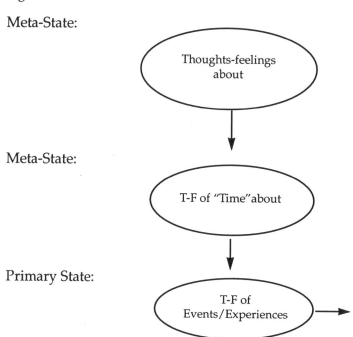

Meta-State:

Primary State:

We do not stop there. Then we have other thoughts-feelings about our thoughts-feelings about "time!"

At the *primary state*, we think-feel: "I feel rushed by what John said about getting this project done." Then, at the meta-state level we think-feel, "I never have enough time." "I hate feeling this time pressure." And at an even higher *meta-meta*-state level, "I feel guilty for these feelings of hatred toward the pressure!"

When we meta-state ourselves in this way, we go into various negative mental-and-emotional states *about* other states and this can loop around several times until we get ourselves into a real quandary of distress. But now we can stop this un-enhancing way of managing "time." Awareness of our mapping gives us a choice, a consciousness of the other alternatives before us.

Now we can meta-state ourselves in a much more empowering way. Try these on for size, "I appreciate my 'tim-ing'—my awareness of 'time,' as I fully realize my ability to alter my representations of 'time' so that they enhance my life." "I fully accept 'time' as a concept and thoroughly enjoy this day and this moment with a hopeful anticipation of the moments to come..."

Time as a Conceptual State

Sir Arthur Eddington has observed,

> "In any attempt to bridge the domains of experience belonging to the spiritual and physical sides of our nature, time occupies the key position." (Fagg, 1985).

An even more provocative statement lies in what Panikkar said in *Time and Sacrifice—the Sacrifice of Time and the Ritual of Modernity,*

> "Time is at the crossing point between consciousness and matter." (*The Study of Time III,* p. 684.)

Figure 11.2 "Time" Chart

The Phenomenology of "Time" in Terms of Logical Levels

Meta-Meta-Levels:

Eternity
Time w/o Limit
Beyond Time
Timelessness

Fictional Time
Imaginary Time
Mythical/Dream Time
Cyclical Time: eternal return

Definitional Time
"Self" as a Time Being

Meta-Level:

Historical Time
Past-Present-Future

Developmental Time
Sense of Development
Growth, Progress
Time Going Somewhere

Mortal Time
Life-Sickness-Death
Finitude/Mortality

Sacred Time
Beliefs @ Time
Going somewhere/
Circular: eternal
return

Psychological Time
Linguistic Time
Narrated Time
Fast/Slow Time
Emotional Time

Meta-Level:
Representational Time

Kinesthetic Time
Sensed as Duration
Internal Rhythms

Visual Time
Represented as Line,
Circle, Boomerang
(Metaphors of Time Rep).

Auditory Time
Voice/Sound of Events
Past, Current, Future

Synesthesia Time
Configuration of Events
sorted as Past, Present
& Future
Stored Time: "memory"

Mathematical Time
Time measured,
sequenced
Clock Time

Primary Level:
Events

Action -- Events Occurring
Times

The World of Process: Changing, Aging, Timlessness
Thermodynamic time: Physical time
Linear: sequential, continuous
Chronos: clock time, rhythm, patterns
Derived from Cosmological time: The Changing, Moving Universe

DISTINGUISHING "TIME" AT DIFFERENT LOGICAL LEVELS

Primary "Times"	Meta-Level "Time"
Events, Happenings, Occurrences in the World of Process derived from Conceptions/ Constant and unending change	Discontinuous & Digital "Time" Constructions of "Time"
Times Change, Rhythm, Movement Thoughts @	"Time" Concept, Abstraction,
Physical Time Psychological Time *Chronos*: chronology, clock time, objective time Quantity of time as measured	Mental-Emotional/ Kairos: Internal subjective time Quality of "Time" as experienced
World of Processes One Dimensional, Unidirectional (goes only in one direction)	World of Representation Multi-Dimensional Time; Can go in many directions
(Events do not go "backward," do not reverse) Concepts/ Memories/ Imagination	can represent events going backward
No Tenses... exists as ongoing existence	Tenses: past, present, future Many narrative configuration

Analysis of the "Time" Chart

This chart of "time" extends our understanding of "time" by formatting and structuring it as involving multiple levels. It also comprises a logical level system. This sorts out the multiordinality of "time" that we discussed in previous chapters by showing and placing the various *kinds of "time"* that we can experience. We offer this as a new way to conceptualize "time" as a multi-ordinal phenomena to NLP as well as psychology in general. Viewing "time" as a model of logical levels acknowledges its multiordinality. "Time" then can refer to different logical levels thereby creating different kinds and dimensions of "time."

Augustine's now classic Eleventh Chapter in his *Confessions* illustrates the confusion of these levels and the problems that it thereby generates,

"I know that my discourse on time is in time; so I know that time exists and that it is measured. But I know neither what time is nor how it is measured. I am in a sorry state, for I do not even know what I do not know." (25:32, quoted by Riceour, 1983, p.15). "If the future and the past do exist, I want to know where they are" (18:23).

The First Logical Level: Representational Time

Since "time" does **not** occur out there in the world only events, actions, movement, rhythms, etc. occur, our first level of mapping that reality involves a simple correspondence mapping. Thus, at this level in our representing of "time," if we map the Territory of events accurately, we will map "time" as moving forward in one direction.

At the primary level of events, "time" only moves forward. After all, events do not go backward, only forward. Things in the world progress, grow, develop, evolve, etc. We never see a full grown tree shrink a layer per year until it becomes a sapling and then a seed. We never see a full grown cow become a calf, we never see a car accident go in reverse.

Though at higher logical levels we will find "time" able to move backwards, it does not do so at this level. At this level we represent physical "time" which we discover as sequential (events happening one after another) and linear. Though some scientists have posited the existence of tachyons, particles with a speed faster than light, this remains an assumption of physicists and, at best, would only apply to the sub-microscopic, not to anything real on the microscopic or macroscopic world.

Primary level "time" then partakes of Eddington's "arrow of time." It moves unidirectionally and irreversibly. This makes the events of "time" at this level, each one, unique and unrepeatable. That leads us to the meta-level awareness that *historical "time"* moves forward toward destiny.

Developmentally, we do not seem born with an activated sense of "time" anymore than we have language, social skills, or other high level human skills at birth. These phenomena in Creatura develop, they emerge. In developmental psychology we know that understanding of one's own age comes to most children about five years of age. At six, most of us develop a sense of "today, yesterday, and tomorrow." At eight, we begin to comprehend clock "time." Yet before the age of eleven, "temporal aspects of history are almost meaningless" (Meerloo, 1970, p. 136).

"Time" as an awareness only arises as we step aside from it and reflect upon it. Yet to do that, we must *represent* it. Thus here we use various modalities to code the numerous concepts we develop that comprise what we call time.

1. We code a sense of endurance and/or rhythm—and usually do this kinesthetically. This refers to "time" as span and duration, as continuity, and as "the order of phenomenon." This also includes biological time that arises from our biological "clocks" or rhythms.

2. We code it visually in terms of various metaphors: as a line, a circle, a boomerang, etc.

3. We code it auditorially.

4. We code it as a synesthesia: a total configuration of these modalities that generate our sense of the continuum: past— present— future.

5. We code time also using various clocks: physical, mechanical, electronic, the seasons, etc. Here we use mathematical codes.

At this level, "time" exists as action, movement, rhythm, and events.

The Second Logical Level: The Meaning of Time

Once we have coded and represented conceptual "time," we then move up another logical level to give it various meanings. This generates various other kinds of "times." Some of this material comes from Edward Hall (1983), *The Dance of Life: The Other Dimension of Time.* There he identified numerous kinds of "time:"

physical, biological, personal, micro, profane, sacred, metaphysical, philosophical and conscious, and unconscious emergent time. Yet in so writing, he also asked the question of classification about all these "times."

"How does one proceed to classify these different kinds of time and do it in a rational way so that the interrelationships can be seen as a coherent system?" (15).

In his work, Hall provided one model for such a classification. Here we offer another—one involving multiple logical levels. Now at the first level meta to primary "time," we have several different kinds of "times." Namely,

1. *Historical meanings.* Our sense of "time" as history, not only the order and sequence of events as "cause" and "influence," but also "time" as history in the sense of the story or narrative of our lives. Here we think of the events of "time" as creating or reflecting a plot or theme.

Regarding historical "time," *only the present now moment actually exists*. What we call the "past" or the "future" exists in the present as thoughts of past events and future potential events.

Ricoeur (1983) writes,

"Augustine will at first appear to turn his back on this certainty that it is the past and the future that we measure. Later, by placing the past and the future within the present, by bringing in memory and expectation, he will be able to rescue this initial certainty from its apparent disaster by transferring onto expectation and onto memory the idea of a long future and a long past..." (8)

"By saying that there is not a future time, past time, and a present time, *but a threefold present, a present of future things, a present of past things, and a present of present things*, Augustine sets us on the path of an investigation into the most primitive temporal structure of action.

It is easy to rewrite each of the three temporal structures of actions in terms of this three-fold present. The present of the future? 'Henceforth, from now on I commit myself to doing that tomorrow.' The present of the past? 'Now I intend to do that because I just realized that...' The present of the future? 'Now I am doing it, because now I can do it.'" (60, emphasis added).

"History" as a sense originally arose from within the Judeo-Christian tradition where the early authors treated events as individual historical events that would not repeat in some kind of "eternal return." From this grew *the concept of history* as we today understand it, a concept that history does not move in cycles, but linearly and unidirectionally forward into an ever-unique future. This separated the deterministic fatalism of many of the ancient religions from the thought of the Western cultures of development and progress. Fagg (1985) added to this these words,

"For both Jews and Christians a sense of linearity undoubt-edly derived from the belief in a creation that was not repeated and in some form of final judgment day, whether the coming of the Messiah for the Jews or Christ's second coming for the christians. (p. 153)

2. *Developmental meanings.* Our sense of "time" as growth, progress, development, etc. We think of developmental "time" when we think of it as moving us along and upwards, as "time" bringing maturity, wisdom, growth.

3. *Meanings of mortality and finitude.* By "mortal time" we refer to our sense of mortality, that we live as finite creatures who will die and we know that as we live this day. This sense of finitude and fallibility highlights our sense of mortality. We do not live forever. We will not always have this experience of life. Mortal "time" obviously raises existential issues and leads to the next meaning of "time."

4. *Sacred meanings.* Our sense of "time" as history and develop-ment and mortality leads many people to believe in "time" as destiny, namely that "history is going somewhere," it operates telelogically, moving us on toward some higher purpose or goal.

This primarily characterizes Western religions, especially Christianity. Other people don't believe that, but hold to a different kind of sacred time. Characteristic more of the Eastern religions, these people view "time" as circular and hence the "eternal return."

Edward Hall (1983) describes sacred time as also including mythic time and *ceremony time*. In his analysis of the Quiche people, he identified how they interwove two calendars. Their civil calender contains eighteen twenty-day months with a civil year of 360 days with five extra days. Their religious calendar, with its 260 days, contains no months as such, but

> "... an assemblage of twenty combinations. These two calen-
> dars interlock into two rotating gears to produce the
> Calendar Round, which only repeats itself every fifty-two
> years." (76).

With this convoluted way of coding or representing of "time" "Quiche time binds them to the village, to ancestors, gods and daily life" (82). In other words, they have so structured and organized "time" that it now, in turn, structures and organizes them. In their case, it primarily binds them to various religious values and events.

5. *Psychological and linguistic meanings.* Our sense of "time" as "time" moving fast or slow, emotional time, stopping "time" as we make snapshots of events, and all of the versions of reality that narrative time can create. In his extensive three-volumes on *Time and Narrative*, Paul Ricoeur (1971) has poetically stated, "Narrative is a guardian of time." By this he referred to the role of story, narrated history, and literature as ways in which we encode "time" and play games with time.

Psychological "time" also shows up in cultural values. Edward Hall (1983) noted how "the cultures of the world can be divided into those in which time heals and those it which which doesn't" (33). Time-healing cultures (like Western societies) find that as we let the past slip away and code it as "the past", it becomes less and less important. Eastern cultures (Indian and Arabic societies, etc.) live in time-toxifying cultures so that not only does the past not go away, but even amplifies the memory of wrongs done.

Hall (1983) further describes *monochronic and polychronic time.* James and Woodsmall (1988) originally used this book to create the NLP "in time" and "through time" distinctions. Yet Hall described M-time and P-time more extensively.

> "Complex societies organize time in at least two different ways: events scheduled as separate items, one thing at a time (North Europe), or Mediterranean model of involvement in several things at once. The two systems are logically and empirically quite distinct—*polychronic (P-time).* The North European system is *monochronic or M-time.* P-time stresses involvement of people and completion of transactions rather than adherence to preset schedules. For P-time people, time is seldom experienced as 'wasted,' considered a point rather than a ribbon or a road." (43).

Psychological "time" would also include fast and slow "time." Our subjective appraisal of the quality and value (to us) of the "time" spent at or in an activity.

The Third Logical Level: Meanings of Meanings

We have noted that Korzybski said that when it comes to humans abstracting to continually higher and higher levels of abstraction, we can find no end to this process. Thus, we not only construct historical and developmental meaning about this concept, but we develop abstract understandings about beginnings and endings, about eternity, etc. Out of that arises various imaginary constructs of time (mythical time, science-fiction time, etc.) as well as transcendental personal time.

General-semanticist Weinberg (1959) described this ongoing abstracting,

> "Time is a second-order duration, the measured duration of the sensing of duration. Time is not felt, duration is. We cannot feel or sense an hour, a year, or a moment. These are measurements, symbols, maps of our non-verbal sense of duration. The non-verbal level is timeless; it has only the unmeasured and unmeasurable *now.* At this level there is no beginning, no end, only flow and change. Beginning and

end are high-order abstractions resulting from our thinking and talking *about* our feelings and sensing, and like all higher-order abstractions they are static; they are symbols and do not apply at the object level of senses and feelings.

Eternity, meaning years without end, is a higher-order abstraction, cannot be felt, and leads to paradox when we try to measure it. But eternity, meaning timelessness, is something that can be felt. When our concentration is wholly upon sensing and feeling without any notion of measurement, without any high-order thinking about what we are experiencing on the non-verbal level, there comes to us that feeling of timelessness and eternity which is profoundly moving and utterly mysterious. It is this sense of "nowness' that the artist tries to capture, convey, invoke, and evoke, and it is in this sense that all great art is timeless. The moment we move away from the feeling of immediacy of experience to the higher level of talking about our experience, we no longer feel its beauty, though we may 'intellectually' know it is beautiful; we are then in the realm of analysis and criticism. I believe that one reason for the mysteriousness of this non-verbal experience is our confusion of the two levels of abstraction and our unawareness of the differences between them. The verbal level is the level of measurement and analysis. The abstractions are relatively static and are not felt. We do not feel the number 2. Now when we apply higher-order abstractions to the lower orders, i.e. when we attempt to measure time and, necessarily, stop the flow of non-verbal abstraction (all measurement requires a beginning, an end, and a stopping of the abstracting process being measured) we may fail to realize that these are symbols about the non-verbal level and not the lower-order abstractions themselves." (Weinberg, *Levels of Knowing and Existence* (201-202).

At the level meta to the the second meta-"time" levels, we have *Eternity "Time," Fictional "Time,"* and *Definitional "Time"* as indicated on the chart. These levels of "time" represent an even higher level of abstraction focusing on the un-ending-ness of events (eternity) as one takes consciousness and attempts to imagine the frame-of-reference beyond all "time" frames! In fictional "time," we may include the kinds of "times" that we imagine and play around with in science fiction movies that involve "time" travel via other dimensions. By definitional "time," I refer to our thoughts-and-feelings about ourself as a being in "time" and yet a being who longs to transcend "time" (the "eternity" planted in our minds!).

Dialectical "Time"

The dialectic between these various "time" uses and dimensions, as in the dialectic between memory (past), attention (present) and anticipation or expectation (future), expresses the conceptual ability at a meta-level for moving back and forth in "time." It explains at that meta-level how we can measure "time"—we compare the sequence, movement, rhythm, etc. of events to other events (the moving of the stars and planets).

Augustine ultimately concluded that "time is in the soul." "Some such different times do exist in the mind, but nowhere else that I can see" (20:26). We have here put it as "in the mind" at various logical levels.

Panikkar's statement that "Time is at the crossing point between consciousness and matter" directs us to the human processing (abstracting) of "time" from the territory into consciousness.

"Time" Non-sense

To illustrate the problems that arise when people confuse logical levels about "time," notice the following statements.

1. "Time, along with ourselves, is *in* nature; nature is not in time. That is, the prevailing current opinion, whether physical, philosophic, religious, seems to be that time does not exist 'out there' beyond the universe, continually flowing on and on. It is one of the entities that is part of he universe, as we are." (Dr. Lawrence Fagg, *Two Faces of Time*, p. 164)

Here Dr. Fagg actually seeks to turn "time" into "an entity"!

Once he has objectified time as a thing, then he talks about it as "in nature." What specifically does he refer to? Can you see, hear, smell, taste, or touch this thing called "time" in nature? Here he uses *conceptual time* at some meta-level and yet talks about it as if at the primary level.

Actually "time" does not flow, does not move, does not exist in nature, "time" in that sense exists solely as a mental construct. What flows, moves, and exists? Events, happenings, movements, changes.

2. *"Eternity."* Fagg asserts that eternity "is something thought to signify everlasting time." (p. 146). Now to have *everlasting time*, you would have to have everlasting events, happenings, changes yet we know that the universe will not last forever. By way of contrast, in the Bible we find statements about "everlasting *life*," but never "everlasting time." Especially for anything that occurs in an age-lasting way (eternal).

Ricoeur (1983) speaks about eternity as "for ever still" in contrast to things "that are never still." He wrote,

> "This stillness lies in the fact that in eternity nothing moves into the past: all is present. Time, on the other hand, is never all present at once."

Figure 11:3

"Eternity"	"Time"
Without Form	Form and structure
Stillness	Movement
No distinctions	Distinctions

What then do we mean by "eternity?" If we mean before or after the presence of the physical universe with its movements, patterns, rhythms, etc. that we use as a "clock" for measuring "time," then eternity takes us, philosophically, to ideas that transcend even our ability to think of reality apart from the universe(!). Sometimes writers use a similar term, "atemporality" to speak of God as existing before or beyond "time." Yet if "time" designates any kind of measuring using events, actions, movements, even then we would have "time." The reason we can't imagine such lies in the fact that we can't even comprehend the kind of actions, events, etc. that would there occur!

3. "Time heals." As a concept, unspecified "time" doesn't heal. How could it? Rather, we need to ask, What events, experiences, processes occur "in" time that we find therapeutic? When we reify "time" and treat it as a thing, then we wait for "time" to heal us. We make ourselves a victim of this thing, rather than map out a process.

4. "The theory of relativity means that we can go back in time." Yes and no. Yes we can return to the past *in our minds, conceptually*. But only in that domain. Not at the primary level. There "times" move on inexorably forward as events after events happen. In that domain and in that level, events do not go backwards.

Conclusion

Obviously, the short word "time," as a nominalized representation of a mental process of abstracting, represents no simple referent. As our thoughts-and-feelings about "time" has grown and developed, it has led to constructing many different dimensions and levels of "time" meanings.

In the previous chapter we have explored many of these "time" aspects. We first focused on how we code the events of our life over "time" and how that generated our "time-line" (or whatever symbolic configuration we use). Recognizing, eliciting, and working with this then leads to many of the "technologies" in NLP for managing it and re-framing it so that we can get "time" to work in a friendly way for us instead of in an antagonistic way against us.

In the last two chapters we offer some new, different, and playful structures with "time." These patterns suggest that we have only begun to touch the hem of the garment with regard to all of the possibilities for representing and relating to the multiordinality of "time." Enjoy, feel amazed, get curious, and use all of your ferocious resolve to reorient yourself to the multi-level nature of "time" so that you fully experience the "time-ness" in your nature!

Chapter 12

Re-Languaging "Time"

Re-Languaging Time as a "Time" Management Skill

What significance does defining and understanding "time" have in the way that we refer to in these chapters? How does it affect our everyday lives?

If we begin with the realization that our *linguistic map* of reality significantly governs how we navigate our way around the territory, then we can easily understand that **how we language "time"** does have ripple effects in our emotions, behavior, and skills. If we have a map of Indianapolis and use it to navigate the streets of Moscow—it probably won't get us anywhere that we want to go. So with our linguistic maps, they need to have at least a somewhat similar structure to the territory that we want to navigate.

- What does all this mean in terms of "time" management?
- What does this have to do with mastering the "time" dragon?

It means that if we mis-represent and misunderstand the very nature and essence of "time" upfront, then all of our "time" management skills, techniques, and workshops will mis-direct us in navigating that territory. If we want to more efficiently handle our schedules, our energies and activities, our consciousness as events transpire, then we need to start with a clear understanding of "time."

Accordingly, **the ultimate "time" management skill** that we can develop involves **languaging "time"** with the kind of words, symbols, beliefs, and values that build an enhancing map for this conceptual reality. In the following we have identified several ways to update our "time" maps so that we can take charge of this facet of our lives and relate to "time" more resourcefully. If you find some of this repeating previous themes, then congratulate yourself on learning and noticing so quickly and thoroughly. We repeat some of it here inasmuch as "repetition is the mother of all learning."

1. "Time" Languaging

The way we language this concept of "time" makes a lot of difference. Whenever we reify a concept, we turn a mental process of thinking, abstracting, conceptualizing (a verb) into a noun. This *nominalizes* (names) the verb so that we formulate the actions in a static, unchanging, and permanent way. And this, *blinds us to its nature* as changing, dynamic, and in process. Such *nominalization* of processes fools us into treating the concept as "real" in an external sense. But if it does not exist externally, objectively, and empirically, then the word has no reference. No "real" reference exists to which we can point. It makes it a pseudo-word, a non-referencing word.

Reifying "time" creates a lot of personal and psychological disorientation, confusion, pseudo-realities, stress, and even pain. Think about it. Think about some of the kind of things we typically say that presuppose **thinking of "time" as a thing:**

> I don't have enough time!
> Where did all the time go?
> I feel a lot of time pressures!
> You need to manage your time better!
> Time is always getting away from me.
> I feel like I wasted a lot of time doing that!
> People should respect my time more!

When we talk this way, we *mis-represent* "time" as a thing, a commodity, and a tangible object because "time," in that sense, does not exist. So what does exist? Processes exist. Thus we can translate those statements without even using the word "time."

I have more things to do than I can accomplish before the end of the day.

I focused so much on that project that I didn't pay any attention to the clock.

I have a lot on my "mind" about all the things I want to/need to accomplish and this creates an inner sense of pressure and stress.

You need to manage your activities/schedule better.

When I don't plan my activities more consciously, I find that things take longer to accomplish than I thought.

I feel that I often fool around doing things that I don't ultimately find valuable and then judge that I have wasted my efforts.

People should respect my activities and choices as much as their own.

Languaging "Time" in an Empowering Way

Since we begin from the premise that language (comprised of words, sentences, syntax, symbols) functions only as a *tool* for coding, representing, transferring, and thinking—as a form of *human technology*, we recognize its value as lying entirely in its usefulness. Does our concept and languaging empower us to relate to events that have occurred, now occur, or that will occur? Do our words, phrases, and metaphors for "time" enable us to live more resourcefully, effectively, disciplined, happy, and confident or does it put us into negative, grumpy, and irritable states?

We will look at this subject later when we explore your particular *representations of "time"* (your "time-lines," Chapter 3). What images, sounds, sensations, etc. do you use to code "time?" What configurations do you use to symbolize your understandings, beliefs, and values about "time?"

2. "Time" Symbolism

What *symbol(s)* do you use to represent "time?" The two most frequently found symbols by which we do our "tim-ing" involve *lines* and *circles*. Many others exist. Some people use boomerangs, lily pads (Andreas 1987), spirals, etc.

The metaphor of "time" as a line provides a fairly useful language-map for "tim-ing." It enables us to do what no animal can do, conceptually *sort and separate* previous, current, and future events. This, in turn, serves as the foundation for thinking, developing awareness of sequences, and effectively responding to sequential events. For sequential events, this kind of map enables us to know the "time" or as we say, "to have an internal sense of time" (clock time). (If you recall, this describes someone who thinks of the "time"-line as outside of their body, hence making one an out-of-time person.)

This ability also facilitates other higher order conceptualizations. It enables us to think in terms of *causality*, cause-effect, consequences, relations, correlations, etc. (another awareness animals seem to lack).

But "time" as a line can create difficulties. A person can get so "time" oriented (in the sense of awareness of sequential calendar events) that s/he can think-and-feel and act in an obsessive and compulsive way about it, "driven by the clock," unable to relax, always "time" conscious, etc. This tends to describe people in Western cultures more than Eastern ones.

"Time" as a Circle

Conversely, the most common symbol in the East for "time" involves a circle or cycle rather than a line. *"Time" seen and experienced as a circle* generates other emotions, experiences, behaviors. This kind of "time" processing, coding, and representing leads to such abilities as the skill of "getting lost in time," living in the "eternal now," losing track of "time," etc. ("In Time" people have their time-line intersecting their body and "random" rather than sequential in their consciousness of "time," see Chapter 2)

This circle metaphor about "time" leads to feeling like one "has all the time in the world," hence, it enables us to access a tensionless state of no pressure, no rush, no push. It leads us into more *philosophical states of mind* rather than pragmatic and task-oriented states of mind. We see this metaphor in the "Philosopher" (the biblical book of Ecclesiastes or Koheleth) when he wrote,

"The sun rises and the sun goes down, and hastens to the place where it rises. The wind blows to the south, and goes round to the north; round and round goes the wind and on its circuits the wind returns ... What has been is what will be, and what has been done is what will be done; and there is nothing new under the sun..." (Eccl. 1:4-10).

When could we use that kind of state of consciousness? When relaxing, kicking back, taking a vacation, enjoying a movie, spending time with a loved one, pleasuring ourselves in a hobby, sport, etc. Can you pull that off? Lots of sequential "out of time people" go on vacations with a mind-set that characterizes the pragmatic, task-oriented mind. Get the picture? "How fast can we get to Disneyland?" "What kind of mileage can we make going through the Magic Kingdom?" So even on vacation we use our "time"-line metaphor/symbolism which puts us in an attitude (positional stance) of getting-things-done efficiently! So who runs things? Us or "Time?" (At such times, "Time" acts like a Dragon to us.)

Others live too long and too much in *"the eternal now,"* philosophically enjoying or fretting over the randomness of the universe. They seem to never shift gears and get into a "get-things-done" "time" frame and state.

Recognizing our *"time"* maps (whether the symbolism of some image or configuration or our linguistics) as maps and testing them for usefulness, enables us to shift these "time" frames as we move from event to event (remember, "time" doesn't move, we move and measure our movements by the concept of "time" hence our "tim-ing"). This gives us the ability to recognize our "time" consciousness and to choose those formats that support the behaviors, emotions, states, and skills that we want.

"Time" Consciousness

Our awareness of "time" generates within us *a "time" consciousness* which enables us to do mental "time" traveling as we have noted. We can, and do, travel to various *"time" zones* (which we designate as "past," present, and "future"). Time-traveling habits can cause us to get stuck in one of those zones to the exclusion of the others so that we seem to "live" in that zone. Those who get "stuck in the places of the past" [mis]use their memories and representations of previous events to play such thoughts-feelings over and over. They carry their "past" with them in this way and often re-trauma- tize themselves for years. Not exactly an enhancing way to live! This represents one of the dangers of misusing the "time" concept.

Our "time" consciousness generates the dimension of **psycholog- ical "time."** This refers to our felt sense about the speed of "time" passing (e.g. events occuring). We "feel" that "time" races, speeds, zips, disappears, vanishes, etc. This occurs whenever we access a state of concentration, focus, or "flow." At least it seems to us (psycho-logically, i.e. mentally-emotionally) that "time" races. Actually, the speed of the planet revolving and moving around the sun does not change. Only *our perception-and-feelings changed.* Psychologically, we experience *fast* "time." Fast "time" occurs when we read an absolutely fascinating book, see a captivating, edge-of-the-seat movie, engage in a highly intense conversation, etc.

Similarly, we experience *slow* "time" whenever we access a state of disinterest or boredom. Then suddenly we become highly aware of (conscious about) the movement of "time" (i.e. the clock). Then it seems like "time" drags, pokes along, and torturously lasts f-o- r-e-v-e-r! We experience slow "time" when we wait in line at the grocery store or in traffic, when we anticipate the visit of a loved one, when we wait for news of someone in an accident. In waiting, we become conscious of the passing of events ("time"). Other factors enter into the structure of "fast" and "slow" "time" (i.e. submodalities) as we indicate in the pattern in chapter twelve.

But afterwards... after a passage of events... another twist in this occurs. William James (1892) described it in this way,

> "A time filled with varied and interesting experiences seems short in passing, but *long as we look back*. On the other hand, a tract of time empty of experiences seems long in passing, *but in retrospect short*... The length in retrospect depends on the multitudinousness of the memories the time affords. Many objects, events, changes, many subdivisions widen the view as we look back. Emptiness, monotony, familiarity, make it shrivel up." (150-151, our emphasis).

So while in the midst of an exciting and captivating experience "time" seems to rush so that it quickly vanishes, but later, as we remember those events, we have much to fill in our awareness and so the "time" seems longer, more protracted. Welcome to *psychological "time!"*

"Time" as a facet of consciousness (a meta-state) also enables us to experience various forms of **spiritual "time."** The Greek word *kairos* describes one form of spiritual "time" (or psychological "time") inasmuch as it speaks about **the inner quality of the moment** and of events in contrast to *chronos* which speaks about external clock-time. We frequently speak about this as "the opportune moment," "the timely moment," "the special moment". *Kairos* describes the significant moment of insight, transformation, love, appreciation, etc. "At that time I woke up to what I was doing with my life...!"

"Eternity" and consciousness of such describe our awareness of the atemporal, the timelessness of something "beyond 'time,'" of our ultimate destiny. These "time" words refer to understandings that we label "spiritual" because they refer to transcendental realities.

3. "Time" Beliefs & Values

That story also highlights some other things about our experience and adventure as "time" creatures in "time" as we take charge of our "tim-ing." As we move from event to event, we all tend to build up various beliefs about time and these indicate various *"time"* values that we develop. Prior to our work together, my friend had developed several very nasty and negative beliefs about "time" that undermined his resourcefulness. Those beliefs had turned "time" into a Dragon that tormented him:

> "Time" is my enemy.
>
> I had a horrible past, therefore I can't expect anything better in the future.
>
> Since I can't see a bright future, I must have some learning disability.
>
> Since I tend to see negative things, I must "be" a negative person—and that's just the way I "am."

Talk about a load of *mental poison!* Toxic through and through! At one point, I turned and said to him, "You don't have a problem with 'time,' you have a problem with *your maps about 'time'!*" He needed clarification on that one.

"The fact that you went through some really crappy experiences with people who hurt you, abused you, neglected you, failed to meet your needs as a young child—you obviously found those *events* obnoxious, toxic, painful, inhuman, and unacceptable. Anybody would! But when you constructed conceptualizations *about* yourself, life, time, God, coping, reaching your potentials, etc., you build negative and toxic ones that took the hurt too seriously and then perpetuated it by building it as a map that you put right in front of you and which you then amplified with some very limiting beliefs about things.

"Anyone who fed their mind with irrational, toxic, ugly, and defeating *beliefs* like those would likewise feel negative, pessimistic, defeated, limited, etc. We just need to purge those toxic ideas so that they stop poisoning you! Your maps of these events and your map of that map just does not serve you well and just does not take you to resourceful places, does it?"

In other words, **the way you code and represent "time"** not only creates your "frame" of mind and "time" zone that you live in, but also your *state*. If you code "time" as **in** you—you enter into an "in time" state where you experience an eternal now, the everlasting moment. If you code "time" as *outside* of you—you enter into an "out-of-time" state where you have a clock-sense of time, know the "time," function well sequentially, etc. If you code "time" in a timeless way (in an atemporal way) you enter into a "beyond time" state wherein you transcend time. Most people experience this as a transcendental spiritual state.

As you think about "time," **so you experience "time."** How do you feel about "time?" Your friend or your enemy? As a pressure and demand or as a space for exploration and adventure? Track back to your "time" thoughts. What do you think about "time?" How do you language yourself about "time?" What changes do you need to make to how you have mapped "time?"

More "Time" Shifting

I (MH) recently conversed with a client who painfully complained, "I just don't have enough time, never have, and I never will." I asked her, "How often do you say this to yourself?" She didn't know for sure, but thought that she probably said it a couple times every hour. "Let's experiment." I said. "I want you to *observe* all of the things you say to yourself about 'time' this next week—keep a notebook, record the number of times you say you don't have enough 'time,' and bring it in." She did. Turned out she repeated that refrain an average of 10 times an hour!

"Another experiment," I said. "This week I want you to take this three-by-five card that says, 'I have plenty of 'time'—all the 'time' that anybody else has, and *I get to enjoy my movements from event to event*." I want you to read this aloud—convincingly—to yourself 10 times every hour for the next week."

She did. "At first it seemed silly and trite. At first I even felt foolish doing it. But eventually I didn't have to look at the card, I just said the words and then I began personalizing them. As I did, something shifted. I felt like I had just landed in Oz because everything suddenly seemed in color, bright, close." "The Uptime state!" I said. "Yes. It was like I had suddenly stepped into the present and stopped using 'half my mind' to anticipate and worry about the future!"

So a simple little **re-languaging** of how you talk about "time" can sometimes make all the difference in the world to how you experience your own "tim-ing." The rabbit in *Alice in Wonderland* had "no time." "I'm late, I'm late, no time, no time" he kept saying to himself. What state did that put him in? He felt pressured, rushed, tense, uptight, late. Have you ever languaged yourself that way? What results did you get?

How about using the line, "This too will pass."? It seems much better than the old lines, "Oh, no, this is horrible!" "This is the end of the world!" "I'm always in a rush!"

Why not do the *"time" experiment* for a week or two on yourself? Keep a notebook to record all of the things you *say to yourself* (and others) about "time." This timely exercise has surprised several people as it has made them more conscious about the unenhancing things they say (and therefore program themselves) about this concept ("tim-ing").

Conclusion

When Dr. Lloyd recently flew into Grand Junction for a visit (MH), one of the first things he shared when he got off the plane went like this, "You remember the old 60s song, 'It's my party and I can cry if I want to, cry if I want to'? I saw a bumper sticker, 'It's my midlife and I can crisis if I want to, crisis if I want to!'"

Well, *"It's your 'tim-ing' and you can do so unresourcefully and to your detriment if you want to,* if you want to! Or you can language it so that it functions as a most useful conceptual map moving you and taking you to places that make your life much more enjoyable, powerful, and enriched."

Chapter 13

Advanced Time-Lining Patterns

The Next Step

The primary "time" and time-line process that we have worked with in this book has involved traditional NLP time-line patterns. Using this we have presented numerous patterns for "time" traveling into the various time zones in order to get unstuck from the places of the past, to release old haunting events that still plague our mind-emotions, gaining new resources from the past, developing a more intense and powerful present moment, focus in the now of today with full "uptime" skills (sensory awareness), creating a bright and compelling future, architecting *tomorrow* today in powerful and enhancing ways.

In this chapter we introduce some new and advanced patterns involving various time-line processes.

Entering Into the Place of Pure Potentiality

This pattern came from the combined work of John Overdurf (1996) and Bob Bodenhamer (1996). We have formulated it here in a new way and with a new design.

The concept. Consider in a meditative way **what** exists or occurs *"before 'time.'"* If primary "time" involves the occurrence of events, happenings, activities, rhythms, etc., then before "time" we have no activity, no event, no rhythm—we only have *thought*. Before "time" then only "the quantum" (Overdurf) or "pure potentiality" (Bodenhamer) exists.

Overdurf takes his concepts from quantum mechanics and quantum physics and describes this, along with Julie Silverthorn, as "the place beyond words." In the quantum, things exist without form and void. Bodenhamer takes his concept from the Judeo-Christian perspective. There a biblical passage suggests the idea of "before being-ness" when one exists not as actuality, but potentiality.

> "Before I formed you in the womb I knew you, and before you were born I consecrated you..." (Jeremiah 1:5)

Here before Jeremiah existed as "Jeremiah" and had any actuality, before he took form as a living-breathing soul, he existed in the mind of God—as a *thought*. Here, too, as in the quantum, things exist without form (formless) in God's "eternity." Bodenhamer has written, "In this state, we existed prior to language, memories, decisions, meta-programs, values, beliefs, and attitudes." In other words, prior to the languaging we do to ourselves as we go *through* *events* and the languaged conclusions we draw *after* we experience various events.

So the place of pure potentiality, the place of quantum, exists *prior* to events, to actuality, to form, to language, etc. It exists as thought, as formless void, as potentiality. In terms of human consciousness—**we find the place of pure quantum potentiality in our thoughts**, especially in our meta-conceptual thoughts.

Figure 13:1

The Place of Pure Quantum Potentiality	The Place of Actuality
Pure Thought — Logos	Actions,Events,Phenomenon
The formless quantum prior to language	Language, labels, beliefs, understandings
No "time" (measuring, sequencing events)	"Time" ... the rhythm of happenings
Pure Potentiality: anything possible	Actuality: constraints of the real
Representational — Imaginary	Empirical
Map-Territory Possibility/ Usefulness	Map-Territory Correspondence, Accuracy

What can we do with this concept of pure potentiality? We have constructed the following pattern as a way to enter into it where you can create for yourself new potentials and possibilities, to move into an area of architecting, so that you can use your power of "pure thought" to relanguage yourself.

The Pattern

1. *Access the Void.* Quiet yourself in a place where you won't experience any distractions and relax comfortably into a nice trance-like state of concentration on the Void. See and hear and then feel the formlessness of you *before* your existence—yourself as

in the formless void of unlanguaged being. Feel yourself moving back further and further into that time before "time," before any events, any happenings, any actualization...

As one lady expressed it, all of her internal representations that had bothered her and made her feel so ugly and depressed she now saw "like clouds evaporating..." as she moved more and more into the place of pure potentiality... no time, no cognitive distortions, no misbeliefs, etc.

2. *Experience the Void fully.* And as you enter into this dimension of the unformed, the unarticulated, the unexpressed, the unactualized ... allow yourself to enjoy it... gently, wondering at how old constructions and formats so enmeshed and so compounded now so gently just come apart ... taking things back to a time when they existed as unformed... And you can wonder, really wonder, about all the potentialities that you now see and hear and feel in all of the component parts...

3. *Construct the Possible.* And as you notice all of the building blocks for effective human experiencing and functioning, for creativity, openness, bonding, love, effectiveness, excitement, passion, learning, helping, inventing, contributing, etc. you can begin to allow the process of reconstructing *a more glorious potential You*—a you that you would like to experience in the way you think and feel and speak and behave and relate... and as you gain greater awareness that in this place of pure potentiality you can construct this coming potential Self with all of the component resources ... and you can... now.

4. *Relanguage the Potential.* Now move forward toward "time" but not into "time" ... yet, but just hesitating as you imagine yourself ready to take a first step into "time" and ready to *language yourself for experiencing resourcefulness*—ready to utter your first Logos... feel all the excitement and anticipation of a new beginning...

5. *Step into "Time" with Your Pure Potentiality.* And now step into "time" languaging yourself with the words that keep your future open, that empower you for flexibility and learning and creativity ... and as you do then zoom up through the days and years of your life bringing these resources with you as you come...

Time Distortion Pattern — Fast & Slow Times

This pattern comes from the genius of Richard Bandler who says "There are two hypnotic phenomenon that are my all time favorites, fast and slow time distortion." This refers to the fact that our *brains* can create two very special kinds of psychological "time"—the sense of "time" moving very fast and the sense of "time" moving very slowly.

The fact that chronological and cosmic "time" does not do this, nor do the events of life, at the macro-level, move any quicker or slower, only *we feel that they do* informs us that all of this occurs inside. It operates as a psycho-logical function of *representation*. And with the NLP attitude and methodology, this inevitably leads us to ask, "*How* does our brain pull this piece of subjectivity off?" "What comprises the internal structure of 'fast' and 'slow' time?" (We have written this as an exercise to do with another person).

The Pattern

1. *Identify the person's time-line.* First begin by noticing and recognizing how the person has his or her "time" organized. How does he or she differentiate between the past and the future?

2. *Assist getting the person into state.* Since an essential part of high quality eliciting involves assisting a person to access state, then present to them various samples of "times" when "time" seemed to move quickly and slowly. Use your voice and tone to speak in a congruent way. Since we need to get people really into state so that they can access the critical information, use your tone, tempo and voice effectively as you mention times when you know from your own experience that "time" seemed to crawl (speak in a veerryyy slloooow tonality).In order to fully get a person back into the state in order to get the best elicitation we also want to stack our presentation so that we use quotes, metaphors, stories, etc. in order to layer a person's internal sense of contexts and context-of-contexts. Why? Because as "time" operates from a meta-level, so fast and slow "time" operate by means of the comparisons we use.

3. *Identify your submodalities of fast time and slow time.* Elicit the person's unique way of representing these different subjective experiences. Take your list of submodalities and go down that list doing a contrastive analysis between when "time" seems "fast" and when it seems "slow."

As you do this, find pleasant instances of slow "time." Reference experiences where "time" moved along very slowly *and* very pleasurably. Think about a day that once occurred when you felt "just wonderful," and which seemed to last forever. Perhaps the first day of a long awaited vacation, when you work all year and then went off on a vacation and during that first day it seemed that "time" just stood still.

In such a memory or imagined representation, find the coding that enables you to feel like you have lots of "time" to do things, when "time" moves very slowly when you move very quickly.

Next find a time when "time" zoomed by. The moment came for something and then before you turned around, the event had ended. It passed as if in no time. You have the feeling, "Where did the time go?" "Two hours have passed? No, it can't be!"

4. *Juxtapose the "time" elicitations and identify the specific submodality differences.* Now take your two kinds of "time" and do a comparison between them. What differences exist between when "time" moves quickly and when it moves slowly? Does the difference lie in the position you use in your mind for the two? Do you have one "time" coded with associated images and the other with dissociated images?

Bandler says that unusual aspects will occur in these representations and that this elicitation will not fit the usual list of submodalities.

"With Time Distortion you may also have a difference between parts of the images. Sometimes the center of the images will be moving quickly, while other parts will be moving slowly, or the side of the images will be moving fast. It's a funny phenomenon. When you're blowing down the freeway going really fast and you pull off into a forty-mile an hour zone, you feel like you're crawling. Do you know what I'm talking about? Whereas if you go from a twenty mile zone into a forty-five you feel like you're going fast."

5. *Utilize the time-line.* Regardless of the configuration of the person's time-line, have them see their time-line out in front of them. Then have the person turn physically and literally, while you do the elicitation so that he or she stands up, turns, and literally *backs up* to the last time they can remember experiencing exquisitely slow time. Check out what it looks like so that they can refresh their memory.

Next have them back up, associatedly, to an instance of fast time. As they back up to these memories—have them let their future disappear in front of them, and then literally pull the events now around them back up as they saw, hear and felt it. And they can pull those events around them until they come fully into that event. "Take a moment and relive fully this event and enjoy the process while you notice all the distinctions."

6. *Re-orient and elicit.* When you complete this, ask the person to realign their time-line so that it goes back and they come into the now "time." Having done this, you can do the conscious elicitation to find out their difference between slow "time" and fast "time."

7. *Distill the information.* Do this time elicitation twice, first when you orient the person back in their time-line to get them into state and second when you bring them back. After you bring them all the way back out, get the submodality information distinctions.

8. *Anchor both fast and slow "time."* As you do, especially pay attention because this can become tricky. When the person does slow "time" and you discover a difference in one submodality, accentuate it and anchor it. Get an anchor on one knee for fast "time" and another on the other knee for slow "time." This will provide you two very powerful anchors.

9. *Identify two experiences*. First identify an experience that you would like to endow with a greater sense of *more "time."* Think of something that goes by too quickly, something that you would like to last a lot longer. Can you think of something like that? Then identify something that you would like to get over a lot quicker.

10. *Access a trance state*. "Allow yourself to close your eyes and go away to another time and place so that you can begin to make preparations to feel yourself *let go* deeper into a trance than you have before... now, so that you can begin to float back on the wings of time and change. And go way, way back. Because what I want to do, speaking to you as a child, involves beginning to get a little bit younger with each breath, a year at a time... becoming younger and younger. Seeing perhaps a birthday or a pleasant event from each year as you *step back* in your mind, getting a little bit younger, and a little bit younger with each breath.

And as you get younger, you can recapture that childlike ability to learn, really learn, and to experience things. Because when you were very young, a month seemed like forever. And as you get older, months seem to just zip by. And when a child, a month seemed like a long time, and an hour took forever. In fact, five minutes seemed to last an eternity....

Now let your unconscious remember how to feel time as slow and fast and to feel it fully (fire anchors). Because your unconscious remembers how you experimented to find out those distinctions, and it can remember fully... now.

And in a moment when I reach over and touch your knee like this (fire anchor for fast time) you will zip back to an event that went really fast... but because you want it to last a lot longer, when I touch this knee (fire anchor for slow time), you can experience time as moving verryyy sloooowlly. It will almost stand still. And as it does you can relive that event in real time of two minutes, but it will seem like an hour.

Spiraling Resource Experiences In Time
—Collapsing Into The Now

The Concept. We adapted and developed this pattern from the one presented by Eric Robbie in *Accessing Your Ferocious Self* (Hall, 1996). It involves imagining a configuration of a spiral or a set of circles.

The Pattern

1. Imagine yourself in a wide-open space in this moment in time fully associated and fully present to your thoughts-and-feelings. As you do, allow yourself to think back to a number of delightfully resourceful experiences of your past—beginning by thinking of such an experience that occurred last year... And once you see and hear and feel that experience, step back into this *moment in time* and imagine that experience circling around you as the planets move around the sun. Watch it circle around you as if you stood in the middle of a spiral.

2. Eventually let it settle back to where you first found it— a year ago, and do the same thing with a resourceful memory from two years ago, and again, one from 3 to 5 years ago. As you find, and re-experience each resource let it become another orbiting event as if a planet of resourcefulness moving around you as in a spiral.

3. Now imagine fully and completely a delightful resource that you want to experience in the coming year, in the year after that, and then in the time between 3 and 5 years from now. Again, let each experience move around you in a circle as another rotating planet of resourcefulness moving around.

4. Next, stepping into the middle of these spiraling, circling resources—just allow yourself to notice them moving around you —at different distances, perhaps moving at different speeds, moving into your past, moving into your future, And as you allow them to rotate as a spiral you know that you can breath deeply and fully in the center of all of these colorful, bright, and exciting resources that surround you and you can wonder, really wonder, what will happen, in just a moment when they collapse into you... fully and completely so that you can again experience them fully from within...

Figure 13:2

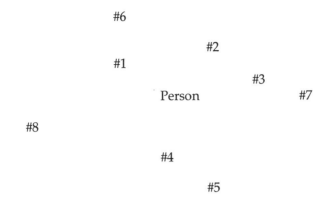

Developing Your Ability to Access the Flow State of the Eternal Now

The Concept. When it comes to primary, "In Time" experience (Chapter 13), concentration obligates *"time" awareness.* Experientially this means that when we access an intense focused concentration on some event, object or person, we lose consciousness of "time" as a concept and enter, phenomenologically, into what we might call "the eternal now." We experience primary level *timelessness.* "Time" stops, or "time" ceases to exist as a filter for our ongoing experience.

This experience of *timelessness* arises because we cease to have any experience of awareness of other events by which to compare the present moment experience. It ceases because (in terms of foreground/background construction), we have entered so much into the foreground, that perceptually the background has disappeared. For us, as a phenomenon, it no longer exists.

Csikszentmihalyi (1990) has described this as the experience of *flow.* It speaks about the kind of concentration that frequently arises from deep hypnosis, trance-states, entranced in a movie, a message, prayer, love making, etc. William Glasser (1967) addressed this flow state as a psycho-neurological "positive addiction." He defined this as involving a simple and repetitive task (event, experience) wherein one enjoys it for itself. This experience lacks a state of evaluative judgment about it (hence no meta-awareness). It has inherent value and significance for us and involves something that can increase our skill as we practice it, and one that we can eventually do without conscious awareness. Glasser included as examples of this meditation, prayer, running, etc. For Glasser the central distinguishing factor of a positive addiction lies in the fact that it leaves the person stronger, more resourceful, relaxed, re-invigorated, more able to get back to the tasks of life in "time." To cultivate your ability of entering into the *eternal now*, the following process describes a lifestyle structure for training yourself in timelessness.

The Pattern

1. Identify a small, simple and enjoyable activity; hitting a ball, walking, running, reading, sewing, etc.

2. In your mind, run through your reasons and motives for why and how you value the activity *in and of itself*. The more inherent values and meanings that you can ascribe to the activity—the more you frame it as *inherently valuable*. This releases you from any need of going meta and evaluating it. It already has value—inherently.

3. Decide to give yourself to this activity for 30 minutes; three or four times a week. This enables you to enjoy the benefits of ongoing repetition. This also enables you to allow the activity to eventually drop out of conscious awareness and to operate at an unconscious level as a "habit." This usually takes between twenty and forty days.

4. Relax and accept the joy of the activity as you experience it.

Developing More Time for Patience — NOW!

The Concept. **Patience** and **impatience** represent emotions of "time." These emotions arise from the thoughts-and-feelings we have about "time" whether schedule time, psychological time, sacred time, or some other meta-level awareness of "time." In the state of **patience** we think, represent, believe and therefore feel that we have plenty of time, or enough time, whereas in

impatience we do the opposite. We think-feel that we don't have enough time, that we have a scarcity of "time," that we need to hurry, rush, go quicker, etc.

These emotions, like all emotions, operates primarily as internal representations *drive* it. When we track back an emotion to the "thought" (the internal coding) out of which it comes—we find representations that encourage impatience, frustration, anger, upsetness, demandingness, etc. To undo this unpleasant and, generally, unuseful emotional state, we need to recode our sense of "time."

The Pattern

1. *Access your representation of "time"* toward or in which you feel impatient, angry, rushed, upset, etc. Identify specifically **what** kind of "time" you have reference to: scheduling time, psychological time, etc.

2. *Discover the impatience.* How do you know you think-feel impatient about this? What lets you know that you feel impatience? Elicit your strategy for adopting this attitude (this position) toward it. Do so using the *meaning* search.

  - "What does it mean to me if I don't get all of these things accomplished?"
  - "What does it mean if I have this and that project demanding a deadline?"
  - "What does it mean that this activity seems boring?"

The structure of impatience necessarily involves a bringing of a state of necessity or demandingness (from yourself or others) upon some primary state of activity or inactivity. This makes it essential to discover the source of that *demandingness.*

3. *Challenge the demandingness.* In NLP we generally find the modal operators of necessity and use the meta-model challenges to deframe the ill-formedness of the structure. In REBT (Rational-Emotive Behavioral Therapy), following Ellis, one argues against the "musts" and "shoulds" and "haves to" one finds philosophically.

- "Why must I accomplish this by Tuesday? I agree that I would prefer to do so, but why 'must' I?"
- "What would happen if I don't get everything done today that I want to get done?"

In exposing the *demandingness*, we often find that we have simply operated from an old impatient program of disliking delay gratification and have conditioned ourselves for low frustration tolerance and that no logical reason argues for the harvest at every moment. Seeing the childishness and immaturity of demandingness helps us deframe it.

4. *Move to a meta-position to accept the feelings of impatience.* By going to a meta-level position and fully *accepting* our thoughts-and-feelings of impatience, we can then relax comfortably in the knowledge of our state. By bringing acceptance, appreciation, calmness, etc. to bear on the impatience, we have meta-stated ourselves into a more resourceful place.

5. *Give yourself more "time."* From the position of acceptance-of-impatience, alter your representations of future "time"—seeing more space, more room, more distance all the while re-languaging yourself, "I have plenty of time and refuse to threaten myself in an erroneous way by thinking of 'time' in terms of scarcity." "I will take effective action to do what I can and leave it at that."

Chrono-phobia Cure Pattern

The Concept. Some people seem to think, and therefore feel, that they "never have enough time available." They rush around always in a hurry, and yet unable to truly show much productivity for the time invested. Consequently, they may develop a constant fear of not enough "time," or that somehow they will "lose" time or "waste" time or miss time. As this habituates, they become *"time" phobics.* If you mention "time" to them, they have a semantic reaction! It "pushes their buttons."

The Pattern

First use the previous pattern, "Developing More Time for Patience." If the person still has not gotten over their meta-level phobia about "time," then have them do the following.

1. *Step back from "time" and from your "self"* and notice the structure of your inner crowding. If the demandingness and pressure about "time" doesn't come from one of the sources in the previous pattern, it undoubtedly arises from an unconscious level wherein you have lots and lots and lots of activities occurring within; conflicting and warring *activities*, each demanding "time." Go inside and ask the following:

- "What part within me wants more time?"
- "What do you want to do during this time?"

2. *Negotiate between the conflicting parts.* Again, go inside and invite these conflicting parts about the meta-outcomes. "When you get what you want, what will that give you? In what way do you evaluate that as having value and importance?" Continue asking about meta-outcomes of those outcomes until both parts have identified an outcome that they can agree upon.

3. *Use the new highest level meta-outcome as an agreement frame for the two parts.* In this way, you can frame the behavior of each part as seeking to accomplish something of value that the other can also appreciate. This cuts out the conflicting and enables the parts to operate and communicate with more respect for each other.

Conclusion

These patterns indicate the *plasticity of "time"* as a construct and therefore as an experience in our lives. By taking charge of our coding and encoding processes at whatever meta-levels necessary, we can make "time" operate as an enhancing factor in our lives rather than living as its victim.

Chapter 14

Linguistic Time-Lining

Conversational Time-Line Processes
Resourcing Your Time-Line Linguistically

"Narrative is the Guardian of time."
(Ricoeur)

In the previous chapters we have provided many visual diagrams, metaphors, and constructions with regard to managing and transforming "time" and time-lines. We have also utilized numerous *linguistic patterns* for expressing and working with this. In this final chapter, we want to focus exclusively on **linguistic time-lining**. In doing this, we aim to identify the kinds of languaging, language distinctions, and language patterns essential in this process. We also have identified several specific time-linings that you can do *conversationally*.

Paul Ricoeur (1971) has written,

> "To have a present, as we have learned from Benveniste, someone must speak. The present is then indicated by the coincidence between an event and the discourse that states it. To rejoin lived time starting from chronicle time, therefore, we have to pass through linguistic time, which refers to discourse." (3:108-09).

These ideas provide additional information regarding why "personality" can transform when we work with "time" and time-line processes. We experience healing and suffering as we do because of the *narrative* we have coded and represented regarding "the events of our lives." We have summarized the "time" of our life using a script, plot, or theme that codes it in a linguistic form. This anchors a meta-level belief system that thereby keeps us in distress and/or limits our choices. "The story of my life can be summarized in one word— failure." (victim, bum, etc.)

Using a one-word or short phrase to generalize the meaning of "time" can create a very limited mental map. At such times, we need a *new narrative*. Yet often, we get and feel stuck because we literally do not know of *anything* else that we could possibly say about our experiences than what we have already said about them which comprises multitudes of ugly and hurtful meanings.

With the configuration and diagram of a time-line that we have used, we have a method by which we can go *above* time, and from there think about time, and recode the happenings that occurred to us *in* time, sometimes prior to "the time" and sometimes from "within" the time.

Here we seek to do it strictly linguistically.

The Concept

Overdurf and Silverthorn (1995) have used the Meta-Model to highlight two facets of our language use. Namely, how much we use language to create boxes that limit us, and how we can learn to use language to free us from such boxes.

White and Epston (1990) in **Narrative Means to Therapeutic Ends** presented a form of Brief Therapy, known as Narrative Therapy. They essentially package a person's experience as *"the story"* that people live and how to think about change or transformation as needing to "de-story" a client. This refers to getting them to stop telling themselves some old dysfunctional story, and to re-story themselves with another plot and theme.

Narrative Therapy offers numerous processes for re-storying a person with new and more powerful and productive stories. In Narrative Therapy, the therapist inquires about who has storied them, what themes, plots, dramas, etc. have someone storied them with, what stories work well and what stories stink. Narrative relates to "time" as a meta-structure. It provides an easy and quick way to summarize classes of events and attribute meaning to those events.

Meerloo (1970) describes therapy itself as "an introduction into continuity" (147). In other words, many people need psychotherapy because they suffer a misalignment to "time," to continuity, to an order patterning of events, etc.

Paul Ricoeur (1983),

> "The notion of time as *lived*, psychological and individual, is expressed through the term vita; the second, based on the concept of writing, is rendered through the term libro. These two notions of writing and lived time merge in the topos of the book of memory, bearing directly on the ways in which narrativity can represent human temporality." (28).

> "I see in the plots we invent the privileged means by which we re-configure our confused, unformed, and at the limit, mute temporal existence." (xi, 1983 Vol. I).

> "My basic hypothesis that between the activity of narrating a story and the temporal character of human experience there exists a correlation that is not merely accidental but that presents a transcultural form of necessity. To put it another way, time becomes human to the extent that it is articulated through a narrative mode, and a narrative attests its full meaning when it becomes a condition of temporal existence." (52).

The episodic dimension of a narrative draws *narrative time* in the direction of a linear representation of "time" by using the linguistic structure of "then, and then..." This describes the simplest form of narrating which results in a story. In this way we *narrate our lives* by sequencing and punctuating events. Yet in doing so we selectively pick and choose events, delete other events, and punctuate them in various ways so that we create a syntax, a strategy, and a meta-structure of meaning via our narrating.

The end result? A story. A narrative, and this narrative operates as "the Guardian of time" (Ricoeur). It encodes it in a large level format and this makes it difficult to change. When we create a narrative or story, we impose a structure on a set of events that enables us to group them together in various ways. It also provides us with rules for eliminating other stories as having any relevance in our mind.

Transforming "Time" by Generating New Sentences

Since personality arises from our use of "time," and since narrative tends to operate as a large-level linguistic structure that guards "time" and structures "time" (the events we've experienced), we invite you to explore your "time" narratives. Use one of the following *sentence stems* and generate 5 to 10 sentence completions. This will invite you to generate some of your current and operational linguistic time-lining "programs."

- *Up until now the story of my life has comprised a story of ...*" (Prompters include: a victim, a failure, bad luck, stress, rejection, ease, success, liked by lots of people, etc.)
- *If I described the plot that the narrative of my life has enacted....* (A tragedy, a drama, a soap-operate, the lone ranger, etc.).
- *Say aloud, Up until now...* I have thought, believed, felt, acted.... Then fully describe and express what has characterized some facet of how you have responded mentally, conceptually, emotionally, verbally, behaviorally, etc.

Once you have identified the "past" linguistically in this way, then complete the statement,

> *"But from this day on... I will increasingly develop into more of a person who...*

The social constructionism in Narrative Therapy underscores that our stories exist as constructions that we have built on the given messages and narratives offered us by our culture, family, and friends. One of the key patterns in that domain involves **externalizing.** This refers to creating a new story about experiences, problems, emotions, etc. as one shifts from telling the story that "I am X..." where X refers to some experience, definition, etc. *The externalizing story* de-constructs the old narrative and invites one to step into a separation of person and behavior. "The Mads have had a long history in sneaking up and tempting me to give way to them." "Yes, Misunderstanding has lured us into treating each other as enemies, but now that we have turned the light on Misunderstanding, we have caught many of its tricks."

Think of a "problem" that you have experienced frequently (an emotion, behavior, circumstance, linguistic label) and externalize it. To an eight year old boy who wetted his bed, whom his mother introduced to me in a counseling session as her "little bed wetter" (internalized story of identity), when I found out that he didn't do it intentionally, but that it sneaks up on him when he least suspects it, I said, "So have you ever stood up to Sneaky Pee and refused to let him get you in trouble?" Yes, he had stood up to Sneaky Pee. As I did some cheer-leading about that, he began to feel more and more pride of his resistance! "Let's figure out some sneaky ways we can do it to this Sneaky Pee!"

Internalizing shows up linguistically in NLP as nominalizations and in general semantics as identification. Externalizing empowers us to tell a whole new story about the events we have come through in "time." It creates a new narrative.

Finding the un-storied narrative in your life offers another linguistic time-lining pattern. We do it in NLP with *counter-examples*. Brief therapy does it with exceptions. Narrative Therapy does it with *unique outcomes* that identify "sparkling events" that provide us the seed for planting the ideas that we can grow into a new narrative. Asking *the how question* frequently brings this out. After identifying a counter-example, we can ask, "How did you do that?"

- How did you not fall into self-pity, but just kept at it?
- How did you resist not losing your cool, and listened to your boss anyway?
- How did you not discount yourself in that instance?
- How did you prevent things from getting even worse with all of that happening?

Since questions about sequences of behaviors and responses *link the past, present, and future together* to create a narrative of drama and action, asking questions that presuppose enhancing responses enables us to assist people in re-narrating their life.

"How long have you cared about improving yourself and making a significant contribution? Have you had any times when you felt that way? Why did you choose to prefer to live your life that way?"

The first question identifies the resource, the second question invites the person to access historical events, the third encourages them to justify, explain, and build up semantic reasons for it. Such questioning encourages people to "thicken the plot" of their preferred life's plot (Freedman and Combs, 1996).

Linguistic Re-Narrating Life

1. *Discover your story.* What story have you lived in up until now? Who storied you with that story? Does it exist as part of your cultural story, racial story, religious story, family story, etc.? How much of the story did you personally buy or create? Tell about the theme of your life and listen to your narrative story. What kind of narrating do you do? Do you tell a story of victimhood or survival, of failing or winning, of connecting or disconnecting, of being loved or rejected, etc.?

2. *Step aside from the story.* Evaluate the usefulness, productivity, value, emotional enjoyment, etc. of that story. Would you recommend living in that story to anyone else? How well has this narrative served you? What doesn't work very well or feel very well about that story? What story would you prefer to tell?

3. *Make up a new story.* Just for fun, make up a wild and woolly story. Use your pretender to its fullest capacity! What positive and bright "sparkling moments" have you experienced that have not fit into your dominant story? What unique outcomes that seem at odds with your problem-saturatured story would you have liked to have grown into your dominant story? How would that have played out? What story would you have wished to have lived? Who do you know that you admire and appreciate; what story do they tell themselves about their self, others, the world, etc.?

4. *Step into the re-story.* Via your imagination, fully and completely step into the re-story and experience it fully in all of your sensory systems. Anchor it. Enrich it with details and find audiences to perform it before.

5. *Future pace.* Now imagine moving out into tomorrow living out that story...

Linguistically De-Storying & Re-Storying Life

These language patterns enable us to "de-story" our life and to "re-story" ourselves. This provides a marvelous route to transformation through a re-storying process. The following language pattern comes from John Overdurf (1995).

The Pattern

1. *Pace a problem* by asking a person or client to go back to a problematic decision that did not turn out very well. Ask them to associate back into the limiting or hurtful decision.

2. *Explore the location (place) where you made that decision.* "Where were you when you were deciding that?"

3. *Move to before the decision.* Invite the person to move (conceptually) to a place prior to the decision. "... And just before that, where were you?" In response to this a person has to move to a prior past place.

4. *Expand the person's sense of choice.* "Now, just allow yourself to notice how many options you have in this place...now. And as you think about your present situation in life, you can allow yourself also to consider all the options and choices that you have now..." (This collapses the non-mirror image reverse with the present problem, Chapter 7.)

5. *Re-associate back to the beginning—in the present.* "Now think of that problem and notice how you feel now?"

6. *Future pace.* "As you think about the next time you may do X, knowing what you know now, notice how much better you feel, not doing it."

The change here occurs at position #3 (using the diagram from Chapter 4) when a person moves neurologically to a position prior to the installation of a decision.

Case Study: *Linguistically De-Storying & Re-Storying Life*

This pattern works extremely well in dealing with regret, as well as loosening up and sometimes eliminating limiting beliefs.

Robert first wished to work on "low self-esteem" and the inability to become involved in a meaningful relationship. Although in his mid-thirties, Robert had never formed a meaningful relationship with a member of the opposite sex. Over a few sessions, we resolved this problem so that Robert started dating and forming meaningful relationships. Recently he informed me that he would soon marry "the girl of his dreams."

Two years after he had resolved that problem, Robert called to work on another difficulty. Although intelligent and a graduate of a prestigious university and also having knowledge of NLP and other trainings, Robert just could not get himself to perform effectively in business. Indeed, he depended upon his mother for providing him with a house and living expenses(!).

From our previous work, I knew that Robert's father had severely abused his mother. On one occasion, his father forced his way into the family's apartment and pointed a pistol in the face of Robert's mother, threatening to kill her. This incident traumatized Robert. Soon afterwards, Robert's mother took Robert and his older brother from North Carolina to Pennsylvania and left them with her parents. She then went back to rebuild her life without Robert's dad with the plan to create a suitable home for Robert and his brother.

Yet to seven-year-old Robert, the trauma from his father's behavior coupled with his mother leaving him with his grandparents produced a deep core belief, "Mother does not love me! If she loved me, she would not have left me with my grandparents." So even though his mother maintained constant contact with Robert, he nonetheless *believed and felt deserted.*

Then to complicate matters, out of that *mis*belief, Robert unconsciously **decided** that if he once got his mother back, he "would become too dependent on her to ever leave me again." His childish thinking went, "If I remain dependent on her for support, she will never leave me again." Obviously, this unconscious part worked well in sabotaging his success as a businessman!

A year later Robert contacted me for another session. He now sold annuities that he marketed through presentations to senior citizen groups that needed some help. He also made an unusual request—would I come by and look at his home and office? "Okay, sure." As I drove into his driveway I noticed an immaculate yard and driveway, the outside of the home as newly painted, and a very attractive place.

Upon entering I discovered a totally remodeled home. Robert had created a prestigious looking reception area, and off to the side, a conference room with conference tables and chairs. Robert also had a fully-equipped office and beyond the reception area he had a training room with professionally prepared visuals and an overhead projector. Downstairs Robert had an apartment for himself. I felt impressed.

"Bob," he said, "I have everything ready to do business. Most of this work I did myself. I have even enlisted a partner. But, I just can't pick up that phone and schedule my first presentation. That's why I need your help."

"What would you say about doing it now?"

"Yes!" he responded and his non-verbals indicated that he had accessed the kinesthetics of the problem as we spoke. As I inquired about his mental map, he immediately flashed back on some old memories of both his father and mother deserting him. As he accessed and felt that pain, I said, "Robert, where were you when you decided not to be successful in business?"

"At the time when my mother left me in Pennsylvania."

"And just before that... *where* were you?"

"Well, I was just a little biddy boy doing what little boys do." As he said this, his physiology shifted dramatically so that his face began to have more normal coloring and he looked more resourceful.

"NOW," I said, "just notice from this place just how many options you have about being successful... As you think about your present situation in life, how many of all the options and choices you have about being successful NOW do you notice?"

"Well, many... I feel unlimited in my business. From here I see that there are no limitations to what I can do. It is unbelievable how successful I can be." His face shone as he spoke, and his voice became more and more enthusiastic.

"NOW I want you to think of that problem that you previously had mentioned to me, and just notice how you feel *NOW...*"

"I can't. There's no problem. I don't have a problem."

"And as you think about the next time you may sabotage your success, knowing what you know now, and noticing how much better you feel, not doing it...."

"I ... I am going to be successful. I can just feel it. ... Hey, what did you do? You did something. I was trying to figure it out but I got so caught up in the changes that I couldn't figure it out. You did something, didn't you?"

"Yes, Robert. I call it linguistic time-lining. The language we shared between us enabled you to go back to *above* and *before* the installation of that old belief and provided you with a context wherein you made some new and far more resourceful choices. Once you made the choices, the language allowed you to collapse the new choices and resources with the old problem and eliminate it. How do you feel now?"

"Great! Just absolutely great!"

Afterwards we talked for a few minutes and agreed that he should spend that evening completing any other integration he may feel the need to complete. We also arranged for a follow up session at a later time.

Twenty minutes after driving home, I received a phone call from Robert. Excitedly he said, "Bob, after you left I decided to go to work. I called three groups and lined up one presentation."

"How long has it been since you had scheduled a presentation?"

"Why, a year or more."

A week later, Robert called to reschedule the appointment due to some business conflicts. As I inquired about things, Robert reported, "The day after that linguistic time-lining, my partner and I went out and made some calls. We made $4800 between us."

"Wow! Sounds like you've got that problem licked!" And he did.

Developing a New Rhythm for "Time"

The Concept. Primary "time" as we have noted, involves the *rhythm* of various activities. Yet how often do we notice or consciously work with our rhythms? Rhythms play an obvious role in some activities, notably in music and dance. Here we keep "time" by finding the beat and getting into that rhythm. We also tend to have conscious awareness of the rhythms of some activity patterns in life: rising and retiring, making love, going to work/leaving work, going to school/leaving for home, etc.

More recently, we have developed increasing awareness of the body rhythms within our biological "clocks." We have diurnal time every twenty-four hours that establishes rhythms of hunger, alertness, sleepiness, etc. We have biorhythmic time established and regulated by neuro-secretory cells in the diencephalon in the central part of the brain near the pineal gland with its autonomic rhythm that establishes life itself.

We also have increased awareness of the danger of violating these rhythms. Such awareness shows up in our understanding of "jet lag," a tyrannical parental clock setting a rhythm for a baby and young child's more natural rhythms. "You are going to eat because it is time to eat!"

Yet we have left out a whole range of activities that we have failed to connect with some kind of rhythm, and to the extent that we do, we can get out-of-sync with the rhythms of that event or the rhythms within larger systems or in other people. Couples frequently complain about "being out of sync." They just don't seem to find each other's beat and learn to enter into that rhythm.

The Pattern

1. *Awareness.* Move to a meta-position to "time" and to the meta-level of "times" and allow yourself to simply begin to experience awareness of the kinds of rhythms and beats within each "time" dimension. Awareness of primary time involves the rhythm of the earth's rotating, the moon's circling, etc. We can easily experience awareness of this. Developing awareness of the rhythms of historical time (past, present, future sequencing) also comes fairly easily, as does developmental time awareness (psycho-social stages, psycho-sexual stages, life stages, etc.).

But what about awareness of the rhythms of mortal time: life, growth, sickness, death? How accepting and/or appreciating do you think-feel about this "time?" And what about awareness of psychological time? Fast time and slow time, the times of your life in terms of story and narrative?

2. *Resource application.* What resources do you need to access and "bring to bear" upon this "time" awareness? To find a beat or rhythm in anything we have to first accept the beat, and accept a willingness to enter into it, and to feel it. Do this with any "time" that you feel out-of-sync with.

3. *Enjoying the beat.* After acceptance and understanding of rhythm comes enjoying the rhythm so that we can truly dance to it and with it. So move to another meta-level and accept the state of joyfulness and "bring it to bear" (meta-state) with that joy... wondering, really wondering, what enhancing meanings can you adopt that will enable you to enjoy the beat and dance to it gracefully...

Developing a Neurological Rhythm for "Time" and "Times"

The Concept. Edward Hall (1983) noted the importance of biological "time" in terms of rhythms, the ebb and flow of tides and seasons.

> "No form of life evolved in a timeless non-rhythmic world.... life developed patterns for sleeping, eating, mating, foraging, hunting, playing, learning, being born, dying... Nothing can grow in a healthy way unless it is a time-controlled, uniform manner: and unregulated (out-of-phase) growth of cells in the body characterizes cancer" (18).

This suggests that perhaps, just perhaps, at the heart of so many forms of psychosomatic illness, distress and disease lies an out-of-phase state of consciousness. And what lies at the heart of living in an *out-of-sync* lifestyle? Not knowing, recognizing, or accepting the *beat* of life's events.

Traditionally in psychology and psychotherapy, the idea of accepting our reality, whether we like it or not, separates the neurotic from the "normal" person. The person "full of nerves" (nervousness, "neurotic") experiences a semantic reaction within mind-body *against* some fact of reality—and so they turn their psychic energies against themselves and against reality. We can hear it in how they language themselves:

"I hate getting older."
"I hate my looks."
"I can't stand the way he looks at me or talks to me."
"I can't stand criticism..."
"It really bothers me when things don't go the way I expect them to go..."
"Why do things have to be so hard? Why can't they be easy?"

The Meta-States Model addresses this by inviting one to "bring to bear" a resourceful state of acceptance, acknowledgement, recognition and even appreciation to any and all primary states and experiences. This realigns our powers so that we find the rhythm, beat or pattern of the experience and then dance with it in a better way. We pace the beat and then lead elsewhere. Then we can dance with "the fact" (our realization of the fact) that we will get older and lose many of our "powers." We dance gracefully with the fact of our mortality, fallibility, fears, angers, etc.

The Pattern

1. *Identify a misalignment or malalignment.* What rhythm, beat, pattern of activities, etc. do you seem or feel out-of-sync with? Examine the various life stages of Erickson's development chart (Chapter 7). What conceptual reality do you seem at odds with?

2. *Identify the beat or rhythm in that area.* For example, in the arena of physical well-being we find that the rhythm of life involves growth and plateaus, development and arrestment of growth for consolidation, sickness and pain, healing and growth, etc. In the arena of relationships, we have closeness and distance, a breathing in and out of coming together into moments of intimacy, and then moving apart as we experience times of distance. In life, every arena has its own unique rhythms and patterns. Thus in the emotional arena, we ride a rollercoaster of positive and negative emotions that move us up and down emotionally. To expect all of life to function as an "up" and then as an "uppity up" (to quote Lucy of the Peanuts cartoons) puts us in an out-of-harmonious relationship to reality.

3. *Accept the rhythm.* Quiet yourself, go inside and access a strong state of acceptance, acknowledgement, or even appreciation and "bring it to bear" on whatever rhythms, patterns, and beats that you find in life that you want to attain a better alignment with.

"Time" Alignment Pattern

The Concept. Meerloo (1970) noted the "time" confusions and "time" sicknesses that people can experience either through drugs like LDS, various brain tumors, or in schizophrenia. Such *chronotaraxis* or temporal ataxia (pages 70-71) can engender all kinds of distortions in personality.

"In schizophrenics, the unity of experiencing reality through different senses is broken. Some of these patients actually have the feeling that they are living in different time fragments. They are not able to connect and integrate these time-lines, 'before' frequently comes 'after.'

One such patient had built up a delusional system on these time failures. He felt never alive after he was hospitalized. His body was dead and timeless; his eyes looked only into the past; but with his hands he could touch the future. He experienced this future as a powerful electronic current containing magic power." (130).

This suggests that we can get out of alignment with our representations of "time" and especially with "past," present and "future" time. So like the Aligned Self pattern in NLP that describes how a person can get out of alignment with their representations of first person (associated and seeing, hearing and feeling out of their own eyes), second person (VAK from the person with whom they communicate) and third person (any other perceptual position), so a person could get disoriented with regard to "past", present and "future".

Meerloo (1970) again,

"A division or split between the personal clock or ego time and the time of the world is part of the pathology seen in schizophrenia. Schizophrenics live in different time worlds" (155).

"We see here a typical schizophrenic time experience in living in a timeless archaic world without rhythm, without night and day—a kind of oceanic experience of time, like that supposedly experienced by the fetus in the womb. Many schizophrenics think about their psychotic episode as an empty eternity; they are aware of their loss of time consciousness. Their weak egos are not able to bring order into their experience. Their inner pilot has lost his bearings." (page 156 emphasis added).

The Pattern

1. *Access your "past," present, and "future" representations.* Notice how fully and completely in terms of your VAK representations you can fully enter into them and experience these "time" zones. Does your time-line move forward sequentially in an ordered way. Or do you find it disordered? If so, what kind of disorder? What kind of randomness, gaps, out-of-sequence patterning do you find?

2. *Center yourself in your "present."* Fully access a sensory-based awareness so that you have all of your eyes, ears, skin, etc. open to the moment. Anchor this state.

3. *Realign your "past" to your present.* From a fully resourceful and centered state in the moment, realign your representations of the past—representing the events that you have transversed—so that you can have access to the memories and learnings that you've made but without empowering the past to determine today.

4. *Realign your "future" to your present.* Now again, from a fully resourceful and centered state in the moment, realign your representations of the future—representing the events and experiences that you anticipate and hope to come—so that you can see them as full of potential, bright, vague enough to leave room for change and alteration, etc.

5. *Move to a meta-position and align.* Again access your strong centered and uptime state in the moment and from there go meta to your entire set of representations about the past and the future and view all of this "time" from a state of acceptance and appreciation of yourself as a time-traveler. You can see yourself moving through "time" from event to event, learning, growing, developing more wisdom, bringing the wisdom of past learnings with you, and developing your skills to architect a bright future for yourself, because you can... now.

Finishing a Past Gestalt

The Concept. In NLP we say that regardless of whether we like it or not, the "past" has ended. It has finished. When it feels like "unfinished business" only our *current thinking* exists as unfinished. No wonder we keep thinking and re-thinking going over and over our representations and meanings of those past events!

Many of the time-line processes in the early chapters offered processes for *finishing an old gestalt* of past emotions, thoughts, decisions, etc. Here we offer a more streamlined linguistic way.

When we analyze what keeps our thinking-and-emoting about those past events alive and dynamic—we almost always finds words. We find that in our self-dialogue, we keep telling ourselves things that energizes and activates the old events,

"Why did that have to happen to me...?"
"Why can't I get over it...?"
"I know that I'll never get over it..."

Here we change the content of our meta-level thoughts *about* the past events so that we can program ourselves for closure.

The Pattern

1. *Move to a meta-position.* Access a state meta to your Historical Time, Psychological Time, Developmental Time, etc. (Figure 11.2).

2. *Re-Language the meaning of those old events.* From this position, out of the problem space, now say words of completion to it. Language it as finished.

"I see those events as unfortunate events that I once experienced..."

"From this day forward I will no longer empower those events or my own thinking about them as having any influence over the kind of person I will become and the kind of experiences that I will have."

"Those exist as just old experiences that I survived and learned from."

Taking Interest To Reframe "Boredom"

The Concept. Since the movement and rhythm of events lies at the very heart of the life processes—neurologically as well as mentally-emotionally and in terms of the concept of "time,"—rhythm, beats, intervals, and frequencies play a crucial role in our subjective experiences. This also means *repetition.* Yet when we consider the attitude of mind-and-emotion that most people in Western societies take toward repetition—we can see the cause of a basic "time" maladjustment—we hate waiting, we despise the "same old thing again and again," we over-value the new, the different, variety, etc.

Thus because underneath rhythm we find *repetition*—sameness, repeating, etc. we find a basic discontent therefore with rhythm in the North European societies. Here we have societies that demand variety and that shun last year's products and fads. This inevitably introduces lots of superficiality and lack of depth into our experiences and that inescapably tends to lead to a dissatisfaction with the old and with the simple things in life. Generally, we prefer the new, improved, updated, never-before seen or heard, the sensational, the greatest, the best, etc.

To so disvalue repetition just because it has occurred before inevitably undermines our ability to find and enjoy the various inherent rhythms in life that allows us to synchronize with reality and experience a quality of depth and satisfaction. Obviously, given this analysis, we need to reframe "boredom," the old, repetition, etc.

The Pattern

1. *Identify a repetitive pattern or rhythm toward which you tend to become bored and uninterested.* What occurs over and over and over again that you tend to hate, dislike, disapprove of, complain about, etc.? Going to work, rising, returning home, doing school work, doing chores, exercising, studying, etc.

2. *Move to a meta-position and just begin to acknowledge the rhythmic patterns.* And as you do you can take a new and profound interest in the value of such rhythmic patterns—noticing how the repeti-

tion installs activities into your neurology at an unconscious level, thus enabling you to experience "unconscious competence." And you can notice how repetition establishes depth and quality—and stability. And how surprised can you allow yourself to feel about these values?

3. *Meta-state yourself with other resources.* As you realize the value of such repetitive processes, you can appreciate, really appreciate, this ... and enjoy it so that you begin to take more interest in such repetitions. This doesn't mean "boredom" or "stagnation," it means power, competence, stability, freedom to move on to other competencies, depth, etc.

Conclusion

Truly "time" plays such a pervasive role in consciousness and therefore in our emotions, perceptions, behaviors, and skills. The ways that we can structure and format this conceptual semantic reality ("time") extend beyond our ability to list. We can develop so many different kinds of relationship to "time," it can function in us for good or ill, health or sickness. The patterns presented here offer but a sampling of the many ways that we can re-structure our coding and relationship to "time." May you thoroughly enjoy your ongoing adventures with "time" and do so in such a way that it allows you to discover ever-new pathways to resourcefulness!

Chapter 15

The Mind Backtracking Technique

Will the Thought in the Back of Your Mind
Please Stand Up?

Back to the experience out of which our map came! In NLP, this describes the heart and passion of using the meta-model. We start with Surface structures and meta-model them in order to get back to the Deep structures.

The Cognitive-Behavioral Psychology model, in which NLP falls, postulates that behind every emotion lies a "thought." This "thought" may involve an understanding, awareness, sensory representation, belief, value, decision, etc. From this awareness that "beneath" (or behind) every emotion lies a thought comes the idea of "back-tracking" to the thought out of which it came. Ellis (1976) in **Rational-Emotive Therapy** (RET) and Beck (1976) each searches with a client to discover the person's evaluative judgment that drives the emotion.

This understanding also fits the diagrams on the levels of abstraction that Korzybski (1941/1994) developed in describing the nervous system's modeling process. We start at the bottom in the unspeakable territory which we can never reach by words and which exists "out there" beyond the nervous system. But then we "abstract," (e.g. summarize, bring in, and transform) from the territory to make our neurological "maps" of that territory. Then, moving up two or three levels, we finally reach the speakable level of words, a linguistic map of various neurological transforms. In *Science and Sanity*, in a section on semantic reactions, Korzybski suggested a semantic experiment to discover the "meaning" of any given term. The effective of the experiment leads a person down further and further into the deep structure, into deeper levels of neurology...

"Here we have reached the bottom and the foundation of all non-elementalistic meanings—meanings of undefined terms, which we "know" somehow, but cannot tell. In fact, we have reached the un-speakable level." (p. 21).

Sometimes we need to go back down to the territory and re-map in more appropriate and accurate ways. This, Bandler and Grinder (1975) built into the meta-model (as a model of human modeling processes) using the deep and surface structures of Chomsky. So dropping down back to the experience out of which we do our mental mapping, describes an insight of the Meta-Model as well as a technique.

As a Technique

This technique involves a backtracking to the neuro-linguistic constructions. In doing so, we imagine "going back" or "dropping down" to a lower or prior level of abstraction. To accomplish what? Typically we use this *"Drop-Down Through"* or *Mind Backtracking Technique* to assist ourselves, or others, in releasing negative emotions, especially those in which we may feel stuck. Via this process the negative emotions will release as we move back or down to previous levels of abstraction.

What lies at the bottom? The Void, the Nothing, the Unspeakable realm, the quantum, God, ultimate reality, etc.

Arising then, first from Korzybski, through the Cognitive Psychology models, then through Bandler and Grinder, Tad James first developed this specific technique as a Time-Line Therapy™ technique. Here we first present Tad's process, then one developed by John Overdurf to streamline the process, then our own development, *Mind Backtracking*.

The Pattern

1. *Find the first event.* "What is the root cause of this problem, the first event which, when disconnected, will cause the problem to disappear? Tell me about the first time you felt this emotion..."

2. *Go back to the first event on your time-line.* "I'd like to ask your unconscious mind to float up... above your time-line, and then to go back into the past... and as you do you can go back to the event itself and drop down into it." [Do not associate yourself or another into the event if it has the qualities or character of a trauma; always run the V/K dissociation pattern first to release the negative emotions.]

3. *Preserve the learnings.* "As you re-visit that event, notice and describe the emotion(s) you now feel? What learnings have you made here that you would want to preserve? What do you need to learn from this event, the learning of which will allow you to let this all go, easily and effortlessly?"

4. *Drop-down through.* "As quickly as you can, allow yourself to drop down through the emotion as you do a kind of kinesthetic 'free-fall' through it and do this as quickly as you can... and say aloud the name of the emotion that you find underneath this first experience..."

5. *Repeat this process again and again.* "And as quickly as you can, just drop through that emotion, the emotion you found underneath the original one. And what do you find underneath that one?" Continue this process until you float down all the way through and come to the "void," or "nothing," to that unspeakable stage of experience and notice, as you do, how you come out the other side to an experience that has a positive kinesthetic to it. Then free-fall another time to a second positive kinesthetic.

[Only go to two positive emotions. If looping occurs more than once, use an inductive language pattern to exit the loop to a deeper level of meaning. End the process when you reach the second positive emotion. You should see and experience an obvious physiological shift. This suggests the chain of emotions below or behind emotions have collapsed together.]

6. *Float above your experience and time-line.* "As you return to the experience that began this experience, float up to your meta-time-line (position #3), and go back in history to well before the beginning of the event, or any of the chain of events that led to that event, and turn and look towards now."

7. *Solidify and test for the disappearance of the negative emotions.* "Now where has the old emotion/s gone? ... Yes, it disappeared." "Now, just float right down into the event and notice just how fully the emotion has completely disappeared from the way you used to experience it... Do you find the emotion totally gone? Good, return back up above to your time-line (position #3)." [Continue to re-run this process until you access the positive kinesthetic.]

8. *Come back to now.* "Now, come back to now, above your time-line only as quickly as you can let go of all the (name the emotion) on the events all the way back to now, assume position #3 with each subsequent event, preserve the learnings, and let go of the (name the emotion) all the way back to now." [Break state.]

9. *Test.* "As you recall some event, any event, in the past where you used to feel that old emotion, go back there and try to see if you can feel it, or you may find that you cannot."

10. *Future pace.* "I want you to go out into the future to an unspecified time in the future which if it had happened in the past, you would have felt (name the emotion) and notice if you can find that old emotion, or you may find that you cannot. OK? Good come back to now."

The Pattern Simplified

John Overdurf and Julie Silverthorn (1996) have simplified this *Drop-Down Through Process* into the following five steps.

1. *Elicit a word which corresponds to emotional state.* Identify a value or unwanted emotional state in the form of some nominalization: anger, fearfulness, timidity, etc.

2. *Invite a person to "just drop down through that emotion . . . until you come to what you find underneath it..."*

3. *Continue the Dropping Down Through.* Continue to repeat this process until you have generated a chain of states that run all the way through to a "void", "nothing," an unspeakable stage, etc. and comes out the other side to a positive kinesthetic state.

4. *End the process when you reach the non-mirror image reverse of the first word* (e.g. the undesired emotional term). Unless you come out immediately to the obvious non-mirror image reverse, go to the second positive kinesthetic. You will find an obvious physiological shift which indicates that the chain has begun to collapse at that point.

5. *Repeat this whole process with another emotional state.* Do this until you have only accessed a positive kinesthetic. You may find that various chains interconnect. In these cases continue running the "branches" of each chain until you reach only a positive kinesthetic.

Demonstrating Dropping-Down Through

For me (BB), the stages of dropping down through that one recent client had with this process involved the following *"chain"* of states:

- Abandonment,
- Scared,
- Lonely,
- Helpless,
- Nothing (a void, here a person will feel or experience "nothing" and so will have a "blank" so to speak),
- Jesus. This client dropped straight into "Jesus." I wrote in my notes, "A big one. She really had a phenomenal experience."

The following represents another case, and a classic example of what we usually get with this process. Often I look at this as a kinesthetic free fall down through the outcome chain that one might get from using the Core Transformation™ process. Here you can take a person back on their time-line and come forward with each painful internal representation. In the process you thereby provide a re-imprint. From another recent client, I got this classic list: 1) Confusion, 2) Shock, 3) Fear, 4) Worry, 5) Fear for dad (different from above), 6) Fear of losing house (different fear, dad arrested for gambling by the police), 7) Nothing. 8) Safety, 9) Christ. At this point the client started laughing out loud.

Some caveats. Like all NLP techniques, this process will not always work. When a person drops down through, he or she may not always get the classic negative emotions, the void, and then two positive. Sometimes you get different mixtures —scramble eggs. Tad recommends that a person follows these directions precisely and to do so only with individuals, not groups.

On my (MH) first experience with this process, I picked a recent incident to which I responded with anger and upset feelings. Then, as I did the kinesthetic free-fall—I first fell into 2) hurt, then I moved into 3) fear, then into a strange emotional state, one wherein I felt a strong sense of life itself feeling 4) unfulfilled, after that, I felt, as *Alice in Wonderland*, falling, falling, falling... I hit the Void of Nothingness. Falling after that took me to the chaos of God's World where I had a sense of his spirit moving upon the waters bringing order out of chaos.

Mind BackTracking

As you can imagine, some people will not like the metaphor of falling or going "down." So for them, playfully using the metaphor of going "behind" enables them to use the same process.

This process may remind you of the *Kinesthetic Stepping Back* technique [I (MH) wrote this in *Spirit of NLP* (1996)]. In that process we take a state of some distress, and step back from it on our time-line so that we can then look at it. There in front of us we see (dissociated, from a spectator's point of view) our Future Self in that distress state! Yet as we have stepped back, we have accessed another state, one with more resources and one in which we can begin to stack and store other resources. "What resource(s) would change that future experience and make it less painful or distressful?"

Once we have accessed those resources, we step back again. Now we see our future self playing and accessing resources for a future distressful state. Here again we can imagine additional resources that would help that future self. And so continuing moving back on one's time-line, associating into more and more resources as moving back, and gaining increasing perspective on the future self.

When a person has backed up numerous times and anchored resources at each spot on a kinesthetic time-line, then the neuro-linguistic programmer could assist with languaging and anchoring, moving the person forward in "time" reanchoring and re-experiencing the resources until coming up to the present (where the process began) now completely re-organized.

Similarly, in backing up or "backtracking" to the cognitive-behav-ioral state out of which the anger/upset came, I landed first at hurt, then fear, etc. Visually I had the experience of running my movie backward—and had a strong kinesthetic sense of quickly zooming back and did so until it came out of a void and then out of God's chaos.

The Mind BackTracking Pattern

With this pattern, we begin with the statement and continue to use this as the driving force:

> "And, behind that thought whirling in your mind lies another thought.... So allow yourself to notice what thought do you find back there?"

Using this directional question that swishes the mind backwards offers a profound and simple way to take a client back to the Void of Nothingness and then on to various resources.

A Demonstration

I (BB) met with a lady that I'll call Susan, female in her mid fifties. I have seen her in therapy several times and because she has come to love NLP, works hard at learning NLP concepts and procedures. Susan also has a deep religious faith. Now, following 38 years of marriage, she has chosen to leave her husband. Her husband has a life history of several affairs and addictive behaviors.

When Susan called, said she had been reading Hall's book ***Dragon Slaying***. And because a dragon had surfaced, she wished to get rid of it. Though she had decided to go ahead and get a divorce, she struggled with the realization of the finality of the separation as well as a divorce after 38 years of marriage. So to backtrack her thinking, I said,

"And, Susan, behind the thought that you are having a hard time dealing with the finality of the separation and divorce after 38 years of marriage swirls another thought in the back of your mind ...(pause)... now as you notice that thought, describe it to me."

"That is the basis of what I came here for today—addiction. I have been totally addicted, sexually, to my husband."

"And, behind, the thought of being totally addicted, sexually, to your husband lies another thought. What is that thought?"

"I am not sure I can trust you with that because you are a man."

"And, behind the thought that you cannot trust me because I am a man swirls another thought. What is that thought?"

"My mother taught me well that I am not to ever trust any man."

"And, Susan, behind the thought that you are not ever to trust a man, what thought lies behind that thought?"

"That I trust my husband and she was right. What am I going to do now? I know all of this?"

"Good question. And behind that question you have another thought, don't you? And what is that thought?"

"I am a very sexual person and I don't know how I am going to deal with this now. And right now I am going to confess something that I have thought about being with another woman. And, I have made a big step by confessing that thought. I can now understand how people can think themselves into homosexuality."

"And, Susan, behind the thought that you have thought of being with another woman whirls another thought. What is that thought?"

"That it is unacceptable to me. I need to know how to accept my sexuality without feeling it is addictive and not feeling like it is bad. I couldn't have sex with my next husband until I get this straight in my mind. Because when I have sex with my first husband it wasn't love. He didn't love me. And, it wasn't love for me either. I was addicted to sex."

"And, Susan, behind that thought lies another thought. What is that thought?"

"I want to have a relationship with a husband that is full of love and full of sexuality."

"And, behind that thought, what thought do you have?"

"That I want us both to be used of the Lord and I know it is out there. The Lord has already told me that there is a husband out there. The Lord has great things for us. I already know that. The devil has been putting these negative thoughts in my mind to stop the Lord from using me. I am not going to let the devil have the victory."

"And, Susan, behind not letting the devil have the victory, what thought is there?"

Susan paused... in her speechlessness I knew she now arrived at the Void.

"I am going to a place of pure potentiality!" (She had experienced this before through the Drop Down Through technique from Time-Line Therapy™.) "This is wonderful!" she exclaimed.

"That is right, Susan, go ahead into the place of pure potentiality. And, being in the place of pure potentiality, what does the Lord tell you?"

"I am going to have another husband and he is going to know NLP. It is going to be unreal how many lives we are going to touch."

Susan got so excited she had to get up and walk around, she was so full...

"Susan, are we through?"

"No, there is one more thing. When I give myself pleasure, I can't enjoy it because I have guilt?"

"Susan, do you speak of masturbation?"

"Yes, but I can't even say it."

"Susan, behind the guilt of giving yourself pleasure, what thought do you have behind that?"

"Maybe I don't deserve pleasure. Maybe because I made such a mess of my marriage. Maybe I don't deserve pleasure because I was just as wrong as my husband was sexually. He probably sensed that in me. No wonder he found other women."

"And, behind that thought that you don't deserve pleasure, what thought is there?"

"I am going to have to accept responsibility for this marriage failing to. Until now I have blamed him, saying he is the guilty one. Now I have to accept part of the guilt."

"And, Susan, what thought do you have behind the thought of accepting your part in the responsibility for the failure of the marriage?"

"I am forgiven for what I did wrong in the marriage. I can't make any more choices for him, and behind that I sense pure potentiality!"

As Susan experienced the place of pure potentiality again, she lit up like a morning glory.

"And I have forgiven myself."

"You have slain that dragon, right?"

"My castle is all white."

Conclusion

How does this process work? It operates by associating into a problem, getting the "thought" that drives it, and then asking a series of backtracking questions about the "thought" (ideas, representations, etc.) behind it that propells it forward into becoming one's frames or generalizations. In doing this, we go (or we take each other) back to the experience out of which it came and ultimately to the Void. When we get there we have arrived at the place of pure potentiality.

As such, it provides a valuable tool for those whose primary representation systems involve something other than the visual modality (e.g. auditory, kinesthetic, and/or auditory digital).

And the value of getting one back (or down) to the *Void*—the unspeakable dimension before abstracting? It opens us up to new potentialities as it gives us new ways to remap. It also gives us a deep neurological or unconscious understanding of the difference between map and territory— "maps are but maps," they never exist as territory.

Though Bob did not future pace or reimprint in this case with Susan, he very well could have brought her forward and have her re-imprint her entire time-line with the resources that she found in that place of pure potentiality. This usually offers an additional reinforcement of the process.

Appendix

There 'Is' No 'Is'

Did you even notice that we wrote this book using the general-semantic extensional device called E-Prime (except for quotes from others)? We did.

E-what? English-primed of the *"to be"* verb family of passive verbs (is, am, are, was, were, be, being, been). Invented by Dr David Bourland, Jr, and popularized by Bourland and Paul Dennithorne Johnston in *To Be or Not: An E-Prime Anthology*, E-Prime and E-Choice empowers people to not fall into the *"is"* traps of language.

The "is" traps? Yes, Alfred Korzybski (1941/1994) warned that the "is" of identity and the "is" of predication present two dangerous linguistic and semantic constructions that map false-to-fact conclusions. The first has to do with identity--how we identify a thing or what we identify ourselves with and the second with attribution, how we frequently project our "stuff" onto others or onto things without realizing it.

Identity as "sameness in all respects," does not even exist. It can't. At the sub-microscopic level, everything involves a "dance of electrons" always moving, changing, and becoming. So no thing can ever "stay the same" even with itself. So nothing "is" in any static, permanent, unchanging way. Since nothing exists as eternal, but since everything continually changes, then nothing "is." To use "is" mis-speaks, mis-evaluates, and mis-maps reality. To say, "She is lazy..." "That is a stupid statement..." falsely maps reality. And Korzybski argued that unsanity and insanity ultimately lie in identifications.

Predication refers to *"asserting"* something. So to say, "This is good," "That flower is red," "He is really stupid!" creates a language structure which implies that something "out there" contains these qualities of "goodness," "redness," and "stupidity."

The "is" suggests that such things exist independent of the speaker's experience. Not so. Our descriptions speak primarily about our internal experience indicating our judgments and values. More accurately we could have said, "I evaluate as good this or that," "I see that flower as red," "I think of him as suffering from stupidity!"

"Is" statements falsely distract and confuse logical levels, and subtly lead us to think that such value judgments exist outside our skin in the world "objectively." Wrong again. The evaluations (good, red, stupid) function as definitions and interpretations in the speaker's mind.

The "*to be*" verbs dangerously presuppose that "things" (actually events or processes) stay the same. **Not!** These verbs invite us to create mental representations of fixedness so that we begin to set the world in concrete and to live in "*a frozen universe.*" These verbs code the dynamic nature of processes statically. "Life is tough." "I am no good at math."

Do these statements not sound definitive? Absolute? "That's just the way it is!" No wonder Bourland calls "is" "am" and "are," etc. "the deity mode." "The fact is that this work is no good!" Such words carry a sense of completeness, finality, and time-independence. Yet discerning the difference between the map and the territory tells us these phenomenon exist on different logical levels. Using E-Prime (or E-Choice) reduces slipping in groundless authoritarian statements which only closes minds or invites arguments.

If we confuse the language we use in describing reality (our map) with reality (the territory), then we identify differing things. And that makes for unsanity. There "is" no is. "Is" non-references. It points to nothing in reality. It operates entirely as an irrational construction of the human mind. Its use leads to semantic mis-evaluations.

Conversely, writing, thinking, and speaking in E-Prime contributes to "consciousness of abstracting" (conscious awareness) that we make maps of the world which inherently differ from the world. E-Prime enables us to think and speak with more clarity and precision as it forces us to take first-person. This reduces the passive verb tense ("It was done." "Mistakes were made."). It restores speakers to statements, thereby contextualizing statements. E-Prime, by raising consciousness of abstracting, thereby enables us to index language. Now I realize that the person I met last week, 'Person last week', "is" not equal in all respects the person that now stands before me, 'Person this week.' This assists me in making critical and valuable distinctions.

E-Choice differs from E-Prime in that with it one uses the "is" of existence (e.g. "Where is your office?" "It is on 7th. Street at Orchard Avenue."), the auxiliary "is" (e.g. "He is coming next week.") and the "is" of name, (e.g. "What is your name?" "It is Michael." "My name is Bob."). Though we wrote this in E-Prime, we have decided to begin to use E-Choice so as to avoid some circumlocutious phrases that we have used in the past(!).

Reference: Hall (1995) *"Elevating NLP to E-Prime"* (Feb. 1995), Anchor Point.

Glossary of NLP Terms

Analogue: Continuously variable between limits, e.g. a dimmer switch for a light. An analogue SBMD varies like light to dark, while a digital SBMD operates as either off or on (we see a picture either associatedly or dissociatedly).

Anchoring: The process by which any stimulus or representation (external or internal) gets connected to and so triggers a response. **Anchors** occur naturally and intentionally (as in analogue marking). Anchoring derives from the Pavlovian stimulus-response reaction, classical conditioning. In Pavlov's study the tuning fork became the stimulus (anchor) that cued the dog to salivate.

Association: Refers to mentally seeing, hearing, and feeling from inside an experience, in contrast with dissociated.

Auditory: The sense of hearing.

Behavior: Any activity. Micro behavior includes thinking, macro behavior—external actions.

Beliefs: Thoughts, conscious or unconscious, which have grown up into a generalization about causality, meaning, self, others, behaviors, identity, etc. Beliefs guide us in perceiving and interpreting reality and stand closely to values.

Calibration: Atuning oneself another's state via reading non-verbal signals previously observed.

Chunking: Size of information you work with. Chunking up refers to going up a level (induction) which leads to higher abstractions. Chunking down refers to going a level (deduction) which leads to more specific examples or cases.

Congruence: State wherein one's IR works together so that what you say corresponds with what you do. Both non-verbal and verbal statements match. A state of unity, fitness, internal harmony, not conflict.

Content: The specifics and details of an event, answers what? and why? Contrasts with process or structure.

Context: The setting, frame or process in which events occur and provides meaning for content.

Cues: Information that provides clues to another's subjective structures, i.e. eye accessing cues, predicates, breathing, body posture, gestures, voice tone and tonality, etc.

Digital: Varying between two states i.e. a light switch—either on or off. A digital submodality: color or black-and-white; an analogue submodality: varying between dark and bright.

Dissociation: Not "in" an experience, but seeing or hearing it from outside as from a spectator's point of view, in contrast to association.

Distortion: Modeling process by which we alter one's representation of something. This can occur to create limitations or resources.

Downtime: Not in sensory awareness, but "down" inside one's "mind" seeing, hearing, and feeling thoughts, memories, awarenesses, a light trance state with attention focused inward.

Ecology: Question about the overall relationship between idea, skill, response and larger environment or system. Internal ecology: the overall relationship between person and thoughts, strategies, behaviors, capabilities, values and beliefs. The dynamic balance of elements in a system.

Elicitation: Evoking a state by word, behavior, gesture or any stimuli. Gathering information by direct observation of non-verbal signals or by asking meta-model questions.

Empowerment: Process of adding vitality, energy, and new resources; vitality at the neurological level.

Eye Accessing Cues: Movements of the eyes in certain directions indicating visual, auditory or kinesthetic thinking (processing).

Epistemology: Study of how we know what we know.

First Position: Perceiving the world from your own point of view, associated, one of the three perceptual positions.

Frame: Context, environment, meta-level, a way of perceiving something.

Future Pace: Process of mentally practicing (rehearsing) an event before it happens. A key process for ensuring the permanency of an outcome.

Gestalt: The overall configuration of something.

Gustatory: Sense of taste.

Hypnosis: State altered from usual states, an inward focus of attention, trance, measurable on an EEG.

Identity: Self-image or self-concept, the person you define yourself, your self-definition.

Incongruence: State wherein parts conflict and war with each other, having reservations, not totally committed to an outcome, expressed in incongruent messages, signals, lack of alignment or matching of word and behavior.

Installation: Process for putting a new mental strategy inside mind-body so it operates automatically, often achieved through anchoring, leverage, metaphors, parables, reframing, future pacing, etc.

Internal Representations (IR): Patterns of information we create and store in our minds, combinations of sights, sounds, sensations, smells and tastes.

Kinesthetic: Sensations, feelings, tactile sensations on surface of skin, proprioceptive sensations inside the body, includes vestibular system or sense of balance.

Logical Level: A higher level, a level about a lower level, a meta-level that drives and modulates the lower level.

Loops: A circle, cycle, a story, metaphor or representation that goes back to its own beginning, so that it loops back (feeds back) onto itself. An open loop: a story left unfinished. A closed loop: finishing a story.

Map of Reality: Model of the world, a unique representation of the world built in each person's brain by abstracting from experiences, comprised of a neurological and a linguistic map, one's IR.

Matching: Adopting facets of another's outputs (behavior, words, etc.) to enhancing rapport.

Meta: Above, beyond, about, at a higher level, a logical level higher.

Meta-Model: A model of 12 linguistic distinctions that identifies language patterns that obscure meaning in a communication via distortion, deletion and generalization. 12 specific challenges or questions by which to clarify imprecise language (ill-formedness) to reconnect it to sensory experience and the deep structure. Meta-modeling brings a person out of trance. Developed by Richard Bandler and John Grinder, the MM serves as the basis of most discoveries in NLP.

Meta-Programs: Mental/perceptual programs for sorting and paying attention to stimuli, perceptual filters that govern attention.

Meta-States: A state about a state, bringing a state of mind-body (fear, anger, joy, learning) to bear upon another state from a higher logical level, generates a gestalt state—a meta-state, developed by Michael Hall (1994).

Metaphor: Indirect communication by a story, figure of speech, parable, similes, allegories, etc. implying a comparison, a "carrying over" of meaning by presenting something on the side, use: to bypass conscious resistance and communicate to unconscious mind directly.

Milton Model: Inverse of the meta-model, using artfully vague language patterns to pace another person's experience and access unconscious resources, a means for inducing trance.

Mirroring: Precisely matching portions of another person's behavior for the purpose of building rapport, becoming a mirror image of another's physiology, tonality and predicates.

Mismatching: Offering different patterns of behavior to another, breaking rapport for the purpose of redirecting, interrupting, or terminating a meeting or conversation, mismatching as a meta-programs.

Modal Operators: Linguistic distinctions in the meta-model that indicate the "mode" by which a person "operates"—the mode of necessity, impossibility, desire, possibility, etc.

Model: A description of how something works, a generalized, deleted or distorted copy of the original.

Modeling: A process of observing and replicating the successful actions and behaviors of others, the process of discerning the sequence of IR and behaviors that enable someone to accomplish a task, the basis of accelerated learning.

Model of the world: A map of reality, a representation of the world via abstraction from our experiences.

Multiple Description: Process of describing the same thing from different viewpoints.

Nominalization: Linguistic distinction in the meta-model, a hypnotic pattern of trance language, a process or verb turned into an (abstract) noun, a process frozen in time.

Outcome: A specific, sensory-based desired result, should meet the well-formedness criteria.

Pacing: Gaining and maintaining rapport with another by joining their model of the world by saying things that fit with and match their language, beliefs, values, current experience, etc.

Parts: Unconscious parts, sub-personalities created through some significant emotional experiences, disowned and separated functions that begin to take on a life of their own, a source of intra-personal conflict when incongruous.

Perceptual filters: Ideas, experiences, beliefs, values, meta-programs, decisions, memories and language that shape and color our model of the world.

Perceptual Position: A point of view, one of three positions: first position—associated, second position—from another person's perspective, third position—from another other position.

Predicates: Words used to assert or predicate about some subject; sensory based words indicating a particular RS (visual predicates, auditory, kinesthetic, unspecified).

Presuppositions: Ideas that we have to take for granted for a communication to make sense, assumptions, that which "holds" (position) "up" (sup) a statement "ahead of time" (pre).

Rapport: Sense of connection with another, a feeling of mutuality, a sense of trust, created by pacing, mirroring and matching, a state of empathy or second position.

Reframing: Changing a frame-of-reference so that things look new or different, presenting an event or idea from a different point of view so it has a different meaning; content or context reframing.

Representation: An idea, thought, presentation of sensory-based or evaluative based information.

Representation System (RS): How we mentally code information using the sensory systems.

Requisite Variety: Flexibility in thinking, emoting, speaking, behaving; the person with the most flexibility of behavior has the most influence.

Resources: Means we can bring to bear to achieve an outcome: physiology, states, thoughts, strategies, experiences, people, events or possessions.

Resourceful State: The total neurological and physical experience when a person feels resourceful.

Second Position: Perceiving the world from another's point of view, in tune with another's sense of reality.

Sensory Acuity: Awareness of the outside world, of the senses, making finer distinctions about the sensory information we get from the world.

Sensory-Based Description: Information directly observable and verifiable by the senses, see-hear-feel language that we can test empirically, in contrast to evaluative descriptions.

Significant Emotional Experience of Pain (SEEP): A high level emotional event during which we tend to make intense learnings that become imprinted, the generation of unconscious parts.

State: Holistic phenomenon of mind-body-emotions, mood, emotional condition, sum total of all neurological and physical processes within individual at any moment in time.

Strategy: A sequencing of thinking-behaving to obtain an outcome or create an experience, the structure of subjectivity ordered in the TOTE.

Submodality: Distinctions within each RS, qualities of internal representations, the smallest building blocks of thoughts, characteristics in each system.

Synesthesia: Automatic link from one RS to another, a V-K synesthesia involves seeing and feeling without a moment of consciousness to think about it, automatic program.

TDS: Transdiverational Search--a linguistic term used in NLP to describe how we "go inside" and search our references to make meaning of things.

Third Position: Perceiving world from viewpoint of an observer's position, one of the three perceptual positions, position where you see both yourself and another.

Time-line: A metaphor describing how we store our sights, sounds and sensations of memories and imaginings, a way of coding and processing the construct "time."

Time-line Therapy™ Techniques: An NLP therapeutic technique developed by Tad James, processes for dealing with problems in one's constructs of past or future events.

Trance: Altered state with an inward focus of attention, hypnosis.

Triple Description: Perceiving experience through first, second and third positions to gain wisdom.

Unconscious: Everything not in conscious awareness.

Uptime: State where attention and senses directed outward to immediate environment, all sensory channels open and alert.

Value: What we consider important and valuable.

Visual: Seeing, imagining, the RS of sight.

Visualization: The process of seeing images.

Well-Formedness Condition: Criteria that enable us to specify an outcome in ways that make it achievable and verifiable, a powerful tool for negotiating win/win solutions.

Bibliography

Andreas, Connairae & Andreas, Steve (1987). *Change Your Mind-- And Keep The Change: Advanced NLP submodalities interventions*. Moab, UT: Real People Press.

Andreas, Connairae & Andreas, Steve (1989). *Heart Of The Mind*. Moab, UT: Real People Press.

Beck, A.T. (1976). *Cognitive Therapy And The Emotional Disorders.* New York: International University Press.

Bodenhamer, Bobby G. (1996). *NLP Master Practitioner Track.* Unpublished materials.

Bodenhamer, Bobby G. (1996). *Jesus' Use Of Cartesian Logic With Inductive Language Patterns.* Unpublished material. Gastonia, NC: NLP Center.

Bodenhamer, Bobby G. (1996). *Advance Communication Course, Levels I, II, & III.* Gastonia, NC: NLP Center.

Bandler, Richard (1985). *Using Your Brain For A Change: Neuro-Linguistic Programming.* UT: Real People Press.

Bandler, Richard (1984). *Magic In Action.* Cupertino, CA. Meta Publications.

Bourland, David D. Jr. and Johnston, Paul Dennithorne. (1991). *To Be Or Not: An e-prime anthology*. San Francisco, CA: International Society for general semantics.

Bourland, David, D. Jr, Johnston; Paul Dennithorne & Klein, Jeremy (1994). *More E-Prime: To be or not II*. Concord, CA: International Society for General Semantics.

Bradshaw, John (1988). *The Family: A revolutionary way of self-discovery*. Beerfield Beach, FL: Health Communications, Inc.

Chomsky, Noam (1957). *Syntactic Structures*. The Hague: Mouton & Co.

Covey, Stephen R. (1989). *The Seven Habits Of Highly Effective People: Restoring the character ethic*. NY: Simon & Schuster.

Csikszentmihalyi, Mihaly (1990). *Flow: The psychology of optimal experience*. New York: HarperPerennial.

Dilts, Robert; Grinder, John; Bandler, Richard & DeLozier, Judith (1980). *Neuro-Linguistic Programming, Volume I: The study of the structure of subjective experience*. Cupertino. CA.: Meta Publications.

Dilts, Robert (1990). *Changing Belief Systems With NLP*. Cupertino, CA: Meta Publications.

Ellis, Albert & Harper, Robert A. (1976). *A New Guide To Rational Living*. Englewood Cliffs, NJ: Prentice-Hall, Inc.

Fagg, W. Lawrence (1985). *Two Faces Of Time*. Wheaton, IL. The Theosophical Publishing House.

Freedman, Jill & Combs, Gene (1993). *The New Language Of Change: Constructive collaboration in psychotherapy*. NY: The Guilford Press.

Freedman, Jill & Combs, Gene (1996). *Narrative Therapy: The social construction of preferred realities*. NY: W.W. Norton.

Glasser, William (1976). *Positive Addiction*. New York: Harper & Row.

Hall, Edward T. (1959). *The Silent Language*. Greenwich, CT: A Fawcett Premier Book.

Hall, Edward T. (1983). *The Dance Of Life: The other dimension of time*. NY: Anchor Press/Doubleday.

Hall, L. Michael (1988a) *Guilt And Pseudo-Guilt* (Jan. 1988), Metamorphosis. Grand Jct. CO: Encounters Publ.

Hall, L. Michael (1990). *Communicating With A Strong-Willed Person*. Grand Jct. CO: Encounters Publ.

Hall, L. Michael (1993). *"The Linguistic Precision Strategy*. Metamorphosis. Grand Jct. CO: ET Publications.

Hall, L. Michael (1990). *Reframing To Transform Meaning*. Metamorphosis. Grand Jct. CO: ET Publications.

Hall, L. Michael (1996). *Languaging: The linguistics of psychotherapy.* Grand Jct. CO: ET Publications.

Hall, L. Michael (1995). *Meta-States: A domain of logical levels, self-reflexiveness in human states of consciousness.* Grand Jct., CO: ET Publ.

Hall, L. Michael (1996). *Becoming A More Ferocious Presenter: Applying the spirit of NLP to presenting.* Grand Jct., CO: ET Publ.

Hall, L. Michael (1996). *Dragon Slaying: Dragons to princes.* Grand Jct., CO: ET Publ.

Hall, L. Michael (1996). *The Spirit Of NLP: The process, meaning and criteria for mastering NLP.* Carmarthen, Wales, U.K.: Anglo-American Books.

James, William (1892/1961). *Psychology: The briefer course.* NY: Harper & Row.

James, Tad (1989). *Master Time Line Therapy™ Training Manual.*

James, Tad & Woodsmall, Wyatt (1988). *Time Line Therapy And The Basis Of Personality.* Cupertino, CA: Meta Publ.

Johnson, Wendell (1946/1989). *People In Quandaries: The semantics of personal adjustment.* San Francisco, CA: International Society for General Semantics.

Kant, Immanuel (1963). *Immanuel Kant's Critique Of Pure Reason.* (Norman K. Smith, Trans.) New York: St. Martin's Press. (Original work published in 1783).

Kodish, Susan P. & Kodish, Bruce I. (1993). *Drive Yourself Sane: Using the uncommon sense of general-semantics.* Englewood, NJ: Institute of General Semantics.

Korzybski, Alfred (1921). *Manhood Of Humanity. Second edition.* Englewood, NJ: Institute of General Semantics.

Korzybski, Alfred (1941/1994). *Science And Sanity: An introduction to non-Aristotelian systems and general semantics, (5th. ed.).* Lakeville, CN: International Non-Aristotelian Library Publishing Co.

Meerloo, Joost A.M. (1970). *Along The Fourth Dimension: Man's sense of time and history.* NY: The John Day Co.

Morris, Richard (1985). *Time's Arrows: Scientific attitudes toward time.* NY: Simon and Schuster.

O'Connor, Joseph & Seymour, John (1991). *Introducing Neuro-Linguistic Programming: The new psychology of personal excellence.* Bodmin, Cornwall, Great Britain: Hartnolls Limited.

Overdurf, John & Silverthorn, Julie (1995). *Beyond Words: Languaging Change Through the Quantum Field.* Audio-Cassettes. PA: Neuro-Energetics.

Ricoeur, Paul (1983, 1985). *Time And Narrative: Volume I, Volume II.* Translated by Kathleen McLaughlin & David Pellauer. Chicago, IL. The University of Chicago Press.

Rogers, George L. (1990) (Ed.). *Benjamin Franklin's "The Art Of Virtue": His formula for successful living.* Eden Prairie, MN: Acorn Printing.

Ryan, K. John (Trans.) (1960). *The Confessions Of St. Augustine.* Garden City, NY: Image Books.

Verny, Thomas (1981). *The Secret Life Of The Unborn Child.* NY: Summit Books.

White, Michael, and Epston, David. (1990). *Narrative Means To Therapeutic Ends*. New York: W. W. Norton.

Weinberg, Harry L. (1959/ 1993). *Levels Of Knowing And Existence: Studies in general-semantics.* Englewood, NJ: Institute of General Semantics.

Yalom, I. (1985). *The Theory And Practice Of Group Psychotherapy* (3rd. ed.). NY: Basic Books.

Index

The Anglo-American Book Company Ltd
Crown Buildings,
Bancyfelin,
Carmarthen, SA33 5ND
Wales.
Telephone: 01267 211880 / 211886

We trust you enjoyed this title from our range of bestselling books for professional and general readership. All our authors are professionals of many years' experience, and all are highly respected in their own field. We choose our books with care for their content and character, and for the value of their contribution of both new and updated material to their particular field. Here is a list of all our other publications.

Figuring Out People
by Bob G. Bodenhamer & L. Michael Hall — Paperback £12.99

Gold Counselling: *A Practical Psychology With NLP*
by Georges Philips — Paperback £14.99

Grieve No More, Beloved: *The Book Of Delight*
by Ormond McGill — Paperback £9.99

Influencing With Integrity
by Genie Z Laborde — Paperback £12.50

Living Organisations: *Beyond The Learning Organisation*
by Lex McKee — Hardback £14.99

The New Encyclopedia Of Stage Hypnotism
by Ormond McGill — Hardback £29.99

The POWER Process: *An NLP Approach To Writing*
by Sid Jacobson & Dixie Elise Hickman — Paperback £12.99

Scripts & Strategies In Hypnotherapy
by Roger P. Allen — Paperback £19.99

Seeing The Unseen: *A Past Life Revealed Through Hypnotic Regression*
by Ormond McGill — Paperback £14.99

Solution States: *A Course In Solving Problems In Business Using NLP*
by Sid Jacobson — Paperback £12.99

The Spirit Of NLP: *The Process, Meaning And Criteria For Mastering NLP*
by L. Michael Hall — Paperback £12.99

Time-Lining: *Patterns For Adventuring In "Time"*
by Bob G. Bodenhamer & L. Michael Hall — Paperback £14.99